REA's Test Prep Books Are The Best!

(a sample of the hundreds of letters REA receives each year)

“ Your excellent [CBEST] book and software—saved the day for me. The reviews and tests were perfect. ”

Student, Sacramento, CA

“ My students report your chapters of review as the most valuable single resource they used for review and preparation. ”

Teacher, American Fork, UT

“ Your book was such a better value and was so much more complete than anything your competition has produced — and I have them all! ”

Teacher, Virginia Beach, VA

“ Compared to the other books that my fellow students had, your book was the most useful in helping me get a great score. ”

Student, North Hollywood, CA

“ Your book was responsible for my success on the exam, which helped me get into the college of my choice... I will look for REA the next time I need help. ”

Student, Chesterfield, MO

“ Just a short note to say thanks for the great support your book gave me in helping me pass the test... I'm on my way to a B.S. degree because of you! ”

Student, Orlando, FL

“ The gem of the book is the tests. They were indicative of the actual exam. The explanations of the answers are practically another review session. ”

Student, Fresno, CA

(more on next page)

(continued from front page)

“ I just wanted to thank you for helping me get a great score on the AP U.S. History... Thank you for making great test preps! ”

Student, Los Angeles, CA

“ Your *Fundamentals of Engineering Exam* book was the absolute best preparation I could have had for the exam, and it is one of the major reasons I did so well and passed the FE on my first try. ”

Student, Sweetwater, TN

“ I used your book to prepare for the test and found that the advice and the sample tests were highly relevant... Without using any other material, I earned very high scores and will be going to the graduate school of my choice. ”

Student, New Orleans, LA

“ What I found in your book was a wealth of information sufficient to shore up my basic skills in math and verbal... The section on analytical ability was excellent. The practice tests were challenging and the answer explanations most helpful. It certainly is the Best Test Prep for the GRE! ”

Student, Pullman, WA

“ I really appreciate the help from your excellent book. Please keep up with your great work.”

Student, Albuquerque, NM

“ I used your *CLEP Introductory Sociology* book and rank it 99% — thank you! ”

Student, Jerusalem, Israel

“ The painstakingly detailed answers in the sample tests are the most helpful part of this book. That’s one of the great things about REA books. ”

Student, Valley Stream, NY

(more on back page)

The Best Test Preparation for the

CBEST

California Basic Educational Skills Test

Written by California and Oregon Educators and CBEST Experts:

Mary F. Andis, Ed.D.
Assistant Professor of Education
California State University, San Bernardino
San Bernardino, CA

Linda Bannister, Ph.D.
Director of University Writing Programs and
Associate Professor of English
Loyola Marymount University
Los Angeles, CA

Mel Friedman, M.S.
Professor of Mathematics
Delaware Valley College
Doylestown, PA

Charles Funkhouser, Ph.D.
Assistant Professor of Education
California State University, San Bernardino
San Bernardino, CA

Marie Ice, Ph.D.
Assistant Professor of Reading/Language Arts
California State University, Bakersfield
Bakersfield, CA

Aida Joshi, Ph.D.
Assistant Professor of Education
University of San Francisco
San Francisco, CA

Adria Klein, Ph.D.
Professor of Education
California State University, San Bernardino
San Bernardino, CA

Kathryn F. Porter, Ph.D.
Associate Professor of Mathematics
St. Mary's College of California
Moraga, CA

Tison Pugh, Ph.D.
(Formerly of the University of Oregon)
Assistant Professor of English
University of Central Florida
Orlando, FL

David M. Rosen, M.A.
(Formerly of the University of Oregon)
Professor of English
Murray State College
Tishomingo, OK

Archibald Sia, Ph.D.
Associate Professor of Elementary Education
California State University, Northridge
Northridge, CA

Mary J. Skillings, Ph.D.
Assistant Professor of Education
California State University, San Bernardino
San Bernardino, CA

Hugo Sun, Ph.D.
Professor of Mathematics
California State University, Fresno
Fresno, CA

Stanley Swartz, Ph.D.
Professor of Education
California State University, San Bernardino
San Bernardino, CA

Research & Education Association
61 Ethel Road West
Piscataway, New Jersey 08854

The Best Test Preparation for the
CALIFORNIA BASIC EDUCATIONAL SKILLS TEST (CBEST)

Year 2003 Printing

Printed in the United States of America

Library of Congress Control Number 2001092075

International Standard Book Number 0-87891-409-9

Research & Education Association
61 Ethel Road West
Piscataway, New Jersey 08854
E-mail: info@rea.com

CONTENTS

CHAPTER 3

Reading Skills Review 67

CHAPTER 4

Mathematics Review 83

CHAPTER 5

Writing Review 133

STUDY SCHEDULE

It is important for you to discover the time and place for studying that works best for you. Some students may set aside a certain number of hours first thing every morning to study, while others may choose to study at night before going to sleep. The fact is, only you will be able to know when and where your studying is most effective. Keep in mind that the most important factor is consistency. Work out a study routine and stick to it!

You may want to follow a schedule similar to the one below. The following schedule consists of an eight-week program. If you need to condense your study time, you can combine two weeks into one, thereby creating a four-week schedule.

Week	Activity
1	Acquaint yourself with the CBEST by reading the Introduction of this book. Take REA's CBEST Diagnostic Exam. Then, carefully read through all the detailed explanations (not just those for your correct answers). Make a note of any sections that are difficult for you, or any questions that remain unclear after reading the explanations. Review the specific field of difficulty in the course review included with this book, or by using the appropriate textbooks and notes.
2	Study your weakest area this week. For example, if you had the most trouble on the measurement and geometry questions in the math section, you would study the geometry in the math review. After reviewing this section completely, retake only the section that covers this subject on the diagnostic test (in the above case, it would be the mathematics section) to see how your score improves.
3	Study your next to lowest scoring area this week. For example, if your essay writing skills were somewhat weak, go to the scoring explanations to determine why each essay earned the score it did. Retake that section from the diagnostic test and note any improvement.
4	Study your strongest area this week. If you are already pleased with your score, you need not repeat this section of the diagnostic test. If you hope to raise your score even further, retake this section of the diagnostic test.

Week	Activity
5	Take CBEST Practice Test I. Make sure that you take this test straight through in one sitting. See if your scores have improved since you last took the test.
6	Restudy any area in which you still show weakness.
7	Take CBEST Practice Test II under the same simulated conditions in which you took the last practice test. Notice any improvement in the amount of time you needed to complete a section. If you can keep up a good pace, you have a better chance of completing all the items on the day of the test.
8	Continue to review all unclear items. You also may take the pencil and paper versions of the tests to practice further. If you are unsure about what grade your essay would receive, seek the advice of a counselor or teacher at school. If you are satisfied with your scores and the time it takes you to complete the sections, you have completed your studying and are ready to take the CBEST with confidence.

The Best Test Preparation for the

CBEST

California Basic Educational Skills Test

Chapter

1

Introduction

About Research & Education Association

Research & Education Association (REA) is an organization of educators, scientists, and engineers specializing in various academic fields. Founded in 1959 with the purpose of disseminating the most recently developed scientific information to groups in industry, government, and universities, REA has since become a successful and highly respected publisher of study aids, test preps, handbooks, and reference works.

REA's Test Preparation series includes study guides for all academic levels in almost all disciplines. Research & Education Association publishes test preps for students who have not yet completed high school, as well as high school students preparing to enter college. Students from countries around the world seeking to attend college in the United States will find the assistance they need in REA's publications. For college students seeking advanced degrees, REA publishes test preps for many major graduate school admission examinations in a wide variety of disciplines, including engineering, law, and medicine. Students at every level, in every field, with every ambition can find what they are looking for among REA's publications.

While most test preparation books present only a few practice tests that bear little resemblance to the actual exams, REA's series presents tests that accurately depict the official exams in both degree of difficulty and types of questions. REA's practice tests are always based upon the most recently administered exams, and include every type of question that can be expected on the actual exams.

REA's publications and educational materials are highly regarded and continually receive an unprecedented amount of praise from professionals, instructors, librarians, parents, and students. Our authors are as diverse as the subject matter represented in the books we publish. They are well-known in their respective disciplines and serve on the faculties of prestigious high schools, colleges, and universities throughout the United States and Canada.

How to Prepare for and Do Your Best on the CBEST

By reviewing and studying this book, you can achieve a top score on the California Basic Educational Skills Test, or CBEST. The CBEST assesses knowledge that you have gained throughout your academic career. Most of the knowledge tested by the CBEST is covered in your college or university teacher preparation programs or through other classes. While the test does not ascertain aspects of teaching such as dedication, rapport with students, and motivation, it does assess basic skills relevant to the teaching profession.

We at REA believe the best way to prep for the CBEST is to replicate the complete CBEST test-taking experience. Toward that end, we provide three full-length exams that accurately reflect the CBEST in terms of format, content, and degree of difficulty. Our practice exams mirror the latest CBEST test forms and include every type of question that you can expect to encounter when you sit for the exam. Following each of our practice exams is an answer key complete with detailed explanations and solutions. Designed specifically to clarify the material for the student, the explanations not only provide the correct answers, but also explain why the answer to a particular question is indeed the best choice. By completing all three practice exams and studying the explanations that follow, you will flesh out your strengths and weaknesses. This in turn will allow you to concentrate progressively on attacking the sections of the exam you find to be toughest.

About REA's Test Experts

To aid us in meeting our objective of providing you with the best possible study guide for the CBEST, REA's test experts have carefully prepared our topical reviews and practice exams. Our authors come armed with specific knowledge of the CBEST. They have thoroughly examined and researched the mechanics of the CBEST to ensure that our model tests accurately depict the exam and appropriately challenge the student. Our experts are highly regarded in the educational community, with most having studied at the doctoral level. They have taught in their respective fields at competitive universities and colleges throughout California and Oregon. They have an in-depth knowledge of the subjects presented in the book, and provide accurate questions that will help you best prepare for the exam. Each question is clearly explained in order to help you achieve a top score on the CBEST.

About the California Basic Educational Skills Test

The CBEST is required by the states of California and Oregon for applicants seeking their first teaching or services credential. In California, unless an applicant already holds a California teaching credential, this test must be taken to obtain an issuance or renewal of an Emergency Credential. This rule does not apply in Oregon.

There are two other cases when the CBEST may be required: (1) for those people who have not taught for 39 months or more and are reentering the teaching profession, and (2) for diagnostic purposes for students entering teacher education programs in their state. To determine if you should take the CBEST, contact the school district where you are considering employment. For questions pertaining to CBEST policies, contact your respective state's teacher credentialing commission:

California Commission on Teacher Credentialing
P.O. Box 944270
Sacramento, CA 94244-2700
Phone: (916) 445-7254
Website: www.ctc.ca.gov

or

Oregon Teacher Standards and Practices Commission
255 Capitol Street N.E., Suite 105
Salem, OR 97310-1332
Phone: (503) 378-3586

The CBEST is given six times a year: in October, December, February, April, June, and August. The test is administered by National Evaluation Systems, Inc., under the direction of the CBEST Program. Questions regarding registration procedures for the CBEST can be referred to:

CBEST Program
National Evaluation Systems, Inc.
P.O. Box 340880
Sacramento, CA 95834-0880
Phone: (916) 928-4001
TDD: (916) 928-4191
Website: www.cbest.nesinc.com

You can also contact your school's education department for information on how to register for the test.

The exam tests reading skills (critical analysis and evaluation and comprehension and research skills), mathematics skills (estimation, measurement, and statistical principles, computation and problem solving, and numerical and graphic relationships), and writing skills (insight into a subject, writing for a specific audience, clarity, consistency of point of view, strength and logic of supporting information, and overall mechanics, spelling, and usage). The CBEST consists of multiple-choice questions and two essay questions. Each multiple-choice question presents five choices (A through E). Examinees are given four hours to take the test. You can divide this time in any way you wish among the three sections.

The test's three sections look like this:

1. **Reading Section:** This section contains 50 multiple-choice questions based on original passages of between 100 and 200 words. In some cases, however, these passages may be short statements of not more than one or two sentences.

2. **Mathematics Section:** This section contains 50 multiple-choice questions. These questions come from three broad categories: arithmetic, algebra, and measurement and geometry. Within these categories, the following types of problems will be tested:

   - Processes Used in Problem Solving—For example, identifying an operation needed to solve a problem or changing a verbal problem into one using math symbols.

   - Solution of Applied Problems—For example, answering word problems including arithmetic, percent, ratio and proportion, algebra, elementary geometry, and elementary statistics.

   - Mathematical Concepts and Relationships—For example, recognizing the definitions of certain terms (such as percent) and relationships shown by graphs.

All of these categories require knowledge of arithmetic,

algebra, and measurement and geometry.

3. **Writing Section:** This section contains two essay questions. You must write on both topics. One topic requires you to analyze a given situation, the other asks you to write about a personal experience.

Following this introduction are test strategies, examples, and suggested study techniques, all of which will help you properly prepare for the CBEST.

About the Diagnostic Test

Our diagnostic test is a full-length model test designed to help you determine your strengths and weaknesses on the material the CBEST will cover. For maximum benefit, simulate actual testing conditions by timing yourself and taking the test where you will not be interrupted.

Take each section separately. After each section, score yourself and review the detailed explanations of answers to determine your strengths and weaknesses. Each section offers a discussion of scoring so that you can understand what grade you must receive to pass the exam.

After you complete each section of the diagnostic test, study the reviews in Reading Skills, Mathematics, and Writing. By reading our Study Schedule, you should be able to refine your own studying plan.

About the Review Sections

This book offers three topical reviews, which correspond to the subject areas you will find on the exam. These include Reading Skills, Mathematics, and Writing. Supplementing your studies with our review will provide focus and structure and will allow you to choose a particular subject or subtopic to study. The reviews are set up to give you exactly what you need to do well on the exam.

Reading Skills Review

In this review you will be taught to recognize literal, inferential, and critical comprehension questions. We give general strategies for answering reading comprehension questions and then you give you ample opportunity to practice these strategies on sample questions.

Mathematics Review

The Mathematics Review offers three mini-reviews on the following topics:

- **Arithmetic**, including integers, prime and composite numbers, odd and even numbers, place value, powers and roots of whole numbers, addition, subtraction, multiplication, and division of integers, common fractions, decimal fractions, percents, and elementary statistics.

- **Algebra**, including algebraic expressions, simplifying algebraic expressions, factoring, solving linear equations, solving inequalities, evaluating formulas, elementary probability, and algebra word problems.

- **Geometry and measurement**, including perimeter and area of rectangles, squares and triangles, circumference and area of circles, volume of cubes and rectangular solids, angle measure, properties of triangles, the Pythagorean Theorem, properties of parallel and perpendicular lines, coordinate geometry, graphs, and the metric system.

You can read a full review on each topic and then be able to practice your skills in a short exercise at the end of this review.

Writing Review

The Writing Review focuses specifically on essay writing for the CBEST. You will learn about the types of topics you can expect to see on the CBEST and sample topics will be given. In addition, you will learn how the essay grade is determined so that you will be able to sharpen your writing ability and achieve a high grade.

Participate in Study Groups

As a final word on how to study for this exam, you may want to study with others. This will allow you to share knowledge and obtain feedback from other members of your study group. Study groups may make preparing for the exam more enjoyable.

Scoring the Exam

The Reading and Mathematics sections in the CBEST are scored the same way: raw scores are determined by adding together all the correct answers without deducting points for incorrect answers.

The Writing section is scored a different way. Each of your essays will be scored by two readers. The criteria by which the readers must grade your work are determined before the reading process begins, and the readers are thoroughly trained to grade using only these criteria. The readers are college professors from public and private institutions in California and Oregon, as well as elementary and secondary school English teachers from these two states.

The two readers will assess each of your essays independently. Each will assign a score from 1 to 4, with 4 being the highest:

4 = Pass
3 = Marginal Pass
2 = Marginal Fail
1 = Fail

The four scores are added, yielding a raw section score that can range from a high of 16 to a low of four.

Every CBEST test form is designed to measure the same cluster of basic skills. Nonetheless, the fact that each CBEST test form may have different questions—with varying degrees of difficulty—makes it necessary to convert the raw scores to a scale that adjusts for those variations. The scaled scores run from a low of 20 to a high of 80 for each of the test's three sections.

Attaining a passing score on the CBEST is not just a matter of simply achieving a minimal overall score, but of doing so on *each section* separately. The scaled passing score on each section is 41, which means that a total score of 123 is required for passing status. While it is possible to pass the CBEST with a scaled score as low as 37 on one or two sections, examinees *cannot pass* the CBEST if they score *below 37* on any one section, no matter how high their total score may be.

Scoring Rule of Thumb: If you correctly answer roughly 70 percent of the items on each section of the test, (i.e., Reading, Mathematics, Writing) you will receive a passing grade for the whole test. It should be noted that the actual raw passing score could vary a point or two each time the test is given because different forms of the test may be administered. For more on scoring the Mathematics section, see page 44. The same standard for a passing score applies equally to the CBEST itself and to REA's practice tests.

CBEST Test-Taking Strategies

How to Beat the Clock

Every second counts and you will want to use the available test time for each section in the most efficient manner. Here's how:

1. Memorize the test directions for each section of the test. You do not want to waste valuable time reading directions on the day of the exam. Your time should be spent on answering the questions.

2. Bring a watch to the exam and pace yourself. Work steadily and quickly. Do not spend too much time on any one question. If, after a few minutes, you cannot answer a particular question, make a note of it and continue. You can go back to it after you have completed easier questions first.

3. As you work on the test, be sure that your answers

correspond with the proper numbers and letters on the answer sheet.

Guessing Strategy

1. If you are uncertain about a question, guess at the answer rather than skipping it. You will not be penalized for answering incorrectly, since wrong answers are not counted toward your final score. This means that you should never leave a blank space on your answer sheet. Even if you do not have time to narrow down the choices, be sure to fill in every space on the answer sheet. You can only gain by this, since you will receive credit for any questions answered correctly—even if purely by luck.

2. You can improve on your guessing strategy by eliminating any choices recognized as incorrect. As you eliminate incorrect choices, cross them out. Remember that writing in test booklets is allowed. By crossing out incorrect choices, you will be better able to focus on the remaining choices.

CBEST

California Basic Educational Skills Test

Diagnostic Test

The First of Three Full-Length Practice Tests

4:45

DIRECTIONS: One or more questions follow each statement or passage in this test. The question(s) are based on the content of the passage. After you have read a statement or passage, select the best answer to each question from among the five possible choices. Your answers to the questions should be based on the stated (literal) or implied (inferential) information given in the statement or passage. Mark all answers on your answer sheet. **Note: You will encounter some passages with numbered sentences, blank spaces, or underscored words and phrases. These cues are provided on the CBEST for your reference in answering the questions that follow the relevant passages.**

Questions 1–5 refer to the following passage:

1 Spa water quality is maintained by a filter to ensure cleanliness and clarity. **2** Wastes such as perspiration, hairspray, and lotions that cannot be removed by the spa filter can be controlled by shock treatment or super chlorination every other week. **3** Although the filter traps most of the solid material to control bacteria and algae and to oxidize any organic material, the addition of disinfectants such as bromine or chlorine is necessary.

4 As all water solutions have a pH which controls corrosion, proper pH balance is also necessary. **5** Based on a 14-point scale, the pH measurement determines if the water is acid or alkaline. **6** High pH (above 7.6) reduces sanitizer efficiency, clouds water, promotes scale formation on surfaces and equipment, and interferes with filter operation. **7** Low pH (below 7.2) is equally damaging, causing equipment corrosion, water which is irritating, and rapid sanitizer dissipation. **8** (When pH is high, add a pH decreaser such as sodium bisulphate [e.g., Spa Down]; when pH is low, add a pH increaser such as sodium bicarbonate [e.g., Spa Up].)

9 The recommended operating temperature of a spa (98°–104°) is a fertile environment for the growth of bacteria and virus. **10** This growth is prevented when appropriate sanitizer levels are continuously monitored. **11** Maintaining a proper bromine level of 3.0 to 5.0 parts per million (ppm) or a chlorine level of 1.0–2.0 ppm can also control bacteria. **12** As bromine tablets should not be added directly to the water, a bromine floater will properly dispense the tablets. **13** Should chlorine be the chosen sanitizer, a granular form is recommended, as liquid chlorine or tablets are too harsh for the spa.

1. Although proper chemical and temperature maintenance of spa water is necessary, the most important condition to monitor is

(A) preventing growth of bacteria and virus.
(B) preventing equipment corrosion.
(C) preventing soap build up.
(D) preventing scale formation.
(E) preventing cloudy water.

2. The ideal operating temperature of a spa is

(A) above 105°.
(B) 3.0 to 5.0.
(C) 7.2 to 7.6.
(D) 98° to 104°.
(E) 1.0 to 2.0.

3. The primary purpose of the passage is to

(A) relate how spa maintenance can negate the enjoyment of the spa experience.
(B) provide evidence that spas are not as practical as swimming pools.
(C) suggest that spa maintenance is expensive and time consuming.
(D) explain the importance of proper spa maintenance.
(E) instruct you on how to care for your spa.

4. Which of these numbered sentences directly states *why* the use of disinfectant is necessary in the spa?

(A) Sentence 3
(B) Sentence 9
(C) Sentence 7
(D) Sentence 11
(E) Sentence 1

5. Which chemical should one avoid when maintaining a spa?

(A) Liquid chlorine
(B) Bromine
(C) Sodium bisulfate
(D) Baking soda
(E) All forms of chlorine

GO ON TO THE NEXT PAGE

Questions 6–10 refer to the following chart:

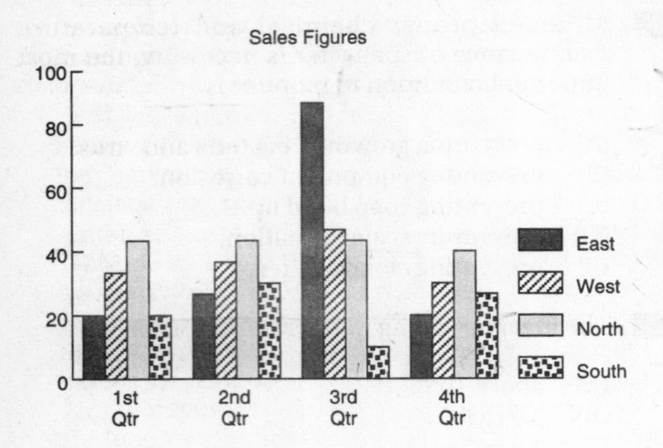

The four divisions of Company X (North, West, South, and East) are represented in the graph by region. The numbers along the left-hand side represent profits from sales in thousands of dollars, while the numbers along the bottom represent the company's fiscal year divided into quarters.

6. Which region shows the most consistent sales figures for the fiscal year?

(A) North
(B) East
(C) West
(D) None of the divisions show consistent sales figures.
(E) Except for one spike in the third quarter, they are all about the same.

7. Which region shows the greatest profit in one quarter?

(A) South
(B) West
(C) East
(D) North
(E) Since it's the same company, all profits are equal.

8. Which division has the overall lowest sales figures for one quarter?

(A) West
(B) North
(C) South
(D) East
(E) None, they all show a profit.

9. Which two divisions made just over $40,000 in one quarter?

(A) East and West in the second quarter
(B) North and South in the first quarter
(C) North and West in the third quarter
(D) South and East in the fourth quarter
(E) South and West in the third quarter

10. Which region shows the most profits for the fiscal year?

(A) East 160
(B) North
(C) West
(D) South
(E) None of the above

Questions 11–14 refer to the following passage:

Learning to communicate well is very important. _______________ communicate articulately, one must understand the meaning embedded in the language. _______________, one must understand a word's connotations (implied meanings) and denotations (literal meanings) in order to communicate clearly. Obviously, articulate communication in the classroom is essential. By being positive role models, teachers can help students develop the skills necessary to put their thoughts and feelings into words. Without <u>articulate</u> communication skills, an individual's thoughts, words, and feelings appear random, confused, and, ultimately, insignificant.

Learning theorists emphasize specific components of learning; behaviorists stress behavior in learning; humanists stress the affective in learning; cognitivists stress cognition in learning. All three of these components occur simultaneously and cannot be separated from each other in the learning process. In 1957, Festinger referred to dissonance as the lack of harmony between what one does (behavior) and what one believes (attitude). Attempts to separate the components of learning either knowingly or unknowingly create dissonances wherein language, thought, feeling, and behavior become diminished of their authenticity. _______________, ideas and concepts lose their content and vitality, and the manipulation and politics of communication assume prominence.

GO ON TO THE NEXT PAGE

11. Which of the following best describes the author's attitude toward the subject discussed?

(A) A blatant disregard
(B) A moral indignation
(C) Passive resignation
(D) An emotional response
(E) An informed concern

12. The primary purpose of the passage is to

(A) stress the importance of higher education.
(B) explain the criteria for learning theories.
(C) assure teachers that articulate communication is required in the classroom.
(D) discuss the relationship between learning and communication, and the role of both in the classroom.
(E) explain the different types of theorists and how they view the classroom differently.

13. What is the most accurate and complete definition of the term articulate as used in the passage?

(A) Talkative
(B) Enunciate clearly
(C) Little
(D) Important
(E) Lucid and well-spoken

14. Which of the grouped words or phrases, if inserted *in order* into the passage's blank lines, would address the logical sequencing of the narrative?

(A) For example, to; Consequently; Nonetheless
(B) In order to; That is; As a result
(C) Thus, to; Moreover; Consequently
(D) Surprisingly; Thus; Initially
(E) Ironically; That is; Finally

Questions 15–17 refer to the following passage:

In 1975, Sinclair observed that it had often been supposed that the main factor in learning to talk is being able to imitate. Schlesinger (1975) noted that at certain stages of learning to speak, a child tends to imitate everything an adult says to him or her, and it therefore seems reasonable to accord to such imitation an important role in the acquisition of language.

Moreover, various investigators have attempted to explain the role of imitation in language. In his discussion of the development of imitation and cognition of adult speech sounds, Nakazema (1975) stated that although the parent's talking stimulates and accelerates the infant's articulatory activity, the parent's phoneme system does not influence the child's articulatory mechanisms. Slobin and Welsh (1973) suggested that the imitation is the reconstruction of the adult's utterances and that the child does so by employing the grammatical rules that he has developed at a specific time. Schlesinger proposed that by imitating the adult, the child practices new grammatical constructions. Brown and Bellugi (1964) noted that a child's imitations resemble spontaneous speech in that they drop inflections, most function words, and sometimes other words. However, the word order of imitated sentences usually was preserved. Brown and Bellugi assumed that imitation is a function of what the child attended to or remembered. Shipley et al. (1969) suggested that repeating an adult's utterances assists the child's comprehension. Ervin (1964) and Braine (1971) found that a child's imitations do not contain more advanced structures than his or her spontaneous utterances; thus, imitation can no longer be regarded as the simple behavioristic act that earlier scholars assumed it to be.

15. The author of the passage would tend to agree with which of the following statements?

(A) Apparently, children are physiologically unable to imitate a parent's phoneme system.
(B) Apparently, children require practice with more advanced structures before they are able to imitate.
(C) Apparently, children only imitate what they already do, using whatever is in their repertoire.
(D) Apparently, the main factor in learning to talk remains being able to imitate.
(E) Apparently, children cannot respond meaningfully to a speech situation until they have reached a stage where they can make symbol-orientation responses.

16. The primary purpose of the passage is to

(A) explain how language is acquired.
(B) discuss theories of the role of imitation in language acquisition.
(C) convince parents of their role in assisting imitation in language acquisition.

GO ON TO THE NEXT PAGE

(D) describe the history of imitation in language acquisition.
(E) discuss the relationships between psychological and physiological processes in the acquisition of language.

17. An inference that parents might make from the passage is that they should

(A) be concerned when a child imitates their language.
(B) focus on developing imitation in their child's language.
(C) realize that their child's imitations may reflect several aspects of language acquisition.
(D) realize that their talking may over-stimulate their child's articulatory activity.
(E) not be concerned, as imitation is too complex for anyone to understand, while being the most sincere form of flattery.

Questions 18 and 19 refer to the following passage:

A major problem with reading/language arts instruction is that practice assignments from workbooks often provide short, segmented activities that do not really resemble the true act of reading. Perhaps more than any computer application, word processing is capable of addressing these issues.

18. The author suggests that a major benefit of computers in reading/language arts instruction is

(A) that the reading act may be more closely resembled.
(B) that short, segmented assignments will be eliminated.
(C) that the issues in reading/language arts instruction will be addressed.
(D) that computer application will be limited to word processing functions.
(E) that reading practice will be eliminated.

19. The way in which a word processing program is capable of resembling the "true act of reading" is

(A) clearly detailed.
(B) highly desirable to educators.
(C) unstated.
(D) suggested as curriculum.
(E) more accessible as computers are less expensive.

Questions 20–22 refer to the following passage:

In view of the current emphasis on literature-based reading instruction, a greater understanding by teachers of variance in cultural, language, and story components should assist in narrowing the gap between reader and text and improve reading comprehension. Classroom teachers should begin with students' meanings and intentions about stories before moving students to the commonalities of story meaning based on common background and culture. With teacher guidance, students should develop a fuller understanding of how complex narratives are when they are generating stories as well as when they are reading stories.

20. Who is the intended audience for the passage?

(A) Parents with young children just entering school
(B) English teachers using literature-based curriculum
(C) Administrators who develop school curriculum
(D) Teachers with multicultural classroom populations
(E) Students of language and literature

21. Where does the passage suggest that meaning begins?

(A) In culture, language, and story components
(B) In comprehension
(C) In students' stories
(D) In the teacher's mind
(E) In students and narratives

22. What is meant by the phrase "variance in culture"?

(A) Different types of stories
(B) Different types of writing techniques
(C) Difference in heritage
(D) Difference in school locations
(E) Difference in educational levels

GO ON TO THE NEXT PAGE

Questions 23–25 refer to the following passage:

To define Jonathan Edwards as a representative of the Colonial period in American Literature (1607–1765) requires a brief definition of that era's key ideologies. In the midst of a continuing conflict between advancing scientific frontiers and diversifying religious exegetical interpretations came advances in technology, industrialization, and colonial expansion. *Reason* and *enlightenment* were the maxims of the day. For the sake of this argument, the term Colonialism will refer to a direct conquest and control of another's land, culture, heritage, government, and so on. Imperialism will denote the ideology of globalization of capitalist productions. Romanticism, with reference to both these issues, will suggest a form of diluted or tranquilized representation, which thereby makes the horrific realities of these colonial practices gentler to endure, both for the oppressor as well as the oppressed.

23. What does the author mean by Romanticism?

(A) He is in love with his subject matter.
(B) It is a form of stylized representation.
(C) It is a form of make-believe or sentimental drivel.
(D) It is a literary period famous for poetry.
(E) It is a time when people were free to express their feelings.

24. The main idea of the passage is

(A) to introduce Jonathan Edwards.
(B) to present the turmoil of the Colonial period.
(C) to define terminology and philosophy.
(D) to comment on the evils of colonial practices.
(E) to endorse colonial expansion.

25. Which of the following is the most complete and accurate definition of the term Colonialism as used in the passage?

(A) A settlement, homestead, or community in the wilderness
(B) A pioneer
(C) Migrating from one place to another
(D) Acquisition and occupation of another's territory, culture, ancestry, etc.
(E) Pilgrim settlements in the New World

Questions 26–29 refer to the following passage:

5:10 25min.

1:07

This theme has been traced through the following significant occurrences in education: Benjamin Franklin's advocacy in 1749 for a more useful type of education; Horace Mann's zealous proposals in the 1830s espousing the tax-supported public school; John Dewey's early twentieth-century attack on traditional schools for not developing the child effectively for his or her role in society; the post-Sputnik pressure for academic rigor; the prolific criticism and accountability pressures of the 1970s; and the ensuing disillusionment and continued criticism of schools through the turn of the millennium. Indeed, the waves of criticism about American education have reflected currents of social dissatisfaction for any given period of this country's history.

As dynamics for change in the social order result in demands for change in the American educational system, so, in turn, insistence has developed for revision of teacher education (witness the more recent Holmes report [1986]). Historically, the education of American teachers has reflected evolving attitudes about public education. With slight modification, the teacher education pattern established following the demise of the normal school during the early 1900s has persisted in most teacher preparation programs. The pattern has been one requiring certain academic and professional (educational) courses, often resulting in teachers prone to teach as they had been taught.

26. The author of this passage would probably agree with which of the following statements?

(A) Teacher education courses tend to have no real value.
(B) Social pressures should cause change in the American school system.
(C) Teacher education programs have changed greatly since normal schools were eliminated.
(D) Critics of American education have strong lobbies and political interests.
(E) Teachers' teaching methods tend to reflect what they have learned in their academic and professional courses.

GO ON TO THE NEXT PAGE

27. Which sentence, when inserted into the blank line, would best present the main idea of the passage?

(A) Seldom has the American school system not been the target of demands for change to meet the social priorities of our times.
(B) Times have been tough lately for the nation's schools.
(C) Teachers' unions have expressed growing concern over the widespread use of so-called high-stakes testing.
(D) Teaching is not the easiest profession.
(E) America's public schools are under siege.

28. One possible sequence of significant occurrences in education noted in the passage is

(A) Mann's tax-supported public schools, post-Sputnik pressures for academic rigor, and the Holmes report.
(B) Franklin's more useful type of education, Dewey's educating children for their role in society, and Mann's tax-supported public schools.
(C) Mann's tax-supported public schools, the Holmes report, and post-Sputnik pressures for academic rigor.
(D) Franklin's more useful type of education, the Holmes report, and accountability pressures of the 1970s.
(E) Mann's tax-supported public schools, accountability pressures of the 1970s, and the post-Sputnik pressures for academic rigor.

29. Which of the following statements implies dissatisfaction with the preparation teachers receive in the United States?

(A) Demands for change in the educational system lead to change in the teacher education programs.
(B) Teacher education requires certain academic and professional education courses.
(C) The education of American teachers reflects the evolving attitudes about public education.
(D) Teachers, like pilots, need renewal training every four years.
(E) Teacher education has changed very little since the days of Benjamin Franklin, while teachers tend to teach as they were taught.

Questions 30–33 refer to the following passage:

HAWK ON A FRESHLY PLOWED FIELD

My lord of the Field, Proudly perched on the sod,
You eye with disdain
And mutter with wings
As steadily each furrow I tractor-plod.
"Intruder!" you glare, firmly standing your ground,
Proclaim this fief yours
By Nature so willed—
Yet bound to the air on my very next round.
You hover and soar, skimming close by the earth,
Distract me from work
To brood there with you
Of changes that Man wrought you land—for his worth.
In medieval days, lords were god over all:
Their word was law.
Yet here is this hawk
A ruler displaced—Man and Season forestall.
My Lord of the Field, from sight you have flown
For purpose untold,
When brave, you return
And perch once again, still liege-lord—but Alone.

Jacqueline K. Hultquist (1952)

30. Which of the following definitions is the most complete and accurate in defining the term liege-lord as used in the passage?

(A) Landlord
(B) King
(C) Proprietor
(D) Hawk
(E) Entertainer

31. What seems to be the author's disposition toward the hawk?

(A) Whimsical
(B) Imaginary
(C) Pensive
(D) Contemptible
(E) Apprehensive

GO ON TO THE NEXT PAGE

32. How does the hawk observe, according to the narrator?

(A) Contentedly
(B) Admiringly
(C) Contemptuously
(D) Adoringly
(E) Complacently

33. Which is the most complete and accurate definition of the term medieval as it is used in the passage?

(A) Archaic
(B) Feudal
(C) Heroic
(D) Antebellum
(E) Olden

Questions 34–37 refer to the following passage:

Reduced to its simplest form, a political system is really no more than a device enabling groups of people to live together in a more or less orderly society. As they have developed, political systems generally have fallen into the broad categories of those which do not offer direct subject participation in the decision-making process, and those which allow citizen participation—in form, if not in actual effectiveness.

Let us consider, however, the type of political system that is classified as the modern democracy in a complex society. Such a democracy is defined by Lipset (1963) as "a political system which supplies regular constitutional opportunities for changing the governing officials, and a social mechanism which permits the largest possible part of the population to influence major decisions by choosing among alternative contenders for political office."

Proceeding from another concept (that of Easton and Dennis), a political system is one of inputs, conversion, and outputs by which the wants of a society are transformed into binding decisions. Easton and Dennis (1967) observed: "To sustain a conversion process of this sort, a society must provide a relatively stable context of political interaction, as a set of general rules of participating in all parts of the political process." As a rule, this interaction evolves around the settling of differences (satisfying wants or demands) involving the elements of a "political regime," which consists of minimal general goal constraints, norms governing behavior, and structures of authority for the input-output function.

In order to persist, a political system would seem to need minimal support for the political regime. To insure the maintenance of such a support is the function of political socialization, a process varying according to political systems but toward the end of indoctrinating the members to the respective political system. "To the extent that the maturing members absorb and become attached to the overarching goals of the system and its basic norms and come to approve its structure of authority as legitimate, we can say that they are learning to contribute support to the regime." The desired political norm (an expectation about the way people will behave) is that referred to as a political efficacy—a feeling that one's action can have an impact on government.

Adapted from Easton, B. and J. Dennis, "The Child's Acquisition of Regime Norms: Political Efficacy," *American Political Science Review*, March 1967.

34. According to the passage, political efficacy is

(A) most likely to be found where citizen participation is encouraged.
(B) most likely to be found where little direct citizen participation is offered.
(C) in an expanding concept of political efficiency.
(D) in a diminishing concept of political efficiency.
(E) in a figurehead of political system.

35. Political socialization is a process that

(A) occurs only in democracies.
(B) occurs only in totalitarian regimes.
(C) occurs in any type of political system.
(D) occurs less frequently in recent years.
(E) occurs when members reject the goals of the system.

36. As used in the passage, which of the following is the most complete and accurate definition of the term conversion?

(A) Transformation
(B) Changeover
(C) Growth
(D) Resolution
(E) Passing

GO ON TO THE NEXT PAGE

37. The major distinction between the concepts of Easton and Dennis as opposed to the concepts of Lipset is

(A) that the concepts of Easton and Dennis are based on the wants of a society, whereas Lipset's concepts are based on change of governing officials.
(B) that Easton and Dennis' concepts are based on arbitrary decisions, whereas Lipset's concepts are based on influencing major decisions.
(C) that Easton and Dennis' concepts must have a set of general rules, whereas Lipset's concepts provide for irregular constitutional opportunities.
(D) that Easton and Dennis' concepts have no inputs, conversion, and outputs, whereas Lipset's concepts allow for no regular constitutional opportunities.
(E) that Easton and Dennis' concepts evolve around the settling of differences, whereas Lipset's concepts permit the largest conflict possible.

Questions 38–41 refer to the following passage:

Because Western European historicism constructs a worldview in its own imaginary image, marginal authors such as María Amparo Ruiz de Burton must reclaim or redefine a non-Eurocentric voice in order not only to be heard, but to reenter mainstream society by reestablishing an ethnic identity. One of the ways of recognizing the influence of Western imperialism is by "acknowledging how effectively it naturalizes its own [imperially constructed] history, how it claims precedence for its own culture by identifying culture with nature," and thus assimilates or eradicates indigenous narrative voice (Deane, 357). One such example would be the attempted eradication of the Native American Indian from the social consciousness by speaking of their culture in the past tense, thus implying an extinction process of natural selection. The continuity of this same narrative ideology proposed by Deane (1995) is reflected and reconstituted in Homi Bhabha's *DissemiNation* (1990) assertion that, "turning Territory into Tradition provides marginal voices [or minority discourse] a place from which to speak" (Bhabha, 300).

38. What does Western European historicism constructs a worldview in its own imaginary image mean?

(A) Western European historicism is literal and should be understood as such.
(B) Western European historicism is precise and careful to record facts just as they happened.
(C) Western European historicism is malleable and periodically adjusted to fit the socioeconomic climate.
(D) Western European historicism is erroneous and the rest of the world is correct.
(E) Western European historicism is accurate and the rest of the world is miscalculated.

39. What does the author mean by a non-Eurocentric voice?

(A) Someone from Europe who cannot speak English
(B) Someone who is born in Europe and moves to America
(C) Someone from America who moves to Europe
(D) Someone from America who cannot speak European
(E) Someone whose worldview is not filtered through the lens of Western European cultural touchstones

40. What does the author mean by the phrase eradicates indigenous narrative voice?

(A) The obliteration of traditional native beliefs
(B) People who cannot speak for themselves
(C) People who live in a certain region speak their own language
(D) The creation of native narrative stories
(E) The removal of one character from a narrative and the replacement of another

41. Which of the following best describes the author's attitude toward the subject discussed?

(A) Morally outraged
(B) Flippant and sarcastic
(C) Frustrated and angry
(D) Informed and involved
(E) Righteously angry and austere

GO ON TO THE NEXT PAGE

Questions 42–44 refer to the following passage:

Beginning readers, and those who are experiencing difficulty with reading, benefit from assisted reading. During assisted reading, the teacher orally reads a passage with a student or students. The teacher fades in and out of the reading act. For example, the teacher lets his or her voice drop to a whisper when students are reading on their own at an acceptable rate and lets his/her voice rise to say the words clearly when the students are having difficulty.

Assisted reading will help students who are threatened by print read word-by-word, or rely on grapho-phonemic cues. These students are stuck on individual language units, which can be as small as a single letter or as large as a phrase or a sentence. As Frank Smith (1977) and other reading educators have noted, speeding up reading, not slowing it down, helps the reader make sense of a passage. This strategy allows students to concentrate on meaning, as the short-term memory is not overloaded by focusing on small language units. As the name implies, assisted reading lets the reader move along without being responsible for every language unit; the pressure is taken off the student. Consequently, when the reading act is sped up, it sounds more like language, and students can begin to integrate the cueing system of semantics and syntax along with grapho-phonemics.

42. As a strategy, assisted reading is best for

(A) beginning readers who are relying on grapho-phonemic cues.
(B) learning disabled readers who are experiencing neurological deficits.
(C) beginning readers who are relying on phono-graphic cues.
(D) remedial readers who are experiencing difficulty with silent reading.
(E) beginning readers who are experiencing difficulties with silent reading.

43. Language units as presented in the passage refer to

(A) individual letters, syllables, or phrases.
(B) individual letters, syllables, or sentences.
(C) individual letters, phrases, or paragraphs.
(D) individual letters, phrases, or sentences.
(E) individual letters, sentences, or paragraphs.

44. According to the passage, to make sense of a passage a reader must

(A) focus on small language units.
(B) overload short-term memory.
(C) slow down when reading.
(D) read word-by-word.
(E) speed up the reading act.

Questions 45–48 refer to the following passage:

The information about the comparison of the technology (duplex versus one-way video and two-way audio) and the comparison of site classes versus regular classes tends to indicate that although there was not much of an apparent difference between classes and technology, student participation and student involvement were viewed as important components in any teaching/learning setting. For the future, perhaps revisiting what learning is might be helpful so that this component of distance learning can be more adequately addressed. The question remains whether or not student participation can be equated with learning. Participation per se does not demonstrate learning. A more <u>rigorous</u> instrument which assesses and determines learning may need to be addressed with future distance learning studies.

45. Student participation and student involvement are viewed as

(A) consequential ingredients in any teaching/learning environment.
(B) inconsequential ingredients in any teaching/learning environment.
(C) only appropriate with regards to distance learning.
(D) an unrelated component of the distance learning process.
(E) not demonstrative of distance learning.

46. Which of the following is the most complete and accurate definition of the term <u>rigorous</u> as used in the passage?

(A) Harsh
(B) Austere
(C) Uncompromising

GO ON TO THE NEXT PAGE

(D) Dogmatic
(E) Precise

47. The author of the passage would tend to endorse which of the following statements?

(A) Learning consists of more than student participation.
(B) Duplex technology is better than one-way video and two-way audio.
(C) Student participation and student involvement is not important to learning.
(D) An instrument that assesses and demonstrates learning is not currently available.
(E) A review of learning is not important, as the topic has been thoroughly researched.

48. The primary purpose of the passage is to

(A) delineate the issues in distance learning.
(B) note student participation in distance learning and question this role in learning.
(C) detail the comparisons of site classes versus regular classes.
(D) share information about duplex technology versus one-way video and two-way audio.
(E) request an assessment instrument that includes a learning component.

Questions 49 and 50 refer to the following passage:

Reading the text *Robinson Crusoe* formalistically however, looking specifically at the animal symbols and what they represent, allows one to see that the book is fraught with a diversified menagerie of animal representations ranging from the sublime Lyon to the perfunctory alley cat, from the domestic dog to the parroting parrot. Each creature, in its own way, serves as a metaphor for imperialistic progressions and absolutist ideologies. That is, *imperialistic,* pertaining to the capital interests surrounding Crusoe's island commodities. The connotation of *absolutism* refers to the pervasive eighteenth-century tensions generated by the theological doctrine that God works absolutely with respect to one's salvation. Additionally, *absolutism* must be seen in conjunction with the social concerns of an expanding colonial government as absolute power, that is, a despotic regime.

49. Which of the following is the most complete and accurate definition of the term metaphor as it is used in the passage?

(A) A figure of speech in which a word or phrase is casually mentioned or alluded to
(B) A figure of speech containing an implied comparison in which a word or phrase ordinarily used for one thing is applied to another
(C) A rhetorical device of repeating a word or phrase at the beginning of successive clauses or sentences
(D) A break or pause in a line of verse
(E) A short, simple story, usually of an occurrence of a familiar kind, from which a moral or religious lesson may be drawn

50. The author of the passage would tend to agree with which of the following statements?

(A) *Robinson Crusoe* is a child's bedtime story about a lonely man on a deserted island who makes friends with the animals.
(B) *Robinson Crusoe* is a complex, yet archaic, story that promotes animal abuse.
(C) *Robinson Crusoe* is a complex story composed of multilevel social and political commentaries.
(D) *Robinson Crusoe* is an outdated, confusing, and hard-to-follow jumble of religious and social commentary.
(E) Robinson Crusoe is not alone on the island. He has animal and human companions to keep him company and remind him of home.

DIAGNOSTIC TEST

ANSWER KEY

Section I: Reading Skills

1. (A)
2. (D)
3. (D)
4. (B)
5. (A)
6. (A)
7. (C)
8. (C)
9. (C)
10. (B)
11. (E)
12. (D)
13. (E)
14. (B)
15. (C)
16. (B)
17. (C)
18. (A)
19. (C)
20. (B)
21. (E)
22. (C)
23. (B)
24. (C)
25. (D)
26. (E)
27. (A)
28. (A)
29. (E)
30. (B)
31. (C)
32. (C)
33. (B)
34. (A)
35. (C)
36. (A)
37. (A)
38. (C)
39. (E)
40. (A)
41. (D)
42. (A)
43. (D)
44. (E)
45. (A)
46. (E)
47. (A)
48. (B)
49. (B)
50. (C)

Detailed Explanations of Answers

DIAGNOSTIC TEST

SECTION 1: Reading Skills

1. **A**

Choices (B), (D), and (E) present minor problems in spa maintenance, whereas choice (C) cannot be prevented. As both temperature and chemicals control bacteria and virus, it becomes a possible source of health problems if ignored.

2. **D**

Choice (A) is above the recommended operating temperature, while (B) is the proper bromine level, (C) the proper pH level, and (E) the chlorine level.

3. **D**

Choices (A), (B), and (C) represent an inference that goes beyond the scope of the passage and would indicate biases of the reader. Although the passage explains spa maintenance, choice (E), the information is not adequate to serve as a detailed guide.

4. **B**

While choice (A), Sentence 3, makes an oblique reference to the necessity for adding disinfectant, only choice (B), Sentence 9, discusses the "fertile environment for the growth of bacteria and virus."

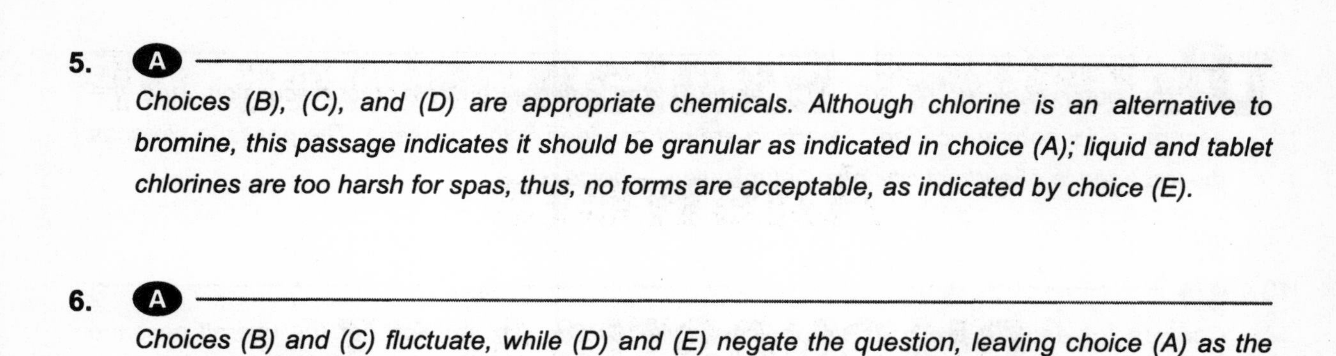

5. **A**

Choices (B), (C), and (D) are appropriate chemicals. Although chlorine is an alternative to bromine, this passage indicates it should be granular as indicated in choice (A); liquid and tablet chlorines are too harsh for spas, thus, no forms are acceptable, as indicated by choice (E).

6. **A**

Choices (B) and (C) fluctuate, while (D) and (E) negate the question, leaving choice (A) as the only viable answer.

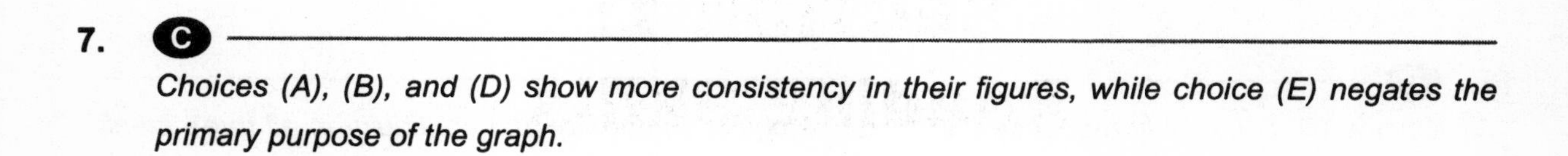

7. **C**

Choices (A), (B), and (D) show more consistency in their figures, while choice (E) negates the primary purpose of the graph.

8. **C**

Choices (B), (D), and (A) all show higher profits; while choice (E) is truthful, it does not directly answer the question.

9. **C**

Choices (A), (B), (D), and (E) present erroneous information, so choice (C) is the only relevant answer.

10. **B**

Choices (A), (C), and (D) have overall yearly profits at a lower cumulative total, while (E) does not address the question.

11. **E**

Choices (A), (B), (C), and (D) all connote extreme or inappropriate attitudes not expressed in the passage. The author presents an informed concern—choice (E).

12. (D)

For the other choices, (A), (B), (C), and (E), the criteria, the role, the discussion, and the assurance for communication or learning are not provided in the passage. The passage stresses the importance of authenticity in communication—choice (D).

13. (E)

Choices (A) and (B) are possible choices while (C) and (D) are not, but the overall passage suggests that communication needs to be clear and well spoken so that student responses may become more significant and authentic—choice (E).

14. (B)

Choice (B) is the only response that ensures logical conformity and continuity in all three blank lines in the passage. Any other of the offered choices would interrupt or distort the passage's sequence or logical thread.

15. (C)

Choices (A), (B), and (E) are not supported by the passage. Choice (D) represents an incorrect conclusion. Choice (C) is supported by the various investigators' explanations.

16. (B)

As stated explicitly in the passage, the various investigators have attempted to explain the role of imitation in language—choice (B). The other choices go beyond the scope of the passage.

17. (C)

The investigators studied different aspects of language while attempting to explain the role of imitation in language, thus, choice (C) is correct. The other choices go beyond the scope of the passage.

18. (A)

The passage explicitly states that computers are capable of addressing the issues of practice and the true act of reading, choice (A). The other choices represent inferences that are not supported by the passage.

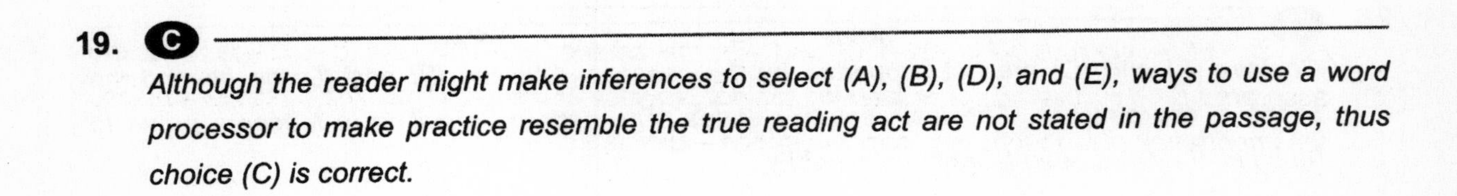

19. **C**

Although the reader might make inferences to select (A), (B), (D), and (E), ways to use a word processor to make practice resemble the true reading act are not stated in the passage, thus choice (C) is correct.

20. **B**

Although audiences in choices (A), (C), (D), and (E) may benefit from the information provided in the passage, the passage explicitly states that a greater understanding of the information in the passage should assist teachers—choice (B).

21. **E**

Although meaning is found in the components of each choice, the passage states that we should begin with students' meanings before moving to the commonalities of story meaning—choice (E).

22. **C**

Choices (A), (B), (D), and (E) might suggest variants or variations, but not of culture.

23. **B**

Romanticism is a form of stylized representation that has its own unique properties and distinctive traits. (A), (C), (D), and (E) do not address these literary properties, thus choice (B) is correct.

24. **C**

While choices (A), (B), (D), and (E) may be truisms, the most comprehensive purpose of the passage is to establish the clear definition of terms and philosophy.

25. **D**

Choices (A), (B), (C), and (E) pertain to colonialism in one form or another, but (D) is reiterated from the passage.

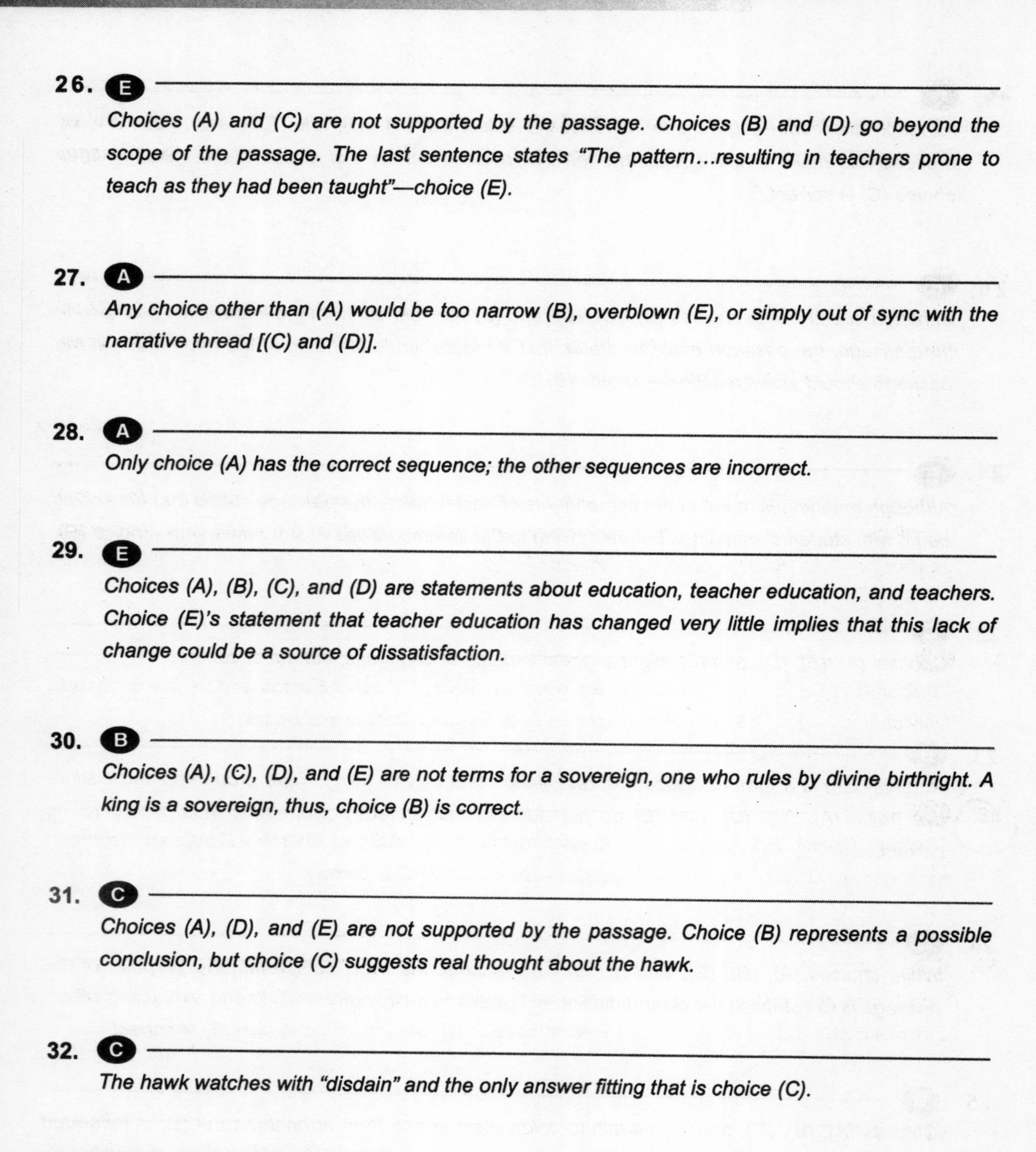

26. **E**

Choices (A) and (C) are not supported by the passage. Choices (B) and (D) go beyond the scope of the passage. The last sentence states "The pattern…resulting in teachers prone to teach as they had been taught"—choice (E).

27. **A**

Any choice other than (A) would be too narrow (B), overblown (E), or simply out of sync with the narrative thread [(C) and (D)].

28. **A**

Only choice (A) has the correct sequence; the other sequences are incorrect.

29. **E**

Choices (A), (B), (C), and (D) are statements about education, teacher education, and teachers. Choice (E)'s statement that teacher education has changed very little implies that this lack of change could be a source of dissatisfaction.

30. **B**

Choices (A), (C), (D), and (E) are not terms for a sovereign, one who rules by divine birthright. A king is a sovereign, thus, choice (B) is correct.

31. **C**

Choices (A), (D), and (E) are not supported by the passage. Choice (B) represents a possible conclusion, but choice (C) suggests real thought about the hawk.

32. **C**

The hawk watches with "disdain" and the only answer fitting that is choice (C).

33. **B**

Choices (A), (C), (D), and (E) are incorrect because of their definitions. Feudal most clearly denotes an association to the Middle Ages.

34. **A**

The passage explicitly states that political efficacy is a feeling that one's actions can have an impact on government—choice (A). Choices (C), (D), and (E) are not supported by the passage. Choice (B) is incorrect.

35. **C**

Choices (A), (B), (D), and (E) are not supported by the passage. The passage states "...political socialization, a process varying according to political systems but toward the end of indoctrinating the members to the respective political system"—choice (C).

36. **A**

Although choices (B), (C), (D), and (E) are possible definitions, the passage explicitly states that "a political system is one of inputs, conversion, and outputs by which the wants of a society are transformed into binding decisions"—choice (A).

37. **A**

Choices (B), (C), (D), and (E) contain an incorrect concept of either Easton and Dennis or Lipset. Only choice (A) has the correct concepts for both Easton / Dennis and Lipset.

38. **C**

Choices (A), (B), (D), and (E) do not encompass the flexibility of Western European historical representations that the passage suggests—thus choice (C) is correct.

39. **E**

Non-Eurocentric voice refers to someone who is not limited to interpreting and evaluating other cultures strictly based on his or her Western European descent—thus, choice (E) is correct.

40. **A**

Eradication of narrative voice is synonymous with the premeditated obliteration of traditional beliefs, oral narratives, and ethnic heritage, thereby making non-Eurocentric voices seem more foreign or undesirable, hence, choice (A) is correct.

41. (D)

The author takes an informed and involved approach to the subject without persuasion or emotional influence, thus, choice (D) is correct.

42. (A)

Choices (D) and (E) are incorrect, as the strategy is for oral reading, not silent reading. Choices (B) and (C) are not supported by the passage—thus, choice (A) is correct.

43. (D)

Choices (A), (B), (C), and (E) include syllable and paragraph elements, which are not supported by the passage. The passage states "...individual language units, which can be as small as a single letter or as large as a phrase or sentence."

44. (E)

Choices (A), (B), (C), and (D) are not supported by the passage. The passage states that "speeding up reading, not slowing it down, helps the reader make sense of a passage."

45. (A)

While choice (E) does reflect the notion that student participation per se does not reflect learning, the passage does tell us that learning remains a consequential ingredient in any teaching/ learning environment—thus, choice (A) is correct.

46. (E)

Choices (A), (B), (C), and (D) are inappropriate for defining an instrument that assesses and demonstrates learning.

47. (A)

Choices (B), (C), (D), and (E) are not supported by the passage.

48. (B)

While choices (A), (C), (D), and (E) are given passing mention in the passage, it focuses on student participation and learning.

49. **B**

Choice (B) is the definition of a metaphor, while choice (A) refers to an allusion, (C) is the definition of an anaphora, (D) is the definition of a caesura, and (E) is the definition of a parable.

50. **C**

Choices (A), (B), (D), and (E) discount the significance of the Crusoe story, and suggest a commentary of the story taken out of historical and social context. Choice (C) is the appropriate answer.

DIRECTIONS: Each of the questions or incomplete statements below is followed by five suggested answers or completions. Select the one that is best in each case.

1. 406.725 is rounded off to the nearest tenth. Find the number.

(A) 406.3
(B) 406.5
(C) 406.7
(D) 406.8
(E) 407.0

2. The mean IQ score for 1,500 students is 100, with a standard deviation of 15. Assuming normal curve distribution, how many students have an IQ between 85 and 115? Refer to the figure shown below.

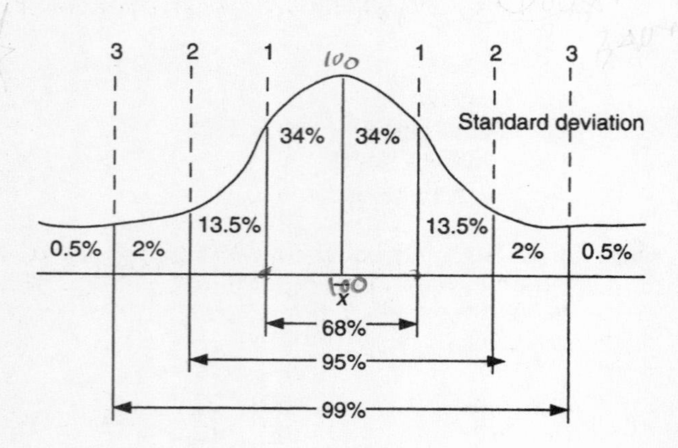

(A) 510
(B) 750
(C) 1,020
(D) 1,275
(E) 1,425

3. The sum of 12 and twice a number is 24. Find the number.

(A) 6
(B) 8
(C) 10
(D) 11
(E) 12

4. Twice the sum of 10 and a number is 28. Find the number.

(A) 4
(B) 8
(C) 12
(D) 14
(E) 24

5. Two college roommates spent $2,000 for their total monthly expenses. The circle graph below indicates a record of their expenses.

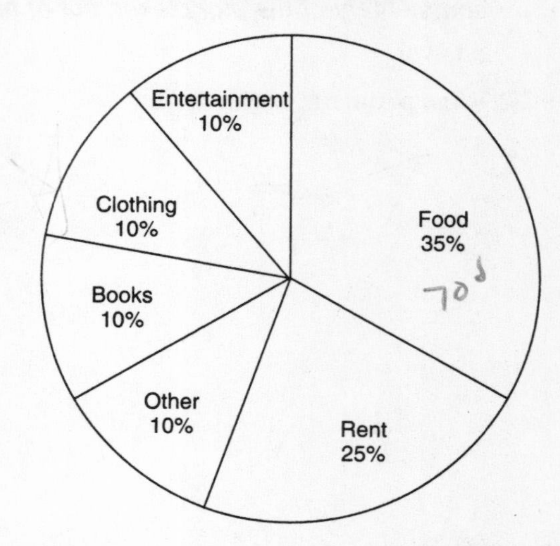

Based on the above information, which of the following statements is accurate?

(A) The roommates spent $700 on food alone.
(B) The roommates spent $550 on rent alone.
(C) The roommates spent $300 on entertainment alone.
(D) The roommates spent $300 on clothing alone.
(E) The roommates spent $300 on books alone.

6. You can buy a telephone for $24. If you are charged $3 per month for renting a telephone from the telephone company, how long will it take you to recover the cost of the phone if you buy one?

(A) 6 months
(B) 7 months
(C) 8 months
(D) 9 months
(E) 10 months

GO ON TO THE NEXT PAGE

7. What is the area of this triangle in square units?

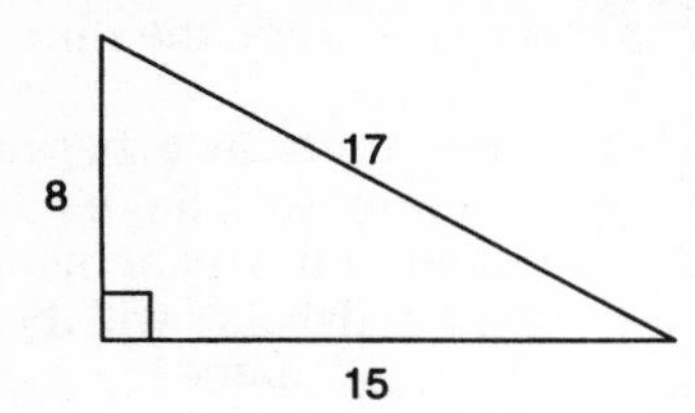

(A) 40
(B) 60
(C) 68
(D) 90
(E) 120

8. What is the perimeter of this figure?

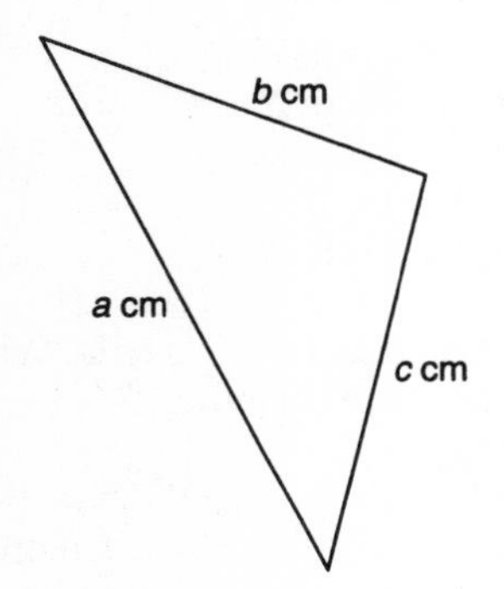

(A) abc cm
(B) abc cm^2
(C) $(a + b + c)$ cm
(D) $(a + b + c)$ cm^2
(E) abc cm^3

9. What is the perimeter of the given triangle?

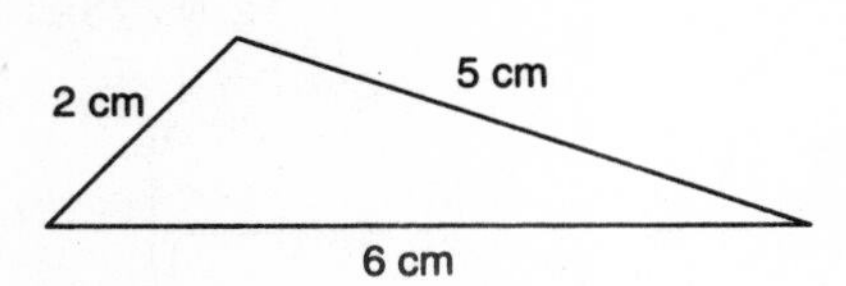

(A) 6 cm
(B) 11 cm
(C) 12 cm
(D) 13 cm
(E) 15 cm

10. Assuming that the quadrilateral in the following figure is a parallelogram, what would be its area?

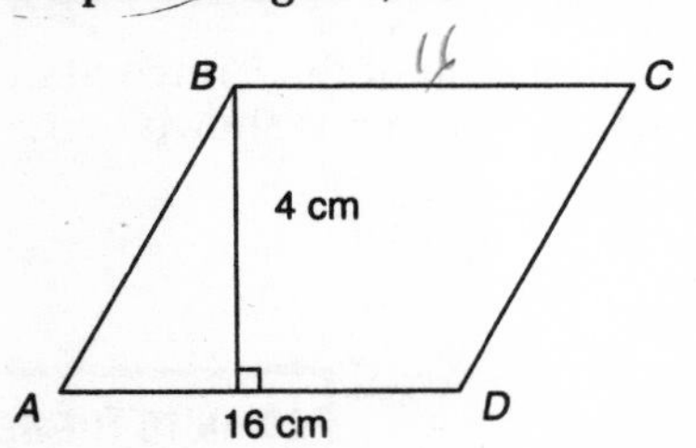

(A) 32 cm
(B) 40 cm
(C) 40 cm^2
(D) 64 cm
(E) 64 cm^2

11. Refer to the figure below to determine which of the following statements is correct.

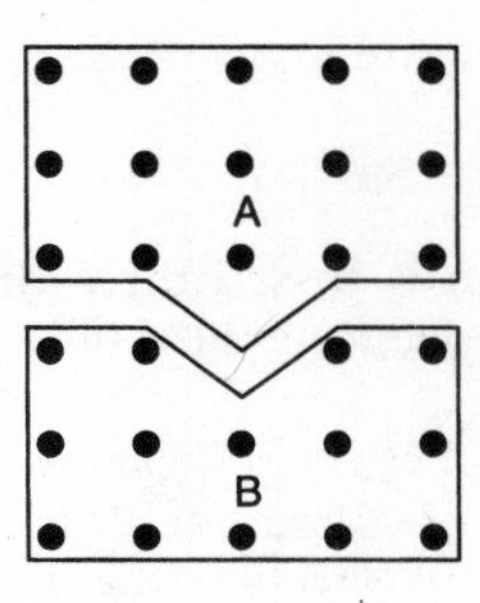

I. Figures A and B have the same area.
II. Figures A and B have the same perimeter.

(A) Only I
(B) Only II
(C) Both I and II
(D) Neither I nor II
(E) Can't be determined

12. If 1 kilogram is equivalent to 2.2 pounds, what is the total weight in kilograms of 3 packages which weigh 5 pounds, 7 pounds, and 10 pounds, respectively?

(A) 3.3
(B) 6.7
(C) 10
(D) 22
(E) 48.4

13. In a math class of 30 students, there are 18 boys and 12 girls. On a particular exam, 50% of the boys and 75% of the girls earned passing grades. What percent of the entire class earned passing grades?

(A) 50
(B) 55
(C) 60
(D) 65
(E) 70

GO ON TO THE NEXT PAGE

14. If an ordinary die is tossed twice, what is the probability that the sum is 10?

(A) $\frac{1}{36}$ (D) $\frac{1}{12}$

(B) $\frac{1}{20}$ (E) $\frac{1}{10}$

(C) $\frac{1}{18}$

15. If a fair coin is tossed three times, what is the probability of getting three tails?

(A) $\frac{1}{2}$ (D) $\frac{1}{6}$

(B) $\frac{1}{3}$ (E) $\frac{1}{8}$

(C) $\frac{1}{4}$

16. This year, Central High School has 1,000 students. If the enrollment next year is 650, what will be the percent decrease?

(A) 35 (D) 55
(B) 40 (E) 65
(C) 50

17. Find the next three terms in this sequence: 1, 4, 9, 16, . . .

(A) 19, 24, 31 (D) 25, 36, 49
(B) 20, 25, 31 (E) 25, 34, 43
(C) 21, 28, 36

18. Assume that one pig eats 4 pounds of food each week. There are 52 weeks in a year. How much food do 10 pigs eat in a week?

(A) 40 lb. (D) 20 lb.
(B) 520 lb. (E) 60 lb.
(C) 208 lb.

19. Suppose that a pair of pants and a shirt cost $65 and the pants cost $25 more than the shirt. What did they each cost?

(A) The pants cost $35 and the shirt costs $30.
(B) The pants cost $40 and the shirt costs $25.
(C) The pants cost $43 and the shirt costs $22.
(D) The pants cost $45 and the shirt costs $20.
(E) The pants cost $50 and the shirt costs $15.

20. There are five members in a basketball team. Suppose each member shakes hands with every other member of the team before the game starts. How many handshakes will there be in all?

(A) 6 (D) 10
(B) 8 (E) 12
(C) 9

21. If all of *X* is in *Y*, and none of *Z* is in *Y*, then which of the following is true?

(A) Some of *X* is in *Z*.
(B) None of *Z* is in *X*.
(C) Some of *Y* is in *Z*.
(D) All of *Y* is in *X*.
(E) Some of *Z* is in *X*.

22. Suppose *P* is false, but *Q* is true. Which one of the following is a true statement?

(A) *P* and *Q* (D) Not *P*
(B) If *Q*, then *P* (E) *P* if and only if *Q*
(C) *P* or *Q*

Use the following chart for Questions 23–25.

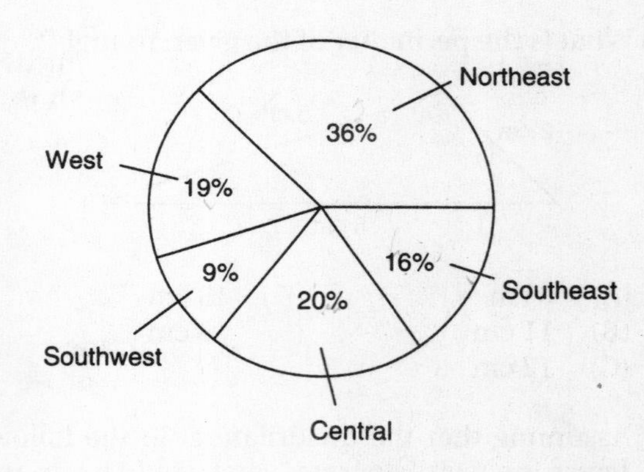

Assume the population of the United States is 250 million, split into percentages as shown in the pie chart.

GO ON TO THE NEXT PAGE

23. In millions, how many people live in the combined regions of Northeast, Southeast, and Central?

(A) 100
(B) 120
(C) 150
(D) 180
(E) 200

24. In millions, how many more people live in the West region than in the Southwest region?

(A) 20
(B) 25
(C) 30
(D) 35
(E) 40

25. In millions, how many people would have to move from the West to the Southeast in order for the populations to be the same in these two regions?

(A) 12.25
(B) 10
(C) 7.5
(D) 5
(E) 3.75

26. Tom bought a piece of land selling for $20,000. If he had to pay 20% of the price as a down payment, how much was the down payment?

(A) $2,500
(B) $3,000
(C) $4,000
(D) $4,500
(E) $5,000

27. A well-equipped computer sells for $3,200 to the general public. If you purchase one in the university, the price is reduced by 20%. What is the sale price of the computer?

(A) $640
(B) $2,000
(C) $2,410
(D) $2,560
(E) $3,180

28. In order for Sue to receive a final grade of C, she must have an average greater than or equal to 70%, but less than 80%, on five tests. Suppose her grades on the first four tests were 65%, 85%, 60%, and 90%. What range of grades on the fifth test would give her a C in the course?

(A) 40 up to but excluding 95
(B) 45 up to but excluding 95
(C) 47 up to but excluding 90
(D) 49 up to but excluding 98
(E) 50 up to but excluding 100

29. Mr. Smith died and left an estate to be divided among his wife, two children, and a foundation of his choosing in the ratio of 8:6:6:1. How much did his wife receive if the estate was valued at $300,000?

(A) $114,285.71
(B) $120,421.91
(C) $85,714.29
(D) $14,285.71
(E) $125,461.71

30. There were 19 hamburgers for 9 people on a picnic. How many whole hamburgers were there for each person if they were divided equally?

(A) 1
(B) 2
(C) 3
(D) 4
(E) 5

31. George has four ways to get from his house to the park. He has seven ways to get from the park to the school. How many ways can George get from his house to school by way of the park?

(A) 4
(B) 7
(C) 28
(D) 3
(E) 11

32. If it takes 1 minute per cut, how long will it take to cut a 15-foot-long piece of timber into 15 equal pieces?

(A) 5
(B) 10
(C) 14
(D) 20
(E) 15

33. Ed has six new shirts and four new pairs of pants. How many combinations of new shirts and pants does he have?

(A) 10
(B) 14
(C) 18
(D) 20
(E) 24

34. The property tax rate of the town of Grandview is $32 per $1,000 of assessed value. What is the tax if the property is assessed at $50,000?

(A) $32
(B) $1,000
(C) $1,562
(D) $1,600
(E) $2,000

GO ON TO THE NEXT PAGE

35. Ralph kept track of his work time in gardening. Refer to the broken-line graph below:

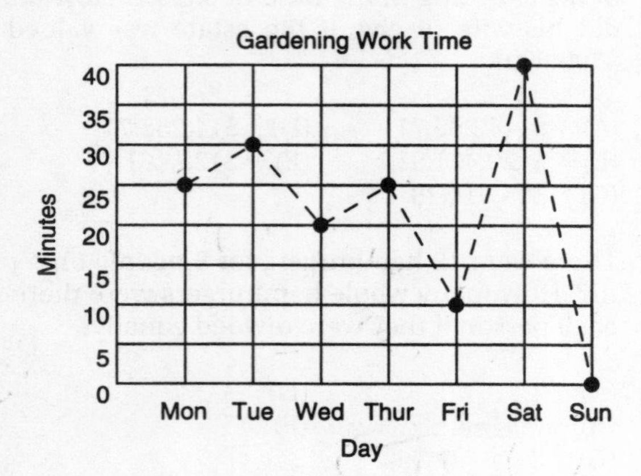

How many minutes did he average per day?

(A) 10 min.
(B) 20 min.
(C) 21:43 min.
(D) 23:05 min.
(E) 25 min.

36. Mary had been selling printed shirts in her neighborhood. She made this pictograph to show how much money she made each week.

Weekly Sales

Week	
1st	$ $ $
2nd	$ $ $ $
3rd	$ $ $ $ $ $
4th	$ $ $ $ $
5th	$ $ $
6th	$ $ $ $

Each $ stands for $12.

How many weeks were sales more than $55?

(A) 1 week
(B) 2 weeks
(C) 3 weeks
(D) 4 weeks
(E) 5 weeks

37. Find the volume of the following figure.

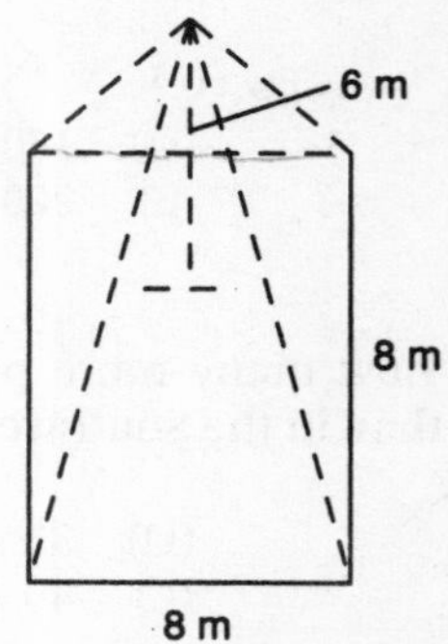

(A) 48 m^2
(B) 64 m^2
(C) 128 m^3
(D) 192 m^3
(E) 384 m^3

38. The result of Mary's spring semester grades follow. Find her grade point average for the term (A = 4, B = 3, C = 2, D = 1, F = 0).

Course	Credits	Grade
Biology	5	A
English	3	C
Math	3	A
French	3	D
P.E.	2	B

(A) 3.80
(B) 3.50
(C) 2.94
(D) 2.00
(E) 1.86

39. In a biology class at International University, the grades on the final examination were as follows:

91	81	65	81
50	70	81	93
36	90	43	87
96	81	75	81

Find the mode.

(A) 36
(B) 70
(C) 81
(D) 87
(E) 96

GO ON TO THE NEXT PAGE

40. One commonly used standard score is a z-score. A z-score gives the number of standard deviations by which the score differs from the mean, as shown in the following example.

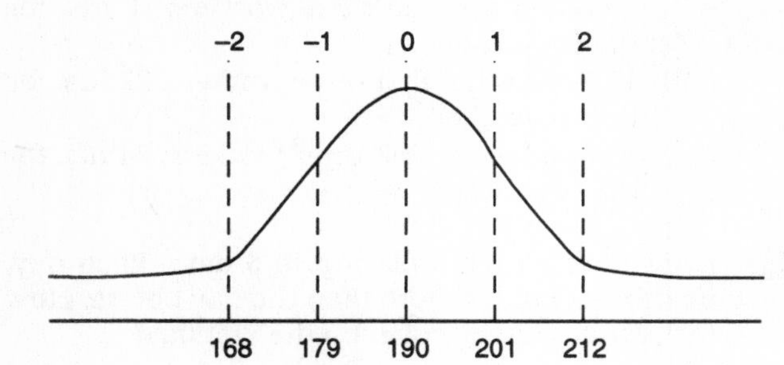

As shown above, the mean $(\bar{x})$ is 190 and the standard deviation(s) is 11. The score of 201 has a z-score of 1 and a score of 168 has a z-score of –2. Consider the mean height of a certain group of people as 190 cm with a standard deviation of 11 cm. Suppose Glenn's height has a z-score of 1.6. What is his height? $\left(\text{Note: } z = \frac{x - \bar{x}}{\text{s.d.}}\right)$

(A) 207.6 cm
(B) 190 cm
(C) 201 cm
(D) 179 cm
(E) 212 cm

41. The cost of gas for heating a house in Riverview, Florida, is $1.83 per cubic foot. What is the monthly gas bill if the customer uses 145 cubic feet?

(A) $265.35
(B) $145.00
(C) $183.00
(D) $79.23
(E) $200.00

42. From 1990 to 1991, the price of an auto rose 5%. From 1991 to 1992, the price of an auto rose 10%. What was the percent increase in the price of an auto from 1990 to 1992?

(A) 7
(B) 9
(C) 12.5
(D) 15
(E) 15.5

43. The wear-out mileage of a certain tire is normally distributed with a mean of 30,000 miles and a standard deviation of 2,500 miles, as shown below.

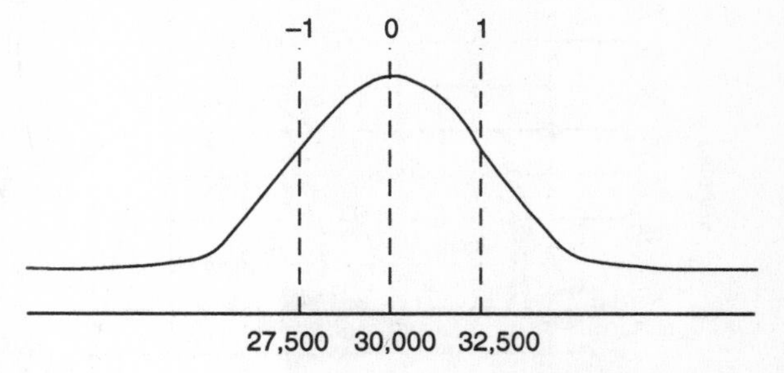

What is the percentage of tires that will last at least 30,000 miles?

(A) 40%
(B) 45%
(C) 50%
(D) 55%
(E) 60%

44.

Class Period	Start Time	End Time
First	8:00 AM	9:40 AM
Second	9:45 AM	
Third		
Fourth		

At a special high school, each day only has four periods. Assuming each period is the same length in time, and that there is a five-minute break between periods, at what time is the last period over?

(A) 2:15 PM
(B) 2:40 PM
(C) 2:55 PM
(D) 3:10 PM
(E) 3:20 PM

GO ON TO THE NEXT PAGE

45. Suppose a person 2 m tall casts a shadow 1 m long. When a tree has an 8 m shadow, how high is the tree?

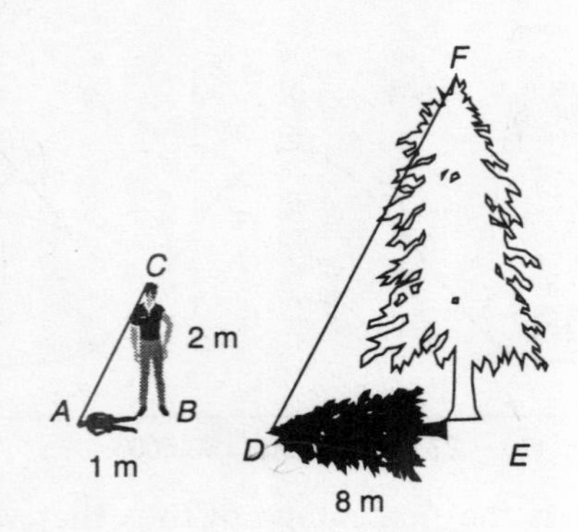

(A) 8 m (D) 16 m
(B) 10 m (E) 18 m
(C) 14 m

46. How many 12 oz. cans of orange juice would it take to give 75 people 8 oz. of orange juice?

(A) 112 cans (D) 900 cans
(B) 75 cans (E) 50 cans
(C) 600 cans

47. A car rental agency charges $139 per week plus $0.08 per mile for an average-size car. How far can you travel to the nearest mile on a maximum budget of $350?

(A) 2,637 miles (D) 1,737 miles
(B) 2,640 miles (E) 4,375 miles
(C) 2,110 miles

48. Suppose 4 people have to split 50 hours of overtime. Twice the number of hours must be assigned to one worker as to each of the other three. Find the number of hours of overtime that will be assigned to each worker.

(A) 10 hrs. for the first three workers; 20 hrs. for the 4th worker
(B) 8 hrs. for the first three workers; 16 hrs. for the 4th worker
(C) 9 hrs. for the first three workers; 18 hrs. for the 4th worker
(D) 11 hrs. for the first three workers; 22 hrs. for the 4th worker
(E) 12 hrs. for the first three workers; 24 hrs. for the 4th worker

49. Peter took a 1,500-mile trip in 5 days. Each day, he drove 30 miles more than the day before. How many miles did he cover on the first day?

(A) 375 miles (D) 240 miles
(B) 294 miles (E) 250 miles
(C) 230 miles

50. Mr. Reagan needs 75 m to enclose his rectangular property. If the length of the property is 5 m more than the width, what are the dimensions of his property? Note the figure below.

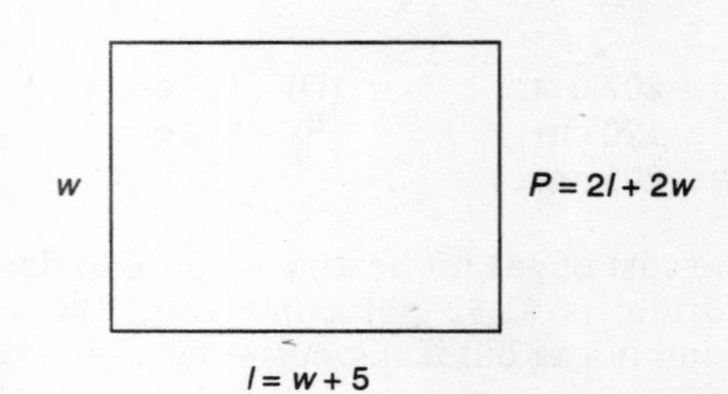

(A) w = 16.25 m; l = 21. 25 m
(B) w = 18.25 m; l = 19.25 m
(C) w = 13.00 m; l = 24.50 m
(D) w = 17.50 m; l = 20.00 m
(E) w = 35.00 m; l = 40.00 m

Diagnostic Test

ANSWER KEY

Section 2: Mathematics

1. (C)
2. (C)
3. (A)
4. (A)
5. (A)
6. (C)
7. (B)
8. (C)
9. (D)
10. (E)
11. (B)
12. (C)
13. (C)
14. (D)
15. (E)
16. (A)
17. (D)
18. (A)
19. (D)
20. (D)
21. (B)
22. (C)
23. (D)
24. (B)
25. (E)
26. (C)
27. (D)
28. (E)
29. (A)
30. (B)
31. (C)
32. (C)
33. (E)
34. (D)
35. (C)
36. (B)
37. (C)
38. (C)
39. (C)
40. (A)
41. (A)
42. (E)
43. (C)
44. (C)
45. (D)
46. (E)
47. (A)
48. (A)
49. (D)
50. (A)

Scoring the Mathematics Section

Your score on this section is based on the total number of questions answered correctly. You will pass the Mathematics section if you answer at least 70% of the test items correctly. To get an idea of how you performed on the section, determine the number of questions you answered correctly out of 50. Generally, if you have answered more than 35 of the items correctly, you will be adequately prepared.

Detailed Explanations of Answers

DIAGNOSTIC TEST

SECTION 2: Mathematics

1. **C**

7 is in the tenth's place. Since the next digit (2) is below 5, drop this digit and retain the 7. The answer, therefore, is 406.7.

2. **C**

The mean IQ score of 100 is given. One standard deviation above the mean is 34% of the cases, with an IQ score up to 115. One standard deviation below the mean is another 34% of the cases, with an IQ score to 85. So, a total of 68% of the students have an IQ between 85 and 115. Therefore, 1,500 x .68 = 1,020.

3. **A**

$$12 + 2x = 24$$
$$2x = 24 - 12$$
$$2x = 12$$
$$x = \frac{12}{2}$$
$$x = 6$$

4. (A)

$(10 + x)2 = 28$

$20 + 2x = 28$

$2x = 28 - 20$

$2x = 8$

$x = \frac{8}{2}$

$x = 4$

5. (A)

$\$2,000 \times .35 = \$700$. The other choices have incorrect computations.

6. (C)

Let x = length of time (# of months) to recover cost.

$3x = 24$

$x = \frac{24}{3}$

x = 8 months

7. (B)

Area $= \left(\frac{1}{2}\right)(8)(15) = 60$

8. (C)

The perimeter is the distance around the triangle which is, therefore, (a + b + c) cm.

9. (D)

The perimeter is the distance around the triangle. Therefore, 2 cm + 6 cm + 5 cm = 13 cm.

10. (E)

The area of a parallelogram is base × height. Therefore, A = bh = (16 cm) × (4 cm) = 64 cm^2*.*

11. **B**

Figure A has an area of about 9 square units while Figure B has an area of about 7 square units. Both Figures A and B have the same perimeter of about 12 units.

12. **C**

$5 + 7 + 10 = 22$ Then $22 \div 2.2 = 10$

13. **C**

$(.50)(18) + (.75)(12) = 9 + 9 = 18$

Then $\left(\frac{18}{30}\right)(100) = 60\%$

14. **D**

There are (6) × (6) = 36 different possibilities, which are known as outcomes. The outcomes 46, 55, and 64 would lead to a sum of 10. Thus, $\frac{3}{36} = \frac{1}{12}$.

15. **E**

Let T = tails, H = heads. There are eight possible outcomes: HHH, HHT, HTH, THH, HTT, THT, TTH, and TTT. Only one outcome has all tails, so the probability becomes $\frac{1}{8}$.

16. **A**

The next year's enrollment will be 350. Then 350 ÷ 1,000 = 35%.

17. **D**

The sequence 1, 4, 9, 16 is the sum of the odd numbers.

1. 1
2. $1 + 3 = 4$
3. $1 + 3 + 5 = 9$
4. $1 + 3 + 5 + 7 = 16$

18. A

Here one must use only the needed information. Do not be distracted by superfluous data. Simple multiplication will do. If one pig eats four pounds of food per week, how much will 10 pigs eat in one week? 10 × 4 = 40 pounds. The problem intentionally contains superfluous data (52 weeks), which should not distract the reader from an easy solution. Ratio and proportion will also work here: $\frac{1}{10} = \frac{4}{x}$, *x = 40 pounds/week.*

19. D

Let the variable S stand for the cost of the shirt. Then the cost of the pair of pants is S + 25 and

$S + (S + 25) = 65$

$2S = 65 - 25$

$2S = 40$

$S = 20$

$20 (cost of shirt)

$20 + $25 = $45 (cost of pants)

20. D

The possible handshakes are illustrated by listing all the possible pairs of players, thus,

AB	AC	AD	AE
BC	BD	BE	
CD	CE		
DE			

(a total of 10 handshakes)

21. B

Graphically:

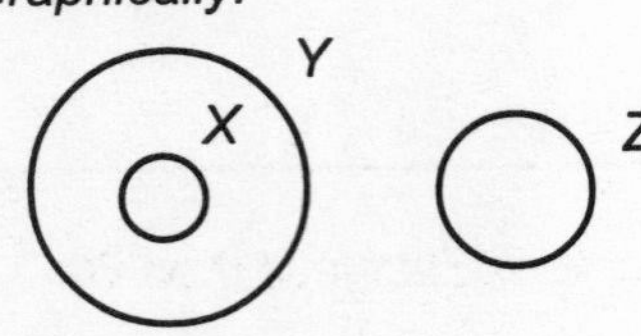

Thus, none of Z is in X.

22. **C**

With the connective "or," if either part is true, the entire statement is true.

23. **D**

36% + 16% + 20% = 72%   Then (.72) (250 million) = 180 million.

24. **B**

19% – 9% = 10%   Then (.10) (250 million) = 25 million.

25. **E**

19% – 16% = 3%. Since 3% ÷ 2 = 1.5%, then a shift of 1.5% from the West to the Southeast would make each region 17.5% of the total U.S. population. Then (.015) (250 million) = 3.75 million.

26. **C**

Let D = down payment

$D = \$20{,}000 \times .20$

$D = \$4{,}000$

27. **D**

20% of $3,200 = $640 amount price reduced

$3,200 – $640 = $2,560 sale price

28. **E**

Let x = 5th grade

$$Average = \frac{65 + 85 + 60 + 90 + x}{5}$$

For Sue to obtain a C, her average must be greater than or equal to 70, but less than 80.

$$70 \le \frac{65 + 85 + 60 + 90 + x}{5} < 80$$

$$70 \le \frac{300 + x}{5} < 80$$

$5(70) \leq 5(300 + x \div 5) < 5(80)$

$350 \leq 300 + x < 400$

$350 - 300 \leq x < 400 - 300$

$50 \leq x < 100$

Thus, a grade of 50, up to but not including a grade of 100, will result in a C.

29. **A**

The ratio 8:6:6:1 implies that for each \$8 the wife received, each child received \$6 and the foundation \$1. The estate is divided into 8 + 6 + 6 + 1, or 21 equal shares. The wife received $\frac{8}{21}$ *of \$300,000, or \$114,285.71; each child received* $\frac{6}{21}$ *of \$300,000, or \$85,714.29; and the foundation received* $\frac{1}{21}$ *of \$300,000, or \$14,285.71. As a check, \$114,285.71 + \$85,714.29 + \$85,714.29 + \$14,285.71 = \$300,000.*

30. **B**

$\frac{19}{9}$ *= 2 whole hamburgers, with one left over.*

31. **C**

$7 \times 4 = 28.$

32. **C**

For a 15-foot log, it will take 14 cuts to make 15 equal pieces. Therefore, it will take 14 minutes for 14 cuts.

33. **E**

$6 \times 4 = 24.$

34. **D**

First, find out how many shares of \$1,000 there are in \$50,000 (\$50,000 ÷ 1,000 = 50). Then multiply the shares by the cost (50 × \$32); the answer is \$1,600.

35. **C**

Find the sum of the seven days. Thus: M = 25; T = 30; W = 20; Th = 25; F = 10; Sat = 40; Sun = 0, or a total of 150 minutes. Find the average by dividing 150 by 7 = 21.43 minutes.

36. **B**

If each [$] stands for $12, only weeks 3 and 4 had a sale of $72 and $60, respectively. The rest are below $55.

37. **C**

The volume of a pyramid is $V=\frac{1}{3}Bh$, *where B is the area of the base and h is the height of the pyramid. Thus,* $V=\frac{1}{3}(64)(6)=\frac{1}{3}(384)=128m^3$.

38. **C**

Total the number of credits earned; in this case, 16 credits. Multiply the credit and the weight for the earned grade per subject (e.g., biology = 5 × 4 = 20). Add the total of the products of the credits and corresponding weights; in this case, 47. Divide 47 by 16 to get the grade point average of 2.94. See the table below.

Biology	=	$5 \times 4 = 20$
English	=	$3 \times 2 = 6$
Math	=	$3 \times 4 = 12$
French	=	$3 \times 1 = 3$
P.E.	=	$\frac{2}{16\ cr} \times 3 = \frac{6}{47\ cr \times gr\ wt}$

$$GPA=\frac{total\ cr \times wt}{total\ cr}$$
$$=\frac{47}{16}$$
$$=2.94$$

39. **C**

The mode is the most frequent score. 81 appeared five times and is, therefore, the mode.

40. **A**

Following the formula $\left(z=\frac{x-\bar{x}}{s.d.}\right)$,

$1.6 = \frac{x - 190}{11}$

$17.60 = x - 190$

$x = 190 + 17.60$

$x = 207.6$ cm (Glenn's height)

41. (A)

Multiply \$1.83 by 145; the answer is \$265.35.

42. (E)

Suppose the price in 1990 was \$1,000. The price in 1991 becomes (1,000) × (1.05) = \$1,050. Finally, the price in 1992 becomes (1,050) × (1.10) = \$1,155. The increase of \$155 represents a $\left(\frac{155}{1,000}\right) \times (100) = 15.5\%$ *increase.*

43. (C)

In a normal distribution, half the data are always above the mean. Since 30,000 miles is the mean, half or 50% of the tires will last at least 30,000 miles.

44. (C)

The end times for successive periods are 1 hour and 45 minutes apart. Therefore, 3 periods = 3 hours + 135 minutes = 5 hours, 15 minutes. Add this 5 hours, 15 minutes to 9:40 AM to get 2:55 PM.

45. (D)

This can be solved using ratio and proportion; thus, 2 is to 1 as x is to 8. $\frac{2}{1} = \frac{x}{8}$, *so x = 16 m.*

46. (E)

First, find out how many ounces of orange juice are needed; multiply 75 × 8 oz. = 600 oz. Then divide 600 by 12 oz. = 50 12-oz. cans needed to serve 75 people with 8 oz. of juice each.

47. **A**

m = number of miles you can travel

$\$0.08m$ = amount spent for m miles traveled at 8 cents per mile,

rental fee + mileage charge = total amount spent

$\$139 + \$0.08m = \$350$

Solution: $139 - 139 + 0.08m = 350 - 139$

$$0.08m = 211$$

$$\frac{0.08m}{0.08} = \frac{211}{0.08}$$

$$m = 2{,}637.5$$

$$m = 2{,}637$$

Therefore, you can travel 2,637 miles (if you go 2,638 miles, you have traveled too far).

48. **A**

Let x = number of hours of overtime for the 1st worker,

x = number of hours of overtime for the 2nd worker,

x = number of hours of overtime for the 3rd worker,

$2x$ = number of hours of overtime for the 4th worker.

$x + x + x + 2x = 50$

$$5x = 50$$

$$x = \frac{50}{5}$$

$x = 10$ hr of overtime for the 1st three workers

$2x = 20$ hr of overtime for the 4th worker

49. **D**

Let m = number of miles covered the 1st day,

$m + 30$ = number of miles covered the 2nd day,

$m + 30 + 30$ = number of miles covered the 3rd day,

$m + 30 + 30 + 30$ = number of miles covered the 4th day,

$m + 30 + 30 + 30 + 30$ = number of miles covered the 5th day.

$m + m + 30$ and so on ... $= 1{,}500$

$$5m + 30\,(10) = 1{,}500$$

$$5m + 300 = 1{,}500$$

$$5m = 1{,}500 - 300$$

$$5m = 1{,}200$$

$$m = \frac{1{,}200}{5}$$

$$m = 240 \text{ mi}$$

50. **A**

Using the formula $P = 2w + 2l$

$$75 = 2w + 2(w + 5)$$

$$75 = 2w + 2w + 10$$

$$75 = 4w + 10$$

$$65 = 4w$$

$$16.25 = w$$

The width is, therefore, 16.25 m and the length is w + 5 or 16.25 + 5 = 21.25 m.

DIRECTIONS: Carefully read the two writing topics below. Plan and write an essay on each, being sure to cover all aspects of each essay. Allow approximately 30 minutes per essay.

Topic 1

There is a current trend in the United States toward smaller families. Sociologists attribute the decline in childbearing to many factors, including the dramatic rise of women in the workforce, delayed marriage, divorce, and the high cost of raising and educating children. Discuss both your view of smaller family size and how smaller families may affect the future of American society.

Topic 2

Write an essay in which you contrast your values and/or personality with the values and/or personality of a member of your family. Explain how two individuals from the same family can be different in the ways you and your relative are different.

Scoring Rubric of the CBEST Writing Exam

Although there are no "right" and "wrong" answers for your essays, it will nevertheless be graded. The graders will read your essay and assign it a score based upon how well it communicates your ideas in a clear, logical, and grammatically correct manner. Your essay will be graded holistically, which means that your score will be determined by grading the essay as a whole, not as parts. Your essay will receive one of the following four scores: Pass (4), Marginal Pass (3), Marginal Fail (2), or Fail (1). The determination of each score is based on the following Six Primary Traits of Good Writing:

- Rhetorical Force
- Organization
- Support and Development
- Usage
- Structure and Conventions
- Appropriateness

The determination of each score is based on the following criteria.

Pass (4)

A score of "4" is assigned to a well-written essay that clearly communicates a coherent and compelling message to its intended audience. This score is achieved by writing an essay with the following characteristics:

1. Rhetorical Force: The essay argues a central idea and maintains its focus on this thesis.
2. Organization: The essay is presented in a logical manner; smooth transitions between ideas help the reader understand the flow of the essay.
3. Support and Development: Specific examples and compelling data support generalizations and assertions.
4. Usage: Word usage is correct and precise.
5. Structure and Conventions: The writer understands how to create sentences of complexity, and only minor flaws in mechanics deter from the essay's readability.
6. Appropriateness: The essay addresses the topic given in the essay prompt, and it does so in a manner and style appropriate for the audience.

Marginal Pass (3)

A score of "3" represents an essay that adequately communicates its message to the intended audience, although several important improvements could be made.

1. Rhetorical Force: The essay showcases a thesis and primarily focuses on this thesis.
2. Organization: The ideas of the essay are organized in an effective and logical manner.
3. Support and Development: Assertions are supported with evidence, although sometimes the evidence is not entirely convincing.
4. Usage: Word choice and usage are competent, but could be improved.

5. Structure and Conventions: Errors in the mechanical conventions of writing are neither serious nor frequent.
6. Appropriateness: The response may not fully respond to the topic given in the essay prompt, but the essay nevertheless sufficiently engages with the questions at issue to create an engaged exchange of ideas.

Marginal Fail (2)

A "2" is a fragmented essay that inadequately communicates its message to the intended audience.

1. Rhetorical Force: Although the writer may present a thesis in the essay, that idea is then lost in the ensuing paragraphs; the reasoning is simplistic and lacks sophistication.
2. Organization: The essay is poorly organized and lacks logical coherence between paragraphs; the author jumps from idea to idea rather than guiding the reader from one idea to the next.
3. Support and Development: Assertions lack supporting evidence and examples; supporting evidence and examples which are present do not effectively contribute to the thesis.
4. Usage: Improperly used words hamper the reader from comprehending the essay.
5. Structure and Conventions: Errors in paragraphing, grammar, and sentence structure impede the essay's readability.
6. Appropriateness: The writing does not engage with the essay prompts, and the essay is inappropriate for its intended audience.

Fail (1)

A score of "1" is assigned to an essay that fails to communicate a meaningful message to its audience.

1. Rhetorical Force: The writer does not provide a thesis to the essay, and the reasoning behind the essay is unconvincing.
2. Organization: The meaning of the essay is difficult to decipher because the organization of ideas appears haphazard rather than logically determined.
3. Support and Development: The writer fails to support generalizations and assertions with adequate evidence.
4. Usage: Errors in word choice and usage make the essay difficult to understand.
5. Structure and Conventions: Frequent mistakes in paragraphing, sentence structure, and grammar impair readability.
6. Appropriateness: The essay fails to engage with the essay prompt, and its tone and language are inappropriate for its audience.

Try to see which of these categories your essay falls into by comparing its characteristics to the ones listed above. You may want to ask a teacher or a trusted friend to read your essay and grade it for you. Also, many colleges have writing labs which offer free tutoring; check to see if your school offers such a service.

Detailed Explanations of Answers

DIAGNOSTIC TEST

SECTION 3: Writing

SAMPLE SCORED ESSAYS WITH EXPLANATIONS

Topic 1 Sample Answers

Essay #1—Pass (Score = 4)

Although today people commonly complain about overcrowding and overpopulation, figures show that the average-sized family has dropped below the number needed for replacement of the population. I favor the trend toward smaller families. We need to move toward creating a world where children are guaranteed the simple things like food and shelter instead of giving birth to generations of starving and homeless people.

There are various reasons for such a steady decline in childbearing that are well worth taking note of. The high cost of raising and educating children, availability of birth control, the desire for greater freedom, and the realization that parenthood may well be a learned behavior rather than an instinct are a few examples.

The first of those points is the most obvious and rational explanation for not having children. The costs of pregnancy, and the first few years of the child's life alone can be staggering, assuming that it's a healthy child. Once you make it past that stage, parents are soon hit with the high cost of education, not to mention getting their child into the "right" school. Another factor to consider is birth control. In the past forty years we have gone from a period where sex was rarely discussed, to one where contraceptives are openly discussed, and distributed. The desire for greater freedom is another important consideration. People who grew up in large families, or whose jobs involve children, often desire the freedom of a marriage without kids. Having a family is quite obviously a lifetime commitment, and often by the time a parent may be ready to make it, it's too late. Last, but possibly the most important, is the growing belief that being a parent may be a learned behavior rather than an instinct. As I grew up I always figured that being a good parent was something that would "come to me" when the time is right. Judging by the high number of cases of abuse and abandonment, this is obviously not the case. It is true that being a good father or mother requires good instinct, but there is a bit more to it than that.

These are all issues worth considering, however they are concerned mostly with individuals, and not the "world family" in general. As I have said, I think we need to concentrate more on the kind of generations we are giving birth to, and the society they will live their lives in. It is ignorant to overlook the fact that we are giving birth to more children than we can possibly provide for. Even more importantly, it is a cruel trick to play on something so young and innocent as a baby.

Scoring Explanation for Essay #1—Pass

Essay #1 is a clear pass because it offers lucid, well-reasoned arguments about smaller family size. The writer's position is clearly stated in the introduction, and several reasons for the steady decline in childbearing are then systematically explored. Although the idea that parenthood is a learned rather than an instinctual behavior is somewhat off the initial thesis about family size, the vast majority of this writer's supporting evidence helps to build a solid foundation for the essay. In addition, the writer coherently links the ideas of the essay together with smooth transitions and logical development.

The author's syntax and grammar are well under control. The text is nearly error-free, and complex sentences are handled with ease. For example, embedded sentences, such as "People who grew up in large families, or whose jobs involve children, often desire the freedom of a marriage without kids" occur often. In addition, the author goes beyond the obvious reactions to the issue of smaller families and draws more thoughtful conclusions, such as the implications of these issues to the "world family." Finally, the essay addresses both crucial aspects the question requires, namely, to express a view on smaller family size and to speculate about how it may affect future society. It accomplishes these goals in a manner and style appropriate to its audience of CBEST graders.

Essay #2—Marginal Pass (Score = 3)

According to sociologists, Americans are having fewer children. Possible reasons to account for this trend may be the increase of women in the work force and the strain of the many problems of adolescents as well as other factors. I feel the trend toward smaller families and childlessness is a definite result of these factors and predict that in the future less importance may be placed on raising a family as part of the "American dream."

To begin with, the norms of society used to reflect that the "woman's place is in the home." Yet, women today are taking charge of their lives and realizing their own ambitions above what society dictates. Most of all they are seeing that children do not automatically have to be a part of their future.

More and more women are placing their own ambitions above what society dictates and do not include children, and each generation is producing less offspring. I, for example, intend to become a nurse and will probably postpone marriage and children. Secondly, people are realizing that there truly is a great deal involved in raising a family. Commitment to the responsibility of having children sometimes slacks when a family experiences difficulty during the child's adolescent years. It is hard enough to deal with the physical, emotional, and psychological changes of young adulthood yet a teenager must also face the pressures of society which may cause personal problems. This factor is one that many couples would rather avoid and, therefore, must refrain from having children altogether in order to do so.

Thirdly, this trend toward smaller family size will most likely continue in the future, affecting society in such a way that the term "family" may not necessarily include children. It seems that many people are living for today and are not concerned about carrying on the family name. Rather, they wish to live a life that is self-fulfilling. This attitude may affect future society in that it would project selfishness as a value onto future generations.

In essence, there is a definite trend toward smaller families and childlessness due to a greater concern for recognizing one's own personal ambitions and transforming them into a successful, fulfilling life. This is particularly true for women who are becoming increasingly active in the work force. Also, raising children is not easy and some couples would rather deal with the difficulties. These and other factors will most likely result in a decrease in the importance of having children as a part of the "American dream."

Scoring Explanation for Essay #2—Marginal Pass

This essay shows adequate reasoning and organization. The introduction sets up a three-part discussion, and the ensuing paragraphs fulfill that commitment in the promised sequence. We read about (1) changing roles for women, (2) the problems involved in raising children (particularly adolescents), and (3) the resulting change in how we understand the concept of family; however, it is not clear why the author addresses the first two of these ideas in one paragraph. The ideas are not sufficiently interrelated to necessitate that they be considered in the same paragraph.

Both general ("More and more women are placing their own ambitions above what society dictates") and specific information ("I, for example, intend to become a nurse") are offered in the discussion. General assertions, however, predominate over specific ones; the author would have done better to include more specific and direct information to support the argument.

The diction and syntax are generally adequate, although some errors in punctuation and a few awkward sentences ("Commitment to the responsibility of having children sometimes slacks when a family experiences difficulty during the child's adolescent years") detract from the essay's readability. Greater attention should have been paid to word choice and sentence structure.

The writer does address the question of how smaller family size will affect future American society, predicting that smaller family size will change the "American Dream," resulting in "living for today," a lack of concern for "carrying on the family name," and selfishness. Unfortunately, the writer appears to confuse the terms "self-fulfillment" and "selfishness," resulting in a hasty generalization about the effect of smaller family size. Despite these problems in the essay's supporting assertions, the very typical strategy of restating the conclusion, and occasional errors in syntax and grammar, the essay deals with the questions and is relatively easy to follow. It is a marginal pass.

Essay #3—Marginal Fail (Score = 2)

The trend toward smaller families and childlessness definitely makes our future society better. In the future, smaller family size will allow the people to live a more carefree and enjoyable lifestyle.

In the passage sociologists point out some good reasons for the decline in childbearing. In today's society the desire of the people to live affluently, the high divorce rates, and the high costs of raising and educating children makes the people to want fewer children or not at all. It may seem selfish but to enjoy oneself one needs to have a choice to not have babies or to have a few just to suit one's lifestyle. Some notices that having a large family give financial problem, the family cannot afford to send all the children to colleges. Also, since divorce rates is high few want to consider having children; they are afraid that it will give them troubles of settling child custody problem.

Because of this major reasons stated in the passage the future society seems to be moving toward a more pleasurable lifestyle. The people tend to look forward to delaying marriage and fulfilling one's desires. Then, of course, what is a bigger problem than childbearing? There is no surprise that an average sized family is greatly reduced . . . it is necessary.

Scoring Explanation for Essay #3—Marginal Fail

The essay's introduction promises a discussion of smaller families resulting in a better society, more "carefree and enjoyable." The bulk of the essay, however, seeks to explain the reasons for the decline in childbearing. The writer has lost sight of his/her original focus or thesis, returning to it only briefly at the end of the essay.

Furthermore, the treatment of the topic is simplistic; the writer primarily explains what is evident from the question and offers little new material. Insufficient information supports the thesis, intriguing as it might be. The writer would have done better to describe in detail how smaller families would, indeed, improve society.

Grammatical errors and several instances of awkward syntax ("the high costs of raising and educating children makes the people to want fewer children or not at all") make the essay difficult to comprehend. Punctuation problems distract as well. Still, the writer did attempt to address the question, although the essay lacks the necessary development to formulate a compelling response to the essay prompt. For these reasons, the essay is a marginal fail.

Essay #4—Fail (Score = 1)

Society in the United States has changed drastic in the ideas of family life. One can contribute this change through a various amount of reasons. One of the pertanent ideas revolve around society becoming more career oriented in their jobs they have been involved with. Another idea is the cost of raising a child and finally the knowledge that has developed over the centuries has played a factor in postponing child birth until last in life.

In the past, having a big family was the desired. Although a family struggled with the demands of raising a large family, they were able to prevale because as the children grow up they could also work with the father or mother, which resulted in an extra source of income. A college education was not a common option. That one could decide to do when they reached the age of 18. At many times a son or daughter would learn it an take over the business.

Today, that idea, has been altered. Couples or even individuals have become more career oriented in their jobs. This idea also stems with stress a greater freedom wanted, and less of a interest to family. The high cost of raising a family is also a factor in less child births. A family or couple can now wait until their late thirties to have a child. Medical advancement has helped in this area of having a family later in life. Through the use of medical procedures, a couple can conceive a child even when they are older in age. Statistics in conceiving a child in the forties age group has risen substantially because of medicine.

With less child births, cities such as Los Angeles won't be as crowded as it was before. Children can get a better education because teachers will be able to devote their attention to a smaller group of students, then a larger-sized group. Lower amounts of poverty striken families will exist. Because of the idea of couples waiting until they are financially stable before raising children. More jobs will also be available due to the decrease in child births. One can also say that the freeway system that people use everyday will in time get better, and more efficient. People today are now thinking twice about bringing up a family. Becoming financially secure first, is a good idea before deciding to have a child.

Scoring Explanation for Essay #4—Fail

Essay #4 fails on a number of counts. The writer introduces an interesting idea by relating medical advancement to childbearing later in life, but this idea is not explored; rather, it is presented repetitively. The writer presents a list of benefits resulting from "less child births" that similarly go uninvestigated; also, this list ranks serious issues ("poverty stricken families") alongside trivial ones ("the freeway system will get more efficient"), resulting in an essay that does not appear to realize the seriousness of its topic. This intellectual confusion derails the beginnings of a promising idea.

The writer's sentence structure shows a serious lack of focus and knowledge of proper syntax. Some sentences are simply awkward (e.g., "Society in the United States has changed drastic in the ideas of family life"), while others are confused and exhibit missing elements or faulty logic (such as "This idea also stems with stress a greater freedom wanted, and less of an interest to family"). The writer simply does not have sufficient control over written English to merit a passing score.

Topic 2 Sample Answers

Essay #1—Pass (Score = 4)

Some people see a glass half-filled with water and say that it is half empty, while other people see the same glass of water and describe it as half-full. The former are pessimists, and the latter are optimists. This crucial distinction applies equally well to my grandmother and me. For her, the world is constantly spiraling downward into oblivion and god-awfulness, while I have a more optimistic and hopeful outlook on life. We have very different perspectives and personalities, yet we come from the same family. Strong families, however, can overcome differences in personalities if they share enough common ground in their values.

I think that my grandmother's viewpoints are generally more pessimistic than my own because her life has been much harder than mine. Her mother died when she was very young, and she also suffered through the years of the Great Depression as a young child. Money was not plentiful in her home, and her father often could not afford to give her the things she desired. I, on the other hand, had a much more secure childhood. Both of my parents are still alive today, and, although we were not extremely well off, my family lived in relative comfort and security. My grandmother often had to fear what tomorrow might bring, while I have lived comfortably as my parents have supported me through childhood and continue to help me in my college years. These differences in our childhood, I think, explain the differences between my grandmother's and my personalities.

Despite the fact that our personalities are so different, my grandmother and I share certain core values. We are both hard workers who strive to do our best, and we support our friends and family members in all their endeavors. We are loyal and loving, and we both believe that a strong family will help its members to succeed. In fact, I think that one of the reasons I am so optimistic is that my grandmother, despite her pessimism in many areas, has shown me that hard work can pay off. Although she may be grumpy and predict doom and gloom far too often, she is a survivor, and she has shown me how to work hard to achieve my goals. Even with our stark differences in personality, we share values which allow us to appreciate and love each other for the people we are, not who we would like each other to be. For my family and me, a strong loving family is one which respects differences in personality while working together to form a community founded upon core values of loyalty, love, and determination.

Scoring Explanation for Essay #1—Pass

Despite the cliché which opens this essay, it is a coherent and compelling response to the essay prompt. The author begins by describing a chief difference in personality between his/her grandmother and him/herself. The essay then considers a possible cause of this difference, noting the differences in each of their backgrounds. The essay concludes by addressing how these two people have different personalities, yet share similar values. Responding to all issues that the essay prompt suggests, the writer investigates the concepts of personalities, values, the causes behind them, and how these factors interrelate with real people to form a family.

The writing in this essay is strong throughout. The writer adeptly handles complex sentences, and the grammar and punctuation assist the passage's readability. The tone is appropriate to the given audience, and the organization of the essay moves smoothly from paragraph to paragraph. With its many strengths, the essay warrants a "4."

Essay #2—Marginal Pass (Score = 3)

People tell me quite often that my brother and I look like twins. We both have brown hair, brown eyes, a fair complexion, and the same features. Though we look like each other, our personalities clash.

Alex is only sixteen years old, and he is very advanced for his age in school. He's intelligent, determined, confident, and always does what he says he's going to do. On my part, I can say that my intelligence is at the average level, and rather than being determined and confident about the things I do, I tend to be somewhat insecure about myself.

I've always wanted to be just like Alex. Throughout my life I've always looked up to him. He's outgoing and open, and I am the shy, quiet type. He's the one who always completes his work on time and never depends on anyone else but himself. I always procrastinate, and I'm lazy.

Also, Alex is the "outgoing" type who plays sports like tennis, football and baseball. Though I was on the tennis team in 1998, I never continued to play on a regular basis. Alex likes to play sports, and I like to watch them on t.v.

My parents can similarly be compared to my brother and I. I share the same personality traits as my father, and Alex shares my mom's personality. My father is the introvert and we are both hesitant to get things done before the last minute. My mother is an open, confident woman and always trusts herself—which can similarly be compared to my brother. My father and I prefer to stay inside while my mom and brother are always on the go. When my mother was our age she was on a running team. She was involved in a lot of sports, and my father was always the one who liked to be alone.

As shown here, my brother and I are different in many ways, and so are my parents.

Scoring Explanation for Essay #2—Marginal Pass

The bulk of this marginally passing essay is spent providing the audience with a series of comparisons (ranging from physical differences to sports preferences) between the writer and his/her brother. These comparisons are offered in sentences that are readable and competent, although not very complex or sophisticated. Very few grammatical errors and only minor punctuation problems deter from easy comprehension of the writer's ideas. Despite the fact that the essay is relatively well written, it fails to show much evidence of critical thinking; rather, it mainly serves as a laundry list of differences between the two siblings.

The last major paragraph of this essay attempts to explain the differences between the siblings by offering corresponding differences between the parents. The author implies, but never clearly states, that the parental characteristics account for those of the children. Thus, the writer attempts to address the question in its entirety but fails to explain these critical ideas explicitly. The conclusion is brief and perfunctory, merely restating the general thrust of the previous paragraph. Because the essay only vaguely addresses the assignment in its entirety, though it is satisfactorily written, the essay is a marginal pass.

Essay #3—Marginal Fail (Score = 2)

Have you ever wondered if someone in your family could possible be from the same family, do to the fact that you are so opposite? My sister Kate and I have to be one of the most opposite sisters in the world. Our likes, values, and personalities contrast terribly. At times I often ask myself: "How could we possibly be related?"

To begin with my sister has red hair, is two inches taller than me and two years younger than me. This is far different from me who is blonde, petite and older. Our looks are the outside appearance of how different we are in the inside.

When it comes to dating, Katie likes to date as many as possible, whereas I like to stick to just one. I am extremely competitive and hate to lose, especially in volleyball. Katie is more carefree and if her team loses it is not that big of a deal. Our bedrooms show a great deal of differences. Katie's room is piled with clothes and many unimportant things. She like to save everything. On the other hand I am very metuculus, and I am annoyed if there is junk laying around. Even when it comes down to the "nitty gritty" of things such as music, clothes, or jewelry Katie and I have opposite taste.

Two individuals from the same family could be different in the ways my sister and me are different, possibly because of different genes in the family. Generations of a family consist of many genes from various relatives, and those genes are passed on contributing to the different personalities of a number of relatives. Every individual is his or her own person and just because people are from the same family, it does not mean that people can not have their own distinct values and personalities different than anyone else in the family.

Scoring Explanation for Essay #3—Marginal Fail

This essay provides a series of contrasts between the writer and her sister, beginning with physical characteristics and ending with tastes in clothing. None of the differences mentioned addresses a contrasting value system, although some minor personality differences are offered. Thus, the question is only partially answered in this essay.

The author does have a lively and unique voice in her essay, but several errors in grammar, syntax, spelling, and word choice inhibit this voice from speaking clearly. One example of an awkward construction appears in the first paragraph: "My sister Kate and I have to be one of the most opposite sisters in the world." Spelling (e.g., "do" for "due," "metuculus" for "meticulous") and punctuation are similarly irregular.

The final paragraph of the essay offers genetic differences as an explanation for the contrasts between the sisters. The author relies on this biological explanation exclusively, although she does not appear to be well-versed with genetics. The author concludes with a wordy restatement of her belief that despite blood ties, family members can differ. The writer is confused, therefore, about how genetics actually do or do not contribute to differences between siblings, and she thus fails to do justice to a promising idea. This problem with reasoning contributes to the essay's marginally failing score.

Essay #4—Fail (Score = 1)

My uncle Gary and I are completely different peoples. First of all, my Uncle Gary is an atheist. I on the other hand am a religious person. I do not go to church every Sunday but I do believe in God. Secondly, my Uncle does not speak to anyone in the family. He has totally sheltered himself from everyone. I love to be with my family at family gatherings. I will admit they get on my nerves sometimes. But I would never want to lose contact with them. Last, but not least, my Uncle is a democrat. I am a Republican. This would be a good discussion topic. If my uncle would ever go to family gatherings. So there you have two completely different people. From the same family.

Scoring Explanation for Essay #4—Fail

This essay suffers from a serious lack of development. Its simplistic listing of differences between the author and his/her uncle only minimally addresses the question. No discussion of these differences is advanced, and the writer concludes without even attempting any explanation beyond: "So there you have two completely different people. From the same family."

Despite the essay's extreme brevity, the author also makes many errors in syntax and grammar. Sentence fragments appear regularly, and the author does not know when to capitalize letters. A lack of attention to the demands of the question, incomplete development, and errors in writing make this essay a clear fail.

Chapter

3

Reading Skills Review

Overview

The reading comprehension segment of the CBEST measures your ability to understand information given through the written word and in charts and graphs. The emphasis is on Critical Analysis, Evaluation, Comprehension, and Research Skills, not on your knowledge of different topics. Test passages vary in difficulty and length. Long passages (up to 200 words) are mixed in with much shorter sections, which can be as brief as one or two lines.

Each of the four components—Critical Analysis, Evaluation, Comprehension, and Research Skills—carries a certain percent value. The Critical Analysis and Evaluation sections are worth 30 percent, or 15 questions, while the Comparison and Research Skills sections are worth 70 percent, or 35 questions.

Definitions of Key Concepts

Critical Analysis

Questions in this section will ask you to explain the significance or meaning of a text by applying sound reasoning to pertinent facts. You may need to identify the author's main idea, or recognize various persuasive techniques used by an author in a written passage. In order to reason and argue convincingly, you must compare and contrast ideas or information presented in different sections of a written passage. You may be asked to identify specific reasons, examples, details, or facts in a reading selection in order to make predictions about the outcome of an event based on that information; or you may be asked to address a text, and find relevant information that logically supports the author's idea. Some questions may ask you if the author presents convincing facts to support his or her ideas. Alternatively, you may be asked to identify inconsistencies in authorial points of view, opinions, or assumptions. For example:

> ***A major problem with reading/language arts instruction is that practice assignments from workbooks often provide short, segmented activities that do not really resemble the true acts of reading. Perhaps more than any computer application, word processing is capable of addressing these issues.***

Given this information, would you say the author would tend to agree that a major benefit of computers in reading/language arts instruction is

(A) that the reading act may be more closely resembled.

(B) that short, segmented assignments will be eliminated.

(C) that the issues in reading/language arts instruction will be addressed.

(D) that computer application will be limited to word processing.

(E) that reading practice will be eliminated.

The correct answer is (A). By looking at the author's reasons, examples, details, or facts in the above reading selection, you can make interpretations concerning that information. The passage explicitly states facts about computers and their ability to address the issues of practice and the true act of reading. Choice (A) supports, or reflects, that same information. The other choices represent inferences that are not supported by the details in the passage.

Evaluation

In this section you may be asked to distinguish between facts and opinions. You might interpret whether a written passage is presenting facts, ideas, or opinions, and evaluate whether or not that information is relevant to the author's argument. You may be asked to identify the statements that either strengthen or weaken the author's claims. For example, what tone does the language create? How do the attitude, opinion, or viewpoints of the passage affect or influence the audience that is reading the selection? Who is the target audience, and so on? You may be asked to determine if the author presents an idea effectively and what drew you to your conclusions. Using the above reading/language quotation as an example, do you think the author's argument for the appropriate use of a word processor to assist in making practice resemble a reading act is

(A) clearly detailed.

(B) desirable.

(C) unstated.

(D) alluded to.

Here you will want to evaluate, estimate, or interpret whether the author is presenting facts, ideas, or opinions, and decide whether or not that information is relevant to the author's argument. Although the reader might make inferences to select choices (A), (B), and (D), the actual ways that a word processor makes practice resemble the act of reading are not stated in the passage. Thus, choice (C) is the correct response.

Comprehension

This section will ask you to demonstrate your understanding of a text. You might be asked to identify the relationships between general and specific ideas in a reading selection, or to arrange those ideas into an outline or other form of graph or chart. You may be asked to determine the sequence of events or steps in a reading selection, recognize the main idea, thesis, or purpose of a passage, or identify accurate paraphrases or summaries of the ideas in a given selection. You might draw conclusions or generalizations from the material presented, or you might be asked to make inferences and recognize implications based on the information given, or you may identify implied relationships between people, ideas, or events. Questions will assess your understanding of high-school-level and college-level reading materials such as, texts, memos, bulletins, newsletters, resource material, and professional journals. You might be asked to distinguish how the meaning of a word, sentence, or paragraph is affected by the context in which it appears, or determine the meanings of figurative or colloquial language in a passage. Here is one example:

In view of the current emphasis on literature-based reading instruction, a greater understanding by teachers of variance in cultural, language, and story components should assist in narrowing the gap between reader and text and improve reading comprehension. Classroom teachers should begin with students' meaning and intentions about stories before moving students to the commonalities of story meaning based on common background and culture. With teacher guidance, students should develop a fuller understanding of how complex narratives can be when the students themselves are generating stories as well as when they are reading stories.

Given the information in the above passage, which of the following choices is the most complete and accurate definition of the term *variance*?

(A) Change

(B) Fluctuations

(C) Diversity

(D) Deviation

(E) Incongruity

Each of the choices is a definition of the word *variance*, so you must look at its context, or the way in which the word is used, to understand its meaning. In this case, choice (C) is the most appropriate.

Research Skills

Questions may require you to use a table of contents, section headings, index, or similar sections of a book to locate specific or relevant information. You may be asked to locate the place in a book, chapter, or article where a specific kind of information can be found, or you might be asked to explain how a reading selection such as a book, chapter, or article is organized. You might also be asked to identify logical conclusions, generalizations, or implied relationships that are supported by information in a table or graph. This section will ask you to gather information from the appropriate source and apply it accordingly. For example, in an anthology of literature, where would you locate the works of a specific author, or a specific work by a specific author?

(A) Table of Contents

(B) Section Heading

(C) Bibliography

(D) Index

The answer is (D), Index. Both (A), Table of Contents, and (B), Section Heading, contain information that may be too broad or general. (C) is a listing of books, so (D), Index, is the most efficient and, therefore, the correct answer.

Key Strategies for Answering the Reading Skills Questions

1. Read all directions carefully.
2. If possible, allocate your time for each question.

Do not spend too much time on any one question. If you can't answer the question easily after reading the passage twice, skip it and move on to the next item.

3. Skim through the questions before reading each passage; this will help you know what key words and ideas you are looking for.

4. Be certain to mark each passage as you read; should you skip an answer and return to it later, a notation will prevent your marking an answer in the wrong place.

5. If you come across unfamiliar words, do not spend too much time attempting to define them until you have read through the entire passage. Reading the phrase or sentence a couple of times and using the context (surrounding words) is valuable in determining meanings of vocabulary words.

6. Always read all the answer choices before choosing the one best answer.

7. Decide whether the question asked is a Critical Analysis, Evaluation, Comprehension, or Research Skills question.

8. Choices of answers that are not relevant, reasonable, or that contradict the information in the passage should be eliminated at the beginning.

The following directions are typical of those you will find on the CBEST.

DIRECTIONS: One or more questions follow each statement or passage in this test. The question(s) are based on the content of the passage. After you have read a statement or passage, select the best answer to each question from among the five possible choices. Your answers to the questions should be based on the stated (literal) or implied (inferential) information given in the statement or passage. Mark all answers on your answer sheet. **Note: You will encounter some passages with numbered sentences, blank spaces, or underscored words and phrases. These cues are provided on the CBEST for your reference in answering the questions that follow the relevant passages.**

Short Passage Sample

Experienced lawyers know that most lawsuits are won or lost before they are ever heard in court. Thus, successful lawyers prepare their cases carefully, undertaking exhaustive research and investigation prior to going to court. Interviews and statements taken from all available witnesses ascertain those who are likely to be called as witnesses for the other side. This time provides opportunities for strategy planning in the building of the case: decisions to be made about expert witnesses to be called (such as doctors, chemists, or others who have special knowledge of the subject matter); books and articles to be read pertaining to the subject matter of the case; and meetings with witnesses to prepare them for possible questions by the opposing lawyers and to review the case. Finally, in preparing the case, a trial memorandum of law is handed to the

judge at the outset of the trial. As a result of this thorough preparation, experienced lawyers know their strong and weak points and can serve their clients well.

Question

The main idea expressed in this passage is to

(A) describe the function of expert witnesses.

(B) explain the importance of pretrial preparation by lawyers.

(C) warn persons who break the law.

(D) verify the importance of the trial memorandum.

(E) refute the belief that all lawyers are trial lawyers.

Detailed Explanation of Answers

Passages such as this one are typically followed by one or two questions. In this case, the passage is followed by a comprehension question. Previewing the questions before reading the passage acquaints you with the writer's overall subject and possibly the author's approach to or point of view on the subject. Usually the main idea of the reading passage is not explicitly stated but becomes apparent as you read. Always ask yourself: What is the most important thing that the author is trying to tell me in this passage?

It is important to read through the entire passage and to mark any key words and phrases that relate to the question. After you have carefully read the passage, reread and consider each possible answer. Avoid giving an answer before you have read all of the choices. Frequently, there are two or more options that are close, but only one is the *best*.

When considering a question that asks for the main idea, you should note the central theme or essential idea being developed in each sentence in the paragraph. It is also important to examine the first word of each of the answers for responses that you can eliminate. In the case of the above passage, choice (C), warn, and choice (E), refute, are not consistent with the rather objective nature of the passage; these two choices can, therefore, be eliminated. Also, these choices are irrelevant to the information in the passage, since the passage does not address people who break the law or the belief that all lawyers are trial lawyers. The remaining choices can be considered based on how central they are to the main idea or if they are subsidiary to the main idea. Choices (A), expert witnesses, and (D), importance of trial memorandum, are mentioned but are subsidiary to the overall theme of the passage. Choice (B) is the best choice. It discusses the preparation done by the lawyers before the trial begins (pretrial).

Longer Passage Sample

Questions 1–5 refer to the following passage:

Mark Twain has been characterized as "an authentic American author" and as "a representative American author." These descriptions seem to suit the man and his writings. He was born Samuel Clemens in 1835, when Missouri and Louisiana were the only states west of the Mississippi River. His birthplace was less than fifty miles from the river. His father, John Clemens, a lawyer and merchant, was rarely far from financial disaster. When Samuel Clemens was four, the family settled in Hannibal, Missouri, beside the great river where Samuel lived out the adventurous life he describes in his best-loved novels. Samuel traveled extensively and tasted life as no other author had done.

He told how travel corresponded with his philosophy on writing, "Now then: as the most valuable capital, or culture, or education usable in the building of novels is personal experience, I ought to be well equipped for the trade." He acquired a wealth of personal experiences for his novels. As a boy of twelve he apprenticed to the printer of his brother's newspaper in Hannibal. Six years later, in 1853, he set out to see the world as a printer in St. Louis, then in Chicago, Philadelphia, Keokuk, and Cincinnati. In 1857 he impulsively apprenticed himself to Horace Bixby, a riverboat pilot, and traveled all 2,348 miles of the Mississippi River. He said of his years on the river, "I got personally and familiarly acquainted with all the different types of human nature that are to be found in fiction, biography, or history."

The Civil War ended his steamboating and he served briefly in a Confederate militia company. Following his stint in the military, he set out with his brother, Orion, by stagecoach over the Rockies. While in the West he tried prospecting and speculating, but found his true calling in journalism. He was greatly influenced by the literary comedians and local colorists of the period, Bret Harte and Artemus Ward. He became more skillful than his teachers in developing his rich characterizations. In 1865 he attained national fame using his pseudonym, Mark Twain, with his story "The Celebrated Jumping Frog of Calaveras County." He also discovered a new vocation as a popular lecturer in San Francisco, keeping his audience convulsed with tales of his adventures. Full public recognition came with the publishing of Innocents Abroad *(1869), a wild and rollicking account of his invasion of the Old World, much of which would seem quite* <u>*languid*</u> *by today's standards. Some of his finest writings were three works filled with lively adventure on the Mississippi River and based on his boyhood,* Tom Sawyer *(1876),* Life on the Mississippi *(1883), and* Huckleberry Finn *(1884). Throughout his career Twain preferred to display his flair for journalistic improvisation rather than*

maintain the artist's concern for form. In his artfully told stories, Mark Twain conveyed his keen powers of observation and perception, his broad understanding of human nature, and his refreshing sense of humor.

Questions 1–5

1. The author's main purpose in writing this passage is to

   (A) suggest when Samuel Clemens started writing.

   (B) survey the variety of jobs Clemens held in his life.

   (C) explain Clemens's philosophy of writing.

   (D) argue that Clemens is one of the best American authors.

   (E) discuss some of the major events that shaped Clemens's writing.

2. From the passage, the author's point of view regarding Clemens's writing is

   (A) literary criticism of his local color style.

   (B) primarily on one of extolling his writing.

   (C) a defense of Clemens's journalistic style.

   (D) indifferent to Clemens's writing style.

   (E) a comparison of Clemens to other writers of the period.

3. In the sentence about *Innocents Abroad,* “a wild and rollicking account of his invasion of the Old World, much of which would seem quite languid by today’s standards,” languid probably means which of the following?

   (A) Similar to

   (B) Difficult

   (C) Tame

   (D) Impossible

   (E) Expensive

4. The passage supports which of the following conclusions about Clemens’s career as a writer?

   (A) Clemens acquired great personal wealth from his writing.

   (B) Clemens was a better journalist than novelist.

   (C) Clemens’s lectures provided material for his writing.

   (D) Clemens’s personal experiences shaped his writing.

   (E) His associations with Bret Harte and Artemus Ward aided Clemens’s professional progress.

5. According to the passage, which of the following best describes Clemens's appeal to his public?

(A) His use of the humorous side of human nature

(B) His descriptions of life on the Mississippi River

(C) His tales of life in the West

(D) Seeing him as the typical American writer

(E) Viewing him as the impulsive traveler

Detailed Explanations of Answers

1. **(E)** The passage mentions a variety of occupations Clemens held and travels he made, which provided the substance of many of his characterizations and settings. Choice (A) is irrelevant to the question and choice (B) is a secondary purpose rather than the primary one, because it digresses from the topic of Samuel Clemens's career as a writer. Choice (D) suggests that the passage is an argument, which is not in keeping with the whole "discussion" tone, and choice (C) is information not given in the passage.

2. **(B)** This choice is supported in the passage with the statement, "He became more skillful than his teachers in developing his rich characterizations." It is also supported in the last sentence of the passage. Choices (A), a literary criticism, (C), a defense of journalistic style, and (E), a comparison, are not suggested by information in the passage. Choice (D) can be eliminated because it contradicts the positive attitude of the passage towards Clemens's writing.

3. **(C)** When test questions involve the meaning of an unfamiliar word, definitions can frequently be determined from the context (surrounding words). Questions of this type are included to

assess how well the reader can extract a word's meaning by looking within the passage for clues. Sometimes the opposite of the meaning is given somewhere in the text. The words "wild and rollicking" are being compared to traveling through Europe by today's standards. Choice (A), similar to today's standards, does not make sense when we compare traveling in the 1800s to today's standards. Choice (B), difficult, can be eliminated since it is a contradiction: traveling is less—not more—difficult today than in the past. Choice (D), impossible, is nonsensical; traveling has never been impossible. Although choice (E), expensive, is a possible correct answer, the context of the passage should cause the reader to look for the opposite of the meaning of "wild and rollicking," which would be "tame."

4. **(D)** Choices (A), (B), and (C) contain information not given in the passage. These can, therefore, be eliminated as irrelevant. Choice (E) could be considered as a possible answer because Bret Harte and Artemus Ward were mentioned as having an influence on Clemens's writing style. However, it is important not to read into this that they assisted him professionally in the development of his writing career. The discussion that Clemens was a world traveler who experienced a wide variety of occupations that provided background for his writing supports choice (D).

5. **(A)** Choices (B) and (C) are possible correct answers because these settings provided the background for some of Clemens's most popular works, but these settings did not necessarily appeal to everyone. Choice (D) is not developed in the text as the reason for Clemens's public appeal. Choice (E) is irrelevant. Clemens's use of humor is discussed in relation to his becoming more skillful than the local colorists who influenced him and also in the last sentence of the passage. Choice (A) is the best answer, since the passage ends by discussing Clemens's humor and gives examples throughout, and because his humor offered widespread appeal.

Chapter

4

Mathematics Review

Overview

The following is intended as a review of the basic mathematical skills assessed on the mathematics section of the CBEST. It is not intended as a substitute for a comprehensive mathematics curriculum. If you're taking the CBEST, this section should provide an efficient means of reviewing a wide range of mathematics topics developed during your schooling.

The mathematics portion of the CBEST assesses cumulative knowledge of the mathematics traditionally taught in elementary and high school and, sometimes, in college. All teachers need to know math, whether or not they teach it as an assigned class.

Three categories of mathematical ability are assessed:

1. Identifying Processes Used in Problem Solving

Questions in this category assess your ability to determine what is required to solve problems or "set up" problems. Questions in this category will not require you to actually solve the problem. Examples of tasks you may be required to perform include identifying an arithmetic operation (addition, subtraction, multiplication, division) that may be required to solve a problem, recognizing that sufficient information is or is not given to solve the problem, translating a word problem into mathematical symbols (or vice versa), or recognizing different ways of solving a problem. The problems in this section may require identifying the arithmetic, geometric, logical, or graphic processes used in solving problems.

2. Solution of Word Problems

Questions in this category assess your ability to solve word or "story" problems. Mathematical topics included in this category are arithmetic, algebra, geometry, and statistics. You also may be asked to evaluate a given formula ("plug in" values and give an answer) or estimate the answer for a problem.

3. Demonstrating an Understanding of Mathematical Concepts and Relationships

Questions in this category assess your ability to understand basic mathematical concepts. Examples include terms (e.g., area, perimeter, volume), order (greater than, less than, equal to), relationships demonstrated by a graph, and elementary probability. Concepts assessed in this category are from arithmetic, algebra, or geometry.

About 40% of the questions on the mathematics section of the CBEST are related to arithmetic. About 20% of the questions are related to elementary geometry. The remaining items are related to other mathematical concepts and skills. None of the questions strictly tests computation as such; however, computational skill is required throughout the test.

Three basic categories of mathematical topics may appear on the mathematics section of the CBEST:

1. **Arithmetic.** Topics included in this category are: integers; prime and composite numbers; odd and even numbers; place value; powers and roots of whole numbers; addition, subtraction, multiplication and division of integers, common fractions, and decimal fractions; percents; and elementary statistics.

2. **Algebra.** Topics included in this category are: algebraic expressions; simplifying algebraic expressions; factoring; solving linear equations; solving inequalities; evaluating formulas; elementary probability; and algebra word problems.

3. **Geometry and Measurement.** Topics included in this category are: perimeter and area of rectangles, squares, and triangles; circumference and area of circles; volume of cubes and rectangular solids; angle measure; properties of triangles; the Pythagorean Theorem; properties of parallel and perpendicular lines; coordinate geometry; graphs; and the metric system.

Part I: Arithmetic

Integers

Natural or counting numbers are 1, 2, 3, ...

Whole numbers are 0, 1, 2, 3, ...

Integers are ...–2, –1, 0, 1, 2, ...

As shown below, a number line is often used to represent integers.

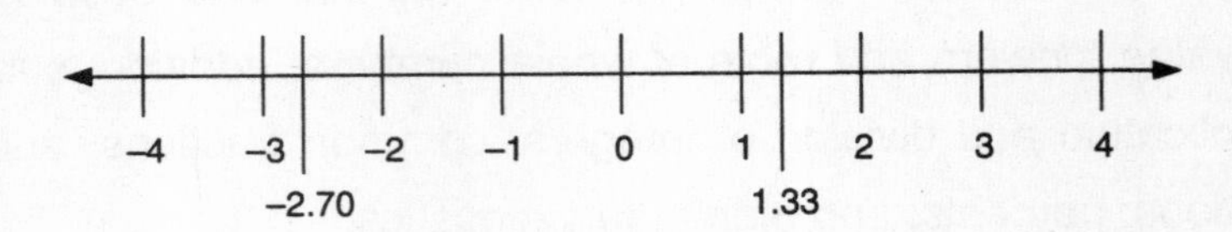

The following are properties of integers:

Example: $2 + 3 = 3 + 2$

Example: $(2 + 3) + 4 = 2 + (3 + 4)$

Example: $2 \times (3 + 4) = (2 \times 3) + (2 \times 4)$
$2 \times 7 = 6 + 8$
$14 = 14$

Example: $2 + 0 = 2$

Example: $2 \times 1 = 2$

Prime and Composite Numbers

When two whole numbers are multiplied, they yield a product. These two whole numbers can be called *factors* or *divisors* of the product. (An exception to this is 0, which can be a factor, but not a divisor, since division by 0 is undefined.)

Example: **$2 \times 3 = 6$**
2 and 3 are factors or divisors of the product 6.

Example: **$0 \times 3 = 0$**
3 is a factor and divisor of the product 0, but 0 is only a factor of the product 0, since $0 \div 0$ is undefined.

A *prime number* is a whole number greater than 1 that has only two different whole number factors, 1 and the number itself.

Example: **5 is a prime number, because it has only two different factors, 1 and 5.**

A *composite number* is a whole number that has three or more whole number factors.

Example: **6 is a composite number, because it has four different factors, 1, 2, 3, and 6.**

Even and Odd Numbers

Even numbers are whole numbers that have 2 as a factor.

Example: **6 is an even number, since $2 \times 3 = 6$.**

Odd numbers are whole numbers that do not have 2 as a factor.

Example: **5 is an odd number, since 2 is not a factor of 5.**

Place Value

Our numeration system uses the *Hindu-Arabic numerals* (0, 1, 2, 3, 4, 5, 6, 7, 8, 9) to represent numbers.

Our numeration system follows a *base 10 place-value scheme*. As we move to the left in any number, each place value is ten times the place value to the right. Similarly, as we move to the right, each place value is one-tenth the place value to the left.

Example: In the number 543.21, the place value of the 5 (100's) is ten times the place value of the 4 (10's). The place value of the 1 ($^1/_{100}$'s) is one-tenth the place value of the 2 ($^1/_{10}$'s).

The concept of place value will be discussed later.

Powers and Roots of Whole Numbers

Exponents and Bases

In the expression 5^3, 5 is called the *base* and 3 is called the *exponent*. The expression $5^3 = 5 \times 5 \times 5$. The base (5) gives the factor used in the expression and the exponent (3) gives the number of times the base is to be used as a factor.

Examples: $4^2 = 4 \times 4$

$3^5 = 3 \times 3 \times 3 \times 3 \times 3$

When the base has an exponent of 2, the base is said to be *squared*. When the base has an exponent of 3, the base is said to be *cubed*.

The Basic Laws of Exponents are

1) $b^m \times b^n = b^{m+n}$

Example: $2^5 \times 2^3 = 2^{5+3} = 2^8$

2) $b^m \div b^n = b^{m-n}$

Example: $2^5 \div 2^3 = 2^{5-3} = 2^2$

3) $(b^m)^n = b^{m \times n}$

Example: $(2^5)^3 = 2^{5 \times 3} = 2^{15}$

Roots

Consider again the expression 5^3. If we carry out the implied multiplication, we get $5^3 = 5 \times 5 \times 5 = 125$. 5 is called the cube root of 125, since $5^3 = 125$. In general, when a base is raised to a power to produce a given result, the base is called the *root* of the given result.

If the power for the base is 2, the base is called the *square root*. If the power for the base is 3, the base is called the *cube root*. In general, if $b^n = p$, then b is the *nth root* of p.

Examples: Since $4^2 = 16$, 4 is the square root of 16.

Since $2^3 = 8$, 2 is the cube root of 8.

Since $3^5 = 243$, 3 is the 5th root of 243.

Arithmetic Operations and Integers

As illustrated in Section 1.1, integers are *signed numbers* preceded by either a "+" or a "–" sign. If no sign is given for the integer, one should infer that the integer is positive (e.g., 3 means +3). As also illustrated in Section 1.1, integers to the left of zero are negative and integers to the right of zero are positive.

The *absolute value* of an integer is the measure of the distance of the integer from zero. Since the measure of distance is always positive, absolute value is always positive: the absolute value of the real number a is denoted by $|a|$ (e.g., $|-3| = 3$, $|3| = 3$).

Addition

When two integers are added, the two integers are called *addends*, and the result is called the sum, as illustrated in the following:

5	+	3	=	8
(addend)		(addend)		(sum)

or

$$\begin{array}{rl} 5 & \text{(addend)} \\ \underline{+\,3} & \text{(addend)} \\ 8 & \text{(sum)} \end{array}$$

When adding two integers, one of the following two situations might occur:

Situation 1: Both integers have the same sign. In this case, add the absolute values of the two addends and give the sum the same sign as the addends.

Examples: **2 + 3 = 5, and**
–2 + (–3) = –5.

Situation 2: The two integers have different signs. In this case, subtract the addend with the smaller absolute value from the addend with the larger absolute value. The sum gets the sign of the addend with the larger absolute value.

Examples: **–2 + 5 = 3, but**
2 + (–5) = –3.

Subtraction

In a subtraction sentence, the top or first number in the subtraction is the *minuend,* the bottom or second number is the *subtra-*

hend, and the result is the *remainder* or *difference*. These quantities are demonstrated in the following:

5	–	3	=	2
(minuend)		(subtrahend)		(remainder)

or

$$\begin{array}{rl} 5 & \text{(minuend)} \\ \underline{-3} & \text{(subtrahend)} \\ 2 & \text{(remainder)} \end{array}$$

When subtracting a negative integer, change the sign of the subtrahend and add the resulting two integers, following the procedures given above.

Examples: 5 – 3 = 2, but
5 – (–3) = 5 + (+3) = 5 + 3 = 8.

Multiplication

When multiplying two integers, the two integers are called *factors,* and the result is called the *product*, as illustrated in the following:

5	×	3	=	15
(factor)		(factor)		(product)

or

$$\begin{array}{rl} 5 & \text{(factor)} \\ \underline{\times 3} & \text{(factor)} \\ 15 & \text{(product)} \end{array}$$

When multiplying two integers, multiply the absolute values of the factors. If the factors have the same sign, the product is positive; if the factors have different signs, the product is negative. If either factor is zero, the product is zero.

Examples: 3 × 5 = 15 and (–3) × (–5) = 15, but
(–3) × 5 = –15 and 3 × (–5) = –15.

Division

When dividing two integers, the number being divided is the *dividend,* the number being divided into another integer is the *divisor*, and the result is the *quotient*, as illustrated in the following:

10	÷	2	=	5
(dividend)		(divisor)		(quotient)

When dividing two integers, divide the absolute values of the dividend and divisor. The sign of the quotient can be obtained by following the same procedures given above.

Examples: $10 \div 2 = 5$ and $(-10) \div (-2) = 5$, but
$(-10) \div 2 = (-5)$ and $10 \div (-2) = (-5)$.

Arithmetic Operations and Common Fractions

A *common fraction* is a number that can be written in the form $\frac{a}{b}$, where a and b are whole numbers. In the expression $\frac{a}{b}$, the dividend a is called the *numerator* and the divisor b is called the *denominator.*

Example: In the expression $\frac{3}{4}$, 3 is the numerator and 4 is the denominator.

A common fraction may not have 0 as a denominator, since *division by 0 is undefined.*

A fraction is in *lowest terms* if the numerator and denominator have no common factors.

Examples: $\frac{1}{2}$, $\frac{3}{4}$, and $\frac{5}{6}$ **are in lowest terms, since the numerator and denominator of each have no common factors.**

$\frac{2}{4}$, $\frac{9}{21}$, and $\frac{20}{24}$ **are *not* in lowest terms, since the numerator and denominator of each have common factors.**

Fractions are *equivalent* if they represent the same number.

Example: $\frac{8}{16}$, $\frac{4}{8}$, $\frac{2}{4}$, and $\frac{5}{10}$ **are equivalent fractions, since each represents** $\frac{1}{2}$.

A *mixed numeral* is a number that consists of an integer and a common fraction.

Example: $5\frac{3}{4}$ **is a mixed numeral since it consists of the integer 5 and the common fraction** $\frac{3}{4}$.

If you wanted to change $\frac{2}{3}$ to a fraction with a denominator of 18, the solution would be $\frac{12}{18}$.

An *improper fraction* is a common fraction whose numerator is larger than its denominator. A mixed numeral can be expressed as an improper fraction by multiplying the denominator of the common fraction part times the integer part and adding that product to the numerator of the common fraction part. The result is the numerator of the improper fraction. The denominator of the improper fraction is the same as the denominator in the mixed numeral.

Example: $5\frac{3}{4} = \frac{23}{4}$**, since $(4 \times 5) + 3 = 23$, and 4 was the denominator of the common fraction part; $\frac{23}{4}$ is an improper fraction, since the numerator 23 is larger than the denominator 4.**

Addition

In order to *add* two fractions, the denominators of the fractions must be the same; when they are, they are called *common denominators.* The equivalent fractions with the smallest common denominator are said to have the *lowest common denominator*.

Examples: $\frac{3}{8} + \frac{2}{8} = \frac{5}{8}$**, but**

$\frac{3}{8} + \frac{1}{4} = \frac{3}{8} + \frac{2}{8} = \frac{5}{8}$**. Note that while 16, 24, 32, and so forth, could have been used as common denominators to obtain equivalent fractions, the lowest common denominator, 8, was used to generate like denominators.**

The procedures regarding the addition of signed numbers given in Section 1.6.1 also apply for the addition of common fractions.

Subtraction

The procedures given for the addition of common fractions together with the procedures for subtraction of signed numbers form the basis for the subtraction of common fractions.

Examples: $\frac{3}{8}-\frac{2}{8}=\frac{1}{8}$, **but**

$\frac{3}{8}-\frac{1}{4}=\frac{3}{8}-\frac{2}{8}=\frac{1}{8}$.

As also suggested,

$$\frac{3}{8}-\left(-\frac{2}{8}\right)=\frac{3}{8}+\frac{2}{8}=\frac{5}{8} \text{ and}$$

$$\frac{3}{8}-\left(-\frac{1}{4}\right)=\frac{3}{8}+\frac{1}{4}=\frac{3}{8}+\frac{2}{8}=\frac{5}{8}.$$

Multiplication

To *multiply* two common fractions, simply find the product of the two numerators and divide it by the product of the two denominators. Reduce the resultant fraction to lowest terms.

Example: $\frac{2}{3}\times\frac{9}{11}=\frac{18}{33}=\frac{6}{11}$

In addition, the procedures regarding the multiplication of integers apply to the multiplication of common fractions.

Division

To find the *reciprocal* of a common fraction, exchange the numerator and the denominator.

Examples: The reciprocal of $\frac{2}{3}$ **is** $\frac{3}{2}$.

The reciprocal of $\frac{21}{4}$ **is** $\frac{4}{21}$.

To *divide* two common fractions, multiply the fraction which is the dividend by the reciprocal of the fraction which is the divisor. Reduce the result to lowest terms.

Examples: $\frac{4}{9} \div \frac{2}{3} = \frac{4}{9} \times \frac{3}{2} = \frac{12}{18} = \frac{2}{3}$

$\frac{7}{8} \div \frac{21}{4} = \frac{7}{8} \times \frac{4}{21} = \frac{28}{168} = \frac{1}{6}$

In addition, the procedures regarding the division of integers apply to the division of common fractions.

Arithmetic Operations and Decimal Fractions

As discussed above, our numeration system follows a base 10 place-value scheme. Another way to represent a fractional number is to write the number to include integer powers of ten. This allows us to represent *decimal fractions* as follows:

$\frac{1}{10} = 10^{-1} = 0.1$ (said "one-tenth")

$\frac{1}{100} = 10^{-2} = 0.01$ (said "one-hundredth")

$\frac{1}{1{,}000} = 10^{-3} = 0.001$ (said "one-thousandth"), and so forth.

Examples: 3.14 is said "three and fourteen hundredths."
528.5 is said "five hundred twenty-eight and five-tenths."

Addition

To *add decimal fractions*, simply line up the decimal points for each decimal numeral to be added, and follow the procedures for the addition of integers. Place the decimal point in the sum directly underneath the decimal point in the addends.

Examples:

89.8	32.456
152.9	6561.22
+ 7.21	+ 2.14
249.91	6595.816

Subtraction

To *subtract decimal fractions*, place zeros as needed so that both the minuend and the subtrahend have a digit in each column. Follow the procedures for addition of decimal fractions, and the procedures for the subtraction of integers.

Examples:

152.9	→	152.90
−7.21		−7.21
		145.69

32.456	→	32.456
−2.14		− 2.140
		30.316

Multiplication

To *multiply decimal fractions*, follow the procedures for multiplying integers, and then place the decimal point so that *the total number of decimal places in the product is equal to the sum of the decimal places in each factor.*

Examples: **(3.14) (0.5) = 1.570, and**
(89.8) (152.9) = 13,730.42

Division

To *divide decimal fractions,*

1) move the decimal point in the divisor to the right, until there are no decimal places in the divisor,

2) move the decimal point in the dividend the same number of decimal places to the right, and

3) divide the transformed dividend and divisor as given above.

4) The number of decimal places in the quotient should be the same as the number of decimal places in the transformed dividend.

Examples: $15.5 \div 0.5 \rightarrow 155 \div 5 = 31$, and
$32.436 \div 0.06 \rightarrow 3243.6 \div 6 = 540.6$

Percent

Percent is another way of expressing a fractional number. Percent always expresses a fractional number in terms of $\frac{1}{100}$ or 0.01. Percents use the "%" symbol.

Examples: $100\% = \frac{100}{100} = 1.00$, and

$25\% = \frac{25}{100} = 0.25.$

As shown in these examples, a percent is easily converted to a common fraction or a decimal fraction. To convert a decimal to a common fraction, place the percent in the numerator and use 100 as the denominator (reduce as necessary). To convert a percent to a decimal fraction, divide the percent by 100, or move the decimal point two places to the left.

Examples: $25\% = \frac{25}{100} = \frac{1}{4}$ **and**

$25\% = 0.25.$

Similarly, $125\% = \frac{125}{100} = 1\frac{25}{100} = 1\frac{1}{4}$ **and**

$125\% = 1.25.$

To convert a *common fraction* to a *percent,* carry a division of the numerator by the denominator of the fraction out to three decimal places. Round the result to two places. To convert a *decimal fraction* to a *percent,* move the decimal point two places to the right (adding 0's as place holders, if needed) and round as necessary.

Examples: $\frac{1}{4} = 1 \div 4 = 0.25 = 25\%$**, and**

$\frac{2}{7} = 2 \div 7 \cong 0.28 = 28\%.$

If you wish to find the *percentage* of a known quantity, change the percent to a common fraction or a decimal fraction, and multiply the fraction times the quantity. The percentage is expressed in the same units as the known quantity.

Example: To find 25% of 360 books, change 25% to 0.25 and multiply times 360, as follows: $0.25 \times 360 = 90$**.**
The result is 90 books.

(Note: The known quantity is the *base,* the percent is the *rate,* and the result is the *percentage.*)

Example: 15 is what percent of 75?

$15 \div 75 = .20 = 20\%$

Example: **45 is 30% of what number?**

$45 \div .30 = 150$

Elementary Statistics

Mean

The average, or *mean,* of a set of numbers can be found by adding the set of numbers and dividing by the total number of elements in the set.

Example: **The mean of 15, 10, 25, 5, 40 is**

$$\frac{15+10+25+5+40}{5} = \frac{95}{5} = 19.$$

Median

If a given set of numbers is ordered from smallest to largest, the *median* is the "middle" number; that is, half of the numbers in the set of numbers are below the median and half of the numbers in the set are above the median.

Example: **To find the median of the set of whole numbers 15, 10, 25, 5, 40, first order the set of numbers to get 5, 10, 15, 25, 40. Since 15 is the middle number (half of the numbers are below 15, half are above 15), 15 is called the median of this set of whole numbers. If there is an even number of numbers in the set, the median is the mean of the middle two numbers.**

Problem: **Find the median for 15, 10, 25, 5, 40, 20.**

Solution: **Rearrange in order to get 5, 10, 15, 20, 25, 40. The median is the average of the third and fourth numbers. 17.5**

Mode

The *mode* of a set of numbers is the number that appears most frequently in the set.

Example: **In the set 15, 10, 25, 10, 5, 40, 10, 15, the number 10 appears most frequently (three times); therefore, 10 is the mode of the given set of numbers.**

There may be no mode or more than one mode for a set of numbers.

Example: **2, 5, 7, 8 (No mode.)**

Example: **6, 3, 5, 6, 5 (5 and 6 are both modes.)**

Range

The *range* of a set of numbers is obtained by subtracting the smallest number in the set from the largest number in the set.

Example: **To find the range of 15, 10, 25, 5, 40, find the difference between the largest and the smallest elements of the set. This gives 40 – 5 = 35. The range of the given set is 35.**

Elementary Probability

The likelihood or chance that an event will take place is called the *probability* of the event. The probability of an event is determined by dividing the number of ways the event could occur by the number of possible events in the given sample. In other words, if a sample space S has n possible outcomes, and an event E has m ways of occurring, then the probability of the event, denoted by $P(E)$, is given by

$$P(E) = \frac{m}{n}.$$

It should be noted that $0 \le P(E) \le 1$.

Problem: **What is the probability of getting "heads" on the toss of a coin?**

Solution: **Since the number of possible outcomes in the toss of a coin is 2 and the number of ways of getting "heads" on a coin toss is 1, P(head) = $\frac{1}{2}$.**

Problem: **What is the probability of drawing an ace from a standard deck of playing cards?**

Solution: **Since the number of aces in a standard deck is 4 and the number of cards in a standard deck is 52, P(ace) = $\frac{4}{52} = \frac{1}{13}$.**

Problem: **In tossing a pair of dice, what is the probability of getting a sum of 10?**

Solution: **There are $6 \times 6 = 36$ possible outcomes. The 3 ways to get a sum of 10 are 5 and 5, 6 and 4, 4 and 6. So the required probability = $\frac{3}{36} = \frac{1}{12}$.**

Part II: Algebra

Algebraic Expressions

An *algebraic expression* is an expression using letters, numbers, symbols, and arithmetic operations to represent a number or relationship among numbers.

A *variable,* or unknown, is a letter that stands for a number in an algebraic expression. *Coefficients* are the numbers that precede the variable to give the quantity of the variable in the expression.

Algebraic expressions are composed of *terms,* or groupings of variables and numbers.

An algebraic expression with one term is called a *monomial;* with two terms, a *binomial;* with three terms, a *trinomial;* with more than one term, a *polynomial.*

Examples: $2ab - cd$ is a binomial algebraic expression with variables a, b, c, and d, and terms $2ab$ and $(-cd)$. 2 is the coefficient of ab and -1 is the coefficient of cd.

$x^2 + 3y - 1$ is a trinomial algebraic expression using the variables x and y, and terms x^2, $3y$, and (-1);

$z(x - 1) + uv - wy - 2$ is a polynomial with variables z, x, u, v, w, and y, and terms $z(x - 1)$, uv, $(-wy)$, and (-2).

As stated above, algebraic expressions can be used to represent the relationships among numbers. For example, if we know there are ten times as many students in a school as teachers, if S represents the number of students in the school and T represents the number of teachers, the total number of students and teachers in the school is $S + T$.

If we wished to form an algebraic sentence equating the number of students and teachers in the school, the sentence would be $S = 10T$. (Note that if either the number of students or the number of teachers were known, the other quantity could be found.)

Simplifying Algebraic Expressions

Like terms are terms in an algebraic expression that are exactly the same; that is, they contain the same variables and the same powers.

Examples: The following are pairs of like terms:
x^2 and $(-3x^2)$, abc and $4abc$, $(x-1)$ and $2(x-1)$.
The following are not pairs of like terms:
x and $(-3x^2)$, abc and $4a^2bc$, $(x-1)$ and (x^2-1).

To simplify an algebraic expression, combine like terms in the following order:

1) Simplify all expressions within symbols of inclusion (e.g., ( ), [ ], { }) using steps 2 through 4 below.

2) Carry out all exponentiation.

3) Carry out all multiplication and division from left to right in the order in which the operations occur.

4) Carry out all addition and subtraction from left to right in the order in which the operations occur.

Factoring Algebraic Expressions

When two numbers are multiplied together, the numbers are called factors and their result is called the product. Similarly, algebraic expressions may be the product of other algebraic expressions.

In factoring algebraic expressions, first remove any monomial factors, then remove any binomial, trinomial, or other polynomial factors. Often one may find other polynomial factors by inspecting for the sum and difference of two squares; that is, $x^2 - y^2 = (x + y)(x - y)$.

Examples: $2a + 2b = 2(a + b)$

$4x^2y - 2xy^2 + 16x^2y^2 = 2xy(2x - y + 8xy)$

$x^2 - 4 = (x + 2)(x - 2)$

$4a^2 - 16b^2 = 4(a^2 - 4b^2) = 4(a + 2b)(a - 2b)$

In factoring polynomials, one often uses what is called the *"FOIL" method (First, Outside, Inside, Last).*

Examples: $x^2 + 3x - 10 = (x - 2)(x + 5)$

$6y^2 - y - 2 = (2y + 1)(3y - 2)$

$ab^2 - 3ab - 10a = a(b^2 - 3b - 10) = a(b + 2)(b - 5)$

Solving Linear Equations

To solve a linear equation, use the following procedures:

1) Isolate the variable; that is, group all the terms with the variable on one side of the equation (commonly the left side) and group all the constants on the other side of the equation (commonly the right side).

2) Combine like terms on each side of the equation.

3) Divide by the coefficient of the variable.

4) Check the result in the original equation.

Problem: Solve $3x + 2 = 5$ for x.
Solution: $3x + 2 = 5$ (add –2 to both sides)

$3x = 3 \left(\text{multiply by } \frac{1}{3}\right)$

$x = 1$

Problem: Solve $a + 3a = 3a + 1$ for a.
Solution: $a + 3a = 3a + 1$ (add $-3a$ to both sides)

$a = 1$

Problem: Solve $3(y - 2) + 5 = 3 + 5y$ for y.
Solution: $3(y - 2) + 5 = 3 + 5y$ (simplify)

$3y - 6 + 5 = 3 + 5y$ (combine like terms)

$3y - 1 = 3 + 5y$ (add 1 to both sides)

$3y = 4 + 5y$ (add $-5y$ to both sides)

$-2y = 4 \left(\text{multiply by } \frac{1}{2}\right)$

$y = -2$

Solving Inequalities

The equivalence properties of integers and the procedures for solving linear equations are used to solve *inequalities.* In addition, the following properties of inequalities should be noted:

If $x < y$ and $z > 0$, then $zx < zy$.
If $x > y$ and $z > 0$, then $zx > zy$.

If $x < y$ and $z < 0$, then $zx > zy$.
If $x > y$ and $z < 0$, then $zx < zy$.

In other words, if both sides of an inequality are *multiplied by a positive number, the sense of the inequality remains the same.* If both sides of an inequality are *multiplied by a negative number, the sense of the inequality is reversed.*

Examples: Since $3 < 5$ and 2 is positive,
$(2)(3) < (2)(5)$ or $6 < 10$.
But since $3 < 5$ and -2 is negative,
$(-2)(3) > (-2)(5)$ or $-6 > -10$.

The above properties are also demonstrated in the following problems:

Problem: Find the values of y for which $2y > y - 3$.
Solution: $2y > y - 3$ (add $-y$ to both sides)
$y > -3$

Problem: Find the values of x for which $x > 4x + 1$.
Solution: $x > 4x + 1$ (add $-4x$ to both sides)

$-3x > 1$ $\left(\text{multiply by } -\frac{1}{3}\right)$

$x < -\frac{1}{3}$

Evaluating Formulas

Formulas are algebraic sentences that are frequently used in mathematics, science, or other fields. Examples of common formulas are $A = l \times w$, $d = r \times t$, and $C = \left(\frac{5}{9}\right)(F - 32°)$. *To evaluate a formula,* replace each variable with the given values of the variables and solve for the unknown variable.

Example: **Since $A = l \times w$, if $l = 2$ ft. and $w = 3$ ft., then $A = 2 \text{ ft.} \times 3 \text{ ft.} = 6$ sq. ft.**

Example: **Since $d = r \times t$, if $r = 32 \text{ m/sec}^2$ and $t = 5$ sec., then $d = (32 \text{ m/sec}^2) \times 5 \text{ sec.} = 160$ m.**

Example: **Since $C = \left(\frac{5}{9}\right)(F - 32)$, if $F = 212°$,**

then $C = \left(\frac{5}{9}\right)(212° - 32°) = 100°$.

Algebra Word Problems

A general procedure for solving word problems was suggested by Polya. His procedure can be summarized as follows:

1) Understand the problem.

2) Devise a plan for solving the problem.

3) Carry out the plan.

4) Look back on the solution to the problem.

When taking the mathematics section of the CBEST, you can use this procedure by translating the word problem into an algebraic sentence and then following the procedures for solving an algebraic sentence. Find a variable to represent the unknown in the problem. Look for key synonyms such as "is, are, were" for "=", "more, more than" for "+", "less, less than, fewer" for "–", and "of" for "x."

Problem: **The sum of the ages of Bill and Paul is 32 years. Bill is 6 years older than Paul. Find the age of each.**

Solution: **If p = Paul's age, then Bill's age is $p + 6$. So that $p + (p + 6) = 32$. Applying the methods from above, we get $p = 13$. Therefore, Paul is 13 and Bill is 19.**

Problem: **Jose weighs twice as much as his brother Carlos. If together they weigh 225 pounds, how much does each weigh?**

Solution: **If c = Carlos' weight, then Jose's weight is $2c$. So $c + 2c = 225$ pounds. Applying the methods above, we get $c = 75$. Therefore, Carlos weighs 75 pounds and Jose weighs 150 pounds.**

Problem: **Julia drove from her home to her aunt's house in 3 hours and 30 minutes. If the distance between the houses is 175 miles, what was the car's average speed?**

Solution: **Distance = rate × time. Since we know $d = 175$ miles and $t = 3\frac{1}{2}$ hr., then 175 miles = $r \times 3\frac{1}{2}$ hr. Solving for the rate (r), we get $r = 50$ mph.**

(It is strongly suggested that individuals who feel they need additional practice in solving word problems using the above procedures seek out additional practice problems in a standard high school first-year algebra textbook.)

Part III: Measurement and Geometry

Perimeter and Area of Rectangles, Squares, and Triangles

Perimeter refers to the measure of the distance around a figure. Perimeter is measured in linear units (e.g., inches, feet, meters). *Area* refers to the measure of the interior of a figure. Area is measured in square units (e.g., square inches, square feet, square meters).

Perimeter of Rectangles, Squares, and Triangles

The *perimeter of a rectangle* is found by adding twice the length of the rectangle to twice the width of the rectangle. This relationship is commonly given by the formula $P = 2l + 2w$, where l is the measure of the length and w is the measure of the width.

Example: **If a rectangle has $l = 10$ m and $w = 5$ m, then the perimeter of the rectangie is given by $P = 2(10 \text{ m}) + 2(5 \text{ m}) = 30$ m.**

The *perimeter of a square* is found by multiplying four times the measure of a side of the square. This relationship is commonly given by the formula $P = 4s$, where s is the measure of a side of the square.

Example: **If a square has $s = 5$ feet, then the perimeter of the square is given by $P = 4(5 \text{ feet}) = 20$ feet.**

The *perimeter of a triangle* is found by adding the measures of the three sides of the triangle. This relationship can be represented by $P = s_1 + s_2 + s_3$, where s_1, s_2, and s_3 are the measures of the sides of the triangle.

Example: If a triangle has three sides measuring 3 inches, 4 inches, and 5 inches, then the perimeter of the triangle is given by $P = 3$ inches + 4 inches + 5 inches = 12 inches.

Area of Rectangles, Squares, and Triangles

The *area of a rectangle* is found by multiplying the measure of the length of the rectangle by the measure of the width of the triangle. This relationship is commonly given by $A = l \times w$, where l is the measure of the length and w is the measure of the width.

Example: If a rectangle has $l = 10$ m and $w = 5$ m, then the area of the rectangle is given by $A = 10 \text{ m} \times 5 \text{ m} = 50 \text{ m}^2$.

The *area of a square* is found by squaring the measure of a side of the square. This relationship is commonly given by $A = s^2$, where s is the measure of a side.

Example: If a square has $s = 5$ ft., then the area of the square is given by $A = (5 \text{ ft})^2 = 25 \text{ ft}^2$.

The area = $\sqrt{s(b - a)(s - b)(s - c)}$, where a, b, c are the three sides and the 3 sides $s = \dfrac{(a + b + c)}{2}$ = semi-perimeter.

The *area of a right triangle* is found by multiplying $\frac{1}{2}$ times the product of the base and the height of the triangle. This relationship is commonly given by $A = \frac{1}{2}bh$, where b is the base and h is the height.

Example: **If a triangle has a base of 3 in. and a height of 4 in., then the area of the triangle is given by**

$$A = \frac{1}{2}(3 \text{ in.} \times 4 \text{ in.}) = \frac{1}{2}(12 \text{ in}^2) = 6 \text{ in}^2.$$

Circumference and Area of Circles

The *radius of a circle* is the distance from the center of the circle to the circle itself. The *diameter of a circle* is a line segment that passes through the center of the circle, the end points of which lie on the circle. The *measure of the diameter of a circle* is twice the measure of the radius.

The number π $\left(\text{approximately } 3.14 \text{ or } 3\frac{1}{7}\right)$ is often used in computations involving circles.

The *circumference of a circle* is found by multiplying π times the diameter (or twice the radius). This relationship is commonly given by $C = \pi \times d$, or $C = 2 \times \pi \times r$.

The *area of a circle* is found by multiplying π by the square of the radius of the circle. This relationship is commonly given by $A = \pi \times r^2$.

Example: **If a circle has a radius of 5 cm, then**
$C = \pi \times 10 \text{ cm} = 3.14 \times 10 \text{ cm} \approx 31.4 \text{ cm}$, **and**
$A = \pi \times (5 \text{ cm})^2 \approx 3.14 \times (5 \text{ cm})^2 = 78.50 \text{ cm}^2$.

Volume of Cubes and Rectangular Solids

Volume refers to the measure of the interior of a three-dimensional figure.

A *rectangular solid* is a rectilinear (right-angled) figure that has length, width, and height. The volume of a rectangular solid is found by computing the product of the length, width, and height of the figure. This relationship is commonly expressed by $V = l \times w \times h$.

Example: The volume of a rectangular solid with $l = 5$ cm, $w = 4$ cm, and $h = 3$ cm is given by $V = 5 \text{ cm} \times 4 \text{ cm} \times 3 \text{ cm} = 60 \text{ cm}^3$.

A *cube* is a rectangular solid, the length, width, and height of which have the same measure. This measure is called the *edge of the cube.* The volume of a cube is found by cubing the measure of the edge. This relationship is commonly expressed by $V = e^3$.

Example: The volume of a cube with $e = 5$ cm is given by $V = (5 \text{ cm})^3 = 125 \text{ cm}^3$.

Angle Measure

An *angle* consists of all the points in two noncollinear rays that have the same vertex. An angle is commonly thought of as two "arrows" joined at their bases.

Two angles are *adjacent* if they share a common vertex, share only one side, and one angle does not lie in the interior of the other.

Angles are usually measured in *degrees.* A circle has a measure of 360°, a half circle 180°, a quarter circle 90°, and so forth. If the measures of two angles are the same, then the angles are said to be *congruent.*

An angle with a measure of 90° is called a *right angle.* Angles with measures less than 90° are called *acute.* Angles with measures more than 90° are called *obtuse.*

If the sum of the measures of two angles is 90°, the two angles are said to be *complementary.* If the sum of the measures of the two angles is 180°, the two angles are said to be *supplementary.*

If two lines intersect, they form two pairs of *vertical angles.* The measures of vertical angles are equivalent; that is, vertical angles are congruent.

Properties of Triangles

Triangles are three-sided polygons.

If the measures of two sides of a triangle are equal, then the triangle is called an *isosceles triangle.* If the measures of all sides of the triangle are equal, then the triangle is called an *equilateral triangle.* If no measures of the sides of a triangle are equal, then the triangle is called a *scalene triangle.*

The sum of the measures of the angles of a triangle is 180°.

The sum of the measures of any two sides of a triangle is greater than the measure of the third side.

If the measure of one angle of a triangle is greater than the measure of another angle of a triangle, then the measure of the side opposite the larger angle is greater than the side opposite the smaller angle. (A similar relationship holds for the measures of angles opposite larger sides.)

If all of the angles of a triangle are acute, then the triangle is called an *acute triangle.* If one of the angles of a triangle is obtuse, then the triangle is called an *obtuse triangle.* If one of the angles of a triangle is a right angle, then the triangle is called a *right triangle.*

Two triangles are *congruent* if the measures of all corresponding sides and angles are equal. Two triangles are *similar* if the measures of all corresponding angles are equal.

Problem: **Find the measures of the angles of a right triangle if one of the angles measures 30°.**

Solution: **Since the triangle is a right triangle, a second angle of the triangle measures 90°. We know the sum of the measures of a triangle is 180°, so that, $90° + 30° + x° = 180°$. Solving for $x°$, we get $x° = 60°$. The measures of the angles of the triangle are 90°, 60°, and 30°.**

The Pythagorean Theorem

In a right triangle, the side opposite the 90° angle is called the *hypotenuse* and the other two sides are called the *legs.* If the hypotenuse has measure c and the legs have measures a and b, the relationship among the measures, known as the *Pythagorean Theorem,* is given by

$$c^2 = a^2 + b^2.$$

Problem: **Find the length of the hypotenuse of a triangle if the measure of one leg is 3 cm and the other leg is 4 cm.**

Solution: **By the Pythagorean Theorem, $c^2 = (3\text{ cm})^2 + (4\text{ cm})^2$, so that $c^2 = (9\text{ cm})^2 + (16\text{ cm})^2$, $c^2 = (25\text{ cm})^2$. Taking the square root of both sides, we get $c = 5$ cm.**

Properties of Parallel and Perpendicular Lines

If lines have a point or points in common, they are said to *intersect.*

Lines are *parallel* if they do not intersect.

Lines are *perpendicular* if they contain the sides of a right angle.

If a third line intersects two other lines, the intersecting line is called a *transversal.*

Two lines crossed by a transversal form eight angles. The four angles that lie between the two lines are called *interior angles.* The four angles that lie outside the two lines are called *exterior angles.*

The interior angles that lie on the same side of the transversal are called *consecutive interior angles.* The interior angles that lie on opposite sides of the transversal are called *alternate interior angles.* Similarly, exterior angles that lie on the same side of the transversal are called *consecutive exterior angles,* and those that lie on opposite sides of the transversal are called *alternate exterior angles.*

An interior angle and an exterior angle that have different vertices and have sides that are on the same side of the transversal are called *corresponding angles.*

Properties of Parallel Lines

The following are true for parallel lines:

Alternate interior angles are congruent. Conversely, if alternate interior angles are congruent, then the lines are parallel.

Interior angles on the same side of the transversal are supplementary. Conversely, if interior angles on the same side of the transversal are supplementary, then the lines are parallel.

Corresponding angles are congruent. Conversely, if corresponding angles are congruent, then the lines are parallel.

Properties of Perpendicular Lines

If two lines are perpendicular, the four angles they form are all right angles.

If two lines are perpendicular to a third line, the lines are parallel.

If one of two parallel lines is perpendicular to a third line, so is the other line.

Coordinate Geometry

The rectangular coordinate system is used as a basis for coordinate geometry. In this system, two perpendicular lines form a plane. The perpendicular lines are called the *x-axis* and the *y-axis*. The coordinate system assigns an *ordered pair of numbers* (x, y) to each point in the plane. The point of intersection of the two axes is called the *origin*, O, and has coordinates (0,0).

As shown in the figure that follows, the *x*-axis has positive integers to the right and negative integers to the left of the origin. Similarly, the *y*-axis has positive integers above and negative integers below the origin.

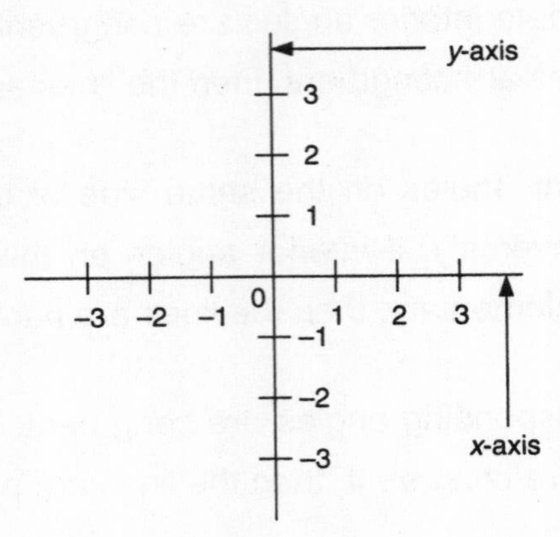

The distance between any two points in the coordinate plane can be found by using the *distance formula.* According to the distance formula, if P_1 and P_2 are two points with coordinates (x_1, y_1) and (x_2, y_2), respectively, then the distance between P_1 and P_2 is given by

$$P_1P_2 = \sqrt{(x_2 - x_1)^2 + (y_2 - y_1)^2}$$

Problem: Compute the distance between the points A and B with coordinates (1, 1) and (4, 5), respectively.

Solution: Using the distance formula,

$$\begin{aligned} \mathbf{AB} &= \sqrt{(4-1)^2 + (5-1)^2} \\ &= \sqrt{3^2 + 4^2} \\ &= \sqrt{9 + 16} \\ &= \sqrt{25} \\ &= 5 \end{aligned}$$

Graphs

To *plot a point* on a graph, first plot the *x*-coordinate, then plot the *y*-coordinate from the given ordered pair.

Problem: Plot the following points on the coordinate plane: A (1, 2), B (2, 1), C (–2, –1).

Solution:

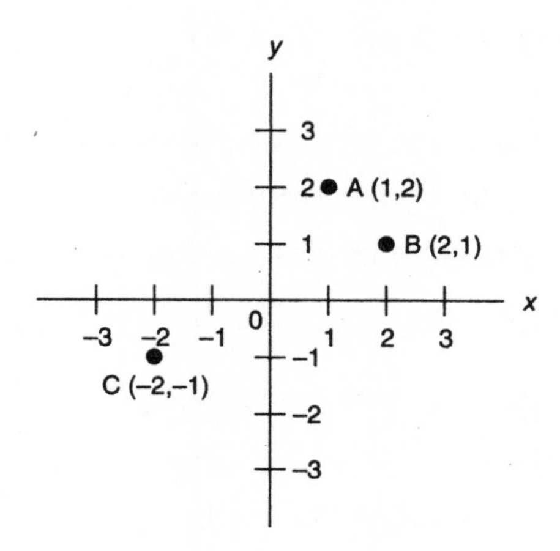

The Metric System

The *metric system of measurement* is closely related to the base 10 place value scheme discussed previously. The prefixes commonly used in the metric system are:

Prefix	**Meaning**
kilo-	thousand (1,000)
deci-	tenth (0.1)
centi-	hundredth (0.01)
milli-	thousandth (0.001)

The basic unit of linear measure in the metric system is the *meter,* represented by m. The relationship among the commonly used linear units of measurement in the metric system is as follows:

1 kilometer (km)	=	1,000 m
1 meter (m)	=	1.0 m
1 decimeter (dm)	=	0.1 m
1 centimeter (cm)	=	0.01 m
1 millimeter (mm)	=	0.001 m

The basic unit of measurement for mass (or weight) in the metric system is the *gram,* represented by g. The relationship among the commonly used units of measurement for mass in the metric system is as follows:

1 kilogram (kg)	=	1,000 g
1 gram (g)	=	1.0 g
1 milligram (mg)	=	0.001 g

The basic unit of measurement for capacity (or volume) in the metric system is the *liter,* represented by L or l. The most commonly used relationship between two metric units of capacity is

1 liter (l) = 1,000 milliliters (ml).

Key Strategies for Answering the Mathematics Questions

1. **Make effective use of your time.** You will have 70 minutes to answer 50 questions on the

mathematics section of the CBEST. This will allow you about a minute and a half to answer each question. If you find yourself taking longer than two minutes on a given question, mark the answer you think is most likely correct, circle the number of the item in the test booklet, and come back to it later if time allows.

2. **Answer all questions on this section of the test.** There is no penalty for guessing on this section of the CBEST, so do not leave any question unanswered. If you are not sure of the correct answer, narrow the choices to the two or three most likely, and choose one. Eliminate answers that could not possibly be correct before you choose.

3. **Read each question carefully.** Be sure you understand what the question is actually asking, not what a casual reading of the question might suggest. Be sure you have separated all the relevant information from the irrelevant information in the question.

4. **Devise a plan for answering the question.** This plan will be especially useful on the word problems and geometry items.

5. **Work the problem backwards to check your answer.** If time allows, check your work by substituting the answer into the original problem. Be certain that the answer meets all the conditions in the original question.

6. **Draw a diagram, sketch, or table to organize your work or to explain the question.** Not all questions that you need an illustration to understand will include an illustration, so make one yourself if necessary. This strategy may be especially useful in the geometry section.

7. **Write in the test booklet.** Mark up diagrams as needed. Write in the margins and other blank spaces. Write information directly into the statement of the problem, especially if you are having trouble setting up a solution.

8. **Look for similar questions.** Similar items may have appeared elsewhere on the test. You also may recall similar questions from classes you have taken previously. Apply suitable strategies from related work to the problem at hand.

Arithmetic Practice Problems

1. $34 + 3 \times 2 - 25 \div 5 =$

(A) 3
(B) 13.8
(C) 34
(D) 35
(E) 69

2. $\frac{4}{5} + \frac{6}{20} =$

(A) $\frac{1}{2}$
(B) $\frac{10}{25}$
(C) $1\frac{1}{10}$
(D) $1\frac{1}{20}$
(E) $1\frac{1}{5}$

3. $.01 \times .4 =$

(A) .4
(B) .04
(C) .004
(D) .0004
(E) 40

4. $\sqrt{100} =$

(A) 10
(B) 50
(C) 200
(D) 500
(E) 10,000

5. $(2^2)^4 =$

(A) $\sqrt{2}$
(B) 2^6
(C) 2^7
(D) 2^8
(E) 2^{16}

6. $\frac{3}{4} \times \frac{8}{9} =$

(A) $\frac{24}{9}$
(B) $\frac{32}{3}$
(C) $\frac{2}{3}$
(D) $\frac{11}{13}$
(E) $\frac{5}{3}$

7. $146.1 - 8.07 =$

(A) 6.54
(B) 65.4
(C) 137.04
(D) 138.03
(E) 148.03

8. What is the mean of 25, 30, 25, 20, 35?

(A) 25
(B) 27
(C) 27.5
(D) 33.75
(E) 34

9. $2(4-1)-(1-7)=$

(A) –2
(B) 0
(C) 10
(D) 12
(E) 18

10. $11\frac{2}{3}-2\frac{5}{6}=$

(A) $9\frac{1}{2}$
(B) $8\frac{2}{3}$
(C) $8\frac{5}{6}$
(D) $9\frac{5}{6}$
(E) $9\frac{2}{3}$

Arithmetic Practice Problem Answers

1. (D)
2. (C)
3. (C)
4. (A)
5. (D)
6. (C)
7. (D)
8. (B)
9. (D)
10. (C)

Algebra Practice Problems

1. $x^2y + xy^2 - 2x^2y + 3xy^2 =$

(A) $3x^2y$
(B) $3xy^2$
(C) $x^2y + 4xy^2$
(D) $-x^2y + 4xy^2$
(E) $4x^2y - xy^2$

2. $(x - 2)(x - 3) =$

(A) $2x - 6$
(B) $6x$
(C) $x^2 - 2x - 6$
(D) $x^2 + 5x + 6$
(E) $x^2 - 5x + 6$

3. Solve $2x + 5 = 9$ for x.

(A) -5
(B) -2
(C) 2
(D) 7
(E) 3

4. $5mn^2 \times 4mn^2 =$

(A) $20m^2n^2$
(B) $20m^2n^4$
(C) $9mn^2$
(D) mn^2
(E) m^2n^4

5. $x^4 - 1 =$

(A) $(x^2 + 1)(x^2)$
(B) $(x^2 - 1)(x^2)$
(C) $(x^2 + 1)(x - 1)(x + 1)$
(D) $(x - 1)(x^3 + 1)$
(E) $(x + 1)(x^3 - 1)$

6. $3m + 2 < 7$

(A) $m \geq \frac{5}{3}$

(B) $m > 2$

(C) $m \leq 2$

(D) $m < \frac{5}{3}$

(E) $m < 2$

7. $2h^3 + 2h^2t - 4ht^2 =$

(A) $2(h^3 - t)(h + t)$

(B) $2h(h + t) - 4ht^2$

(C) $2h(h - 2t)^2$

(D) $2h(h + 2t)(h - t)$

(E) $4h(ht - t^2)$

8. $0 < 2 - y < 6$

(A) $-4 < y < 2$

(B) $-2 < y < 4$

(C) $-4 < y < 0$

(D) $0 < y < 4$

(E) $-4 < y < -2$

9. $7b^3 - 4c^2 - 6b^3 + 3c^2 =$

(A) $b^3 - c^2$

(B) $7b - c$

(C) $-11b^2 - 3c^2$

(D) 0

(E) $13b^3 - c$

10. Solve $3x - 10 = 5 - 2x$ for x.

(A) -3

(B) -2

(C) 2

(D) 3

(E) No solution

Algebra Practice Problem Answers

1. (D)
2. (E)
3. (C)
4. (B)
5. (C)
6. (D)
7. (D)
8. (A)
9. (A)
10. (D)

Measurement and Geometry Practice Problems

1. Find the perimeter of a rectangle with l = 3 m and w = 4 m.

   (A) 12 m^2
   (B) 14 m
   (C) 14 m^2
   (D) 9 m
   (E) 16 m

2. Find the area of a circle with a diameter of 10 cm.

(A) 10π cm

(B) 20π cm^2

(C) 25π cm

(D) 25π cm^2

(E) 100π cm^2

3. Find the area of a square with a perimeter of 12 cm.

(A) 9 cm^2

(B) 12 cm^2

(C) 48 cm^2

(D) 96 cm^2

(E) 144 cm^2

4. A triangle has angles = x, $2x$, and $3x$. Solve for x.

(A) 15°

(B) 25°

(C) 30°

(D) 45°

(E) 90°

5. The circumference of a circle is 18π cm. Find the area of the circle.

(A) 18π cm^2

(B) 81 cm^2

(C) 36 cm^2

(D) 36π cm^2

(E) 81π cm^2

6. Find the volume of a solid with l = 4 cm, w = 3 cm, and h = 6 cm.

(A) 8 cm^3

(B) 9 cm^3

(C) 36 cm^3

(D) 72 cm^3

(E) 108 cm^3

7. $\angle a$ and $\angle b$ are supplementary angles and $\angle a = 3\angle b$. Find $\angle b$.

(A) 22.5° (B) 45°

(C) 90° (D) 135°

(E) 270°

8. Find the area of a triangle with b = 6 cm and h = 8 cm.

(A) 14 cm^2

(B) 24 cm^2

(C) 36 cm^2

(D) 48 cm^2

(E) Not enough information given.

9. Find the length of the hypotenuse of a triangle with one leg = 6 cm and the other leg = 8 cm.

(A) $\sqrt{28}$ cm (D) $\sqrt{45}$ cm

(B) 7 cm (E) 10 cm

(C) $\sqrt{70}$ cm

10. Find the perimeter of a square with s = 8 m.

(A) 16 m

(B) 24 m

(C) 32 m

(D) 40 m

(E) Not enough information given

Measurement and Geometry Practice Problem Answers

1. (B)
2. (D)
3. (A)
4. (C)
5. (E)
6. (D)
7. (B)
8. (B)
9. (E)
10. (C)

Chapter 5

Writing Review

Overview

The writing portion of the CBEST assesses your ability to compose two effective essays within a one-hour time limit. You must write your essays on the two topics printed in the test booklet. In one essay you must analyze a given situation or a particular statement; in the other, you will write about a personal experience. These essays test your ability both to compose effective prose and to communicate your ideas to your intended audience. You will not need to demonstrate any specialized knowledge; rather, your personal observations and experiences will provide you with sufficient material to write these essays.

An example of the first type of essay topic is:

Topic 1

"Describing how individuals are different is the easier task; discovering how individuals are alike is the more important task."

On the basis of your own experience, explain why you agree or disagree with this idea.

In the second essay, you will be asked to write about a personal experience. An example of this second type of topic is:

Topic 2

Describe two incidents in your life that significantly influenced your decision to choose the career you are pursuing.

Essay writing demonstrates your ability to think critically and to use language logically and clearly. The 30-minute time limit for each essay allows you little time to rewrite and reflect on your writing. Therefore, your performance on the CBEST writing test will demonstrate your ability to organize and support your ideas quickly. This type of writing is illustrative of the kind of thinking all teachers need to effectively present concepts and ideas to their students.

The time limit challenges you to write quickly and to write well. In most writing situations, writers have the luxury of time to organize their thoughts and to polish their work to a professional level; they can work through multiple drafts to increase the subtlety and sophistication of their words. In a timed writing scenario, however, you must recognize that you do not have these optimal conditions.

It is essential, therefore, that you organize your thoughts prior to writing your essay. *Take a few minutes at the outset of this portion of the CBEST to make an outline of your ideas.* Write down a thesis statement, and then brainstorm a few reasons why you believe your thesis statement to be true. For each of these reasons, think of an illustrative example that supports your point of view. Taking a few minutes to write such an outline will help you to organize your thoughts, to develop your essay in a clear and logical manner, and to maintain your thesis throughout the essay. This strategy is the single most effective step you can take to help you write a coherent and compelling essay.

Note the similarities between an analytical essay (given in the first essay topic) and a personal experience essay (given in the second essay topic). In both types of essays, you must articulate a reasonable and interesting thesis, provide reasons why your thesis is an intelligent response to the essay prompt, explore illustrative examples, and end with a conclusion that summarizes the argument and gives a sense of its relevance. Within the parameters of the CBEST, the differences between an analytical essay and a personal experience essay are almost non-existent because you cannot include relevant research on the given topic for the analytical essay; the test does not allow you time to do library or other types of research to provide the foundation of your analysis. Therefore, for both the analytical and the personal experience essay, concentrate on providing examples and observations from your personal experiences in order to create a compelling thesis that responds to the question put before you by the test.

Six Primary Traits of Good Writing

The CBEST essays are graded holistically, which means that the grader examines your essay as a complete entity unto itself. Essays that do not pass are then scored diagnostically. The diagnostic scoring offers feedback to the test-taker about the weaknesses of the essay. (See the Essay Scoring section for more information on this topic.) The following **Six Primary Traits of Good Writing** are evaluated during diagnostic scoring:

1. **Rhetorical Force:** Can you clearly convey the

central idea of your essay? Does your essay exemplify logical reasoning and coherency of argument? Do you maintain a consistent point of view throughout the essay? Is your thesis powerful, interesting, and free of clichés?

2. **Organization:** Do your ideas follow a logical sequence? Do you provide smooth transitions between ideas? Do the introduction, the supporting paragraphs, and the conclusion all work to support the same thesis?

3. **Support and Development:** Do you provide supporting information that helps the reader to understand your thesis? Is the supporting information relevant and meaningful?

4. **Usage:** Do you use words carefully and correctly? Does your writing show close attention to how words work together to build sentences?

5. **Structure and Conventions:** Is your writing free of grammatical errors? Do you spell, punctuate, and capitalize correctly?

6. **Appropriateness:** Do you choose a topic appropriate to your audience? Does the thesis of your essay demonstrate your understanding of the question at hand? Does your style highlight your comprehension of who your audience is?

Paying close attention to these Six Primary Traits of Good Writing will help you polish your writing and, since writing reflects your thought processes, your thinking.

Review of Essay Writing Concepts and Skills

An essay is a group of related paragraphs organized around a single topic. This topic should be as fully developed as possible, given the time limitations of the test. All the sentences in each paragraph and all the paragraphs in the essay are focused on this topic. **Essays that tend to receive the highest score on the CBEST, "a pass," have five or six relatively short paragraphs.** The structure of a typical five-paragraph essay consists of an opening paragraph that contains a thesis statement, three supporting paragraphs, and a concluding paragraph. Although the five-paragraph format is not the only way to organize your essay, it is a useful template with which to begin.

The opening (introductory) paragraph performs three functions. First, the opening paragraph defines the audience. In other words, it sets the tone or style of your writing for the rest of the essay. Obviously, you would write in a very different style for an audience of children or students; choose an appropriate tone and style for your audience of CBEST graders. Second, the opening paragraph attracts the attention of the readers so that they will want to know what you have to say. Finally, it contains a thesis statement which presents the focus of your essay; it tells the reader your opinion on a given topic and suggests the direction your essay will then take. The thesis statement is often (although not always) the final sentence of the introductory paragraph.

The body of the essay follows the opening paragraph. Here you present several major points to support the thesis statement. Each major point is developed into a supporting paragraph. The number of supporting paragraphs will vary according to the nature of your topic and ideas, but three is a common number of major points in a timed-test exercise of this type. Each supporting paragraph should have a topic sentence and supporting information or statements that expand or explain the topic sentence of the paragraphs. Supporting paragraphs are important to the cohesiveness of your essay because they explain, narrate, describe, or argue the key points of the thesis statement in the opening paragraph. Be careful to provide smooth transitions between the body paragraphs; highlight the logical connection between the body paragraphs by telling the reader how these ideas are related.

The concluding paragraph of the essay often summarizes the thesis statement and the topic sentences of the supporting paragraphs; it also rephrases the main idea and explores it in more depth. A conclusion should also give the reader a sense of the importance of the ideas presented in the essay. Although you are writing the essay because it is part of a test, give the reader a sense of why the ideas presented in your essay are important to you and why they should be important to the reader as well.

A summary of this multi-paragraph essay structure follows:

Opening Paragraph: Includes the thesis statement, sets the style or tone of writing appropriate for the audience, and captures the attention of the reader.

Supporting Paragraphs: *Each* supporting paragraph includes a topic sentence, which is the first major point related to the thesis. Then, give an illustrative example that demonstrates to the reader the validity of your opinion. (You may include as many supporting paragraphs as you need to set forth your major points. Three or four paragraphs should be sufficient, given the 30-minute time limit of the CBEST.)

Concluding Paragraph: Includes a restatement and/or summary of the essay, and an appropriate logical conclusion.

Key Strategies for Answering the Essay Questions

Use the strategies described below in order to prepare for the essay section of the CBEST.

Preparing for the Test

1. Practice writing essays about the example topics given in this book. Limit yourself to 30 minutes so that you become accustomed to working under timed conditions.

2. Practice brainstorming and making outlines to help you structure your ideas.

3. Study a list of the most frequently misspelled words so that you can avoid such mistakes.

4. Review the basic rules of good grammar and mechanics. Many college handbooks or office references are good sources. Also, know your own error patterns and practice editing your own writing. Working with a tutor at a college writing lab can help you both to identify errors you often make and to develop strategies for spotting and correcting them.

On the Day of the Test

1. **Wear a watch** so that you can keep track of the time. You have one hour to write two essays, so

allow 30 minutes to write each one. Give yourself five to seven minutes to write an outline, and spend the remaining time writing the essay. Pace yourself carefully, as no one will make time announcements during the test.

2. **Take two No. 2 soft-lead pencils with good erasers.** You will need two pencils in case one breaks. You are not allowed to have paper, other than the test booklet, during the test. However, you may make notes at the bottom of the test booklet page on which the assigned topics appear. You should jot notes in the bottom margin as you brainstorm and outline. The CBEST requires that you use a No. 2 pencil, so do not bring a pen.

3. **Make sure that your handwriting is legible!** After graders have looked at many tests, they are tired and possibly grumpy. Do not give them an "incentive" to lower your grade by making them struggle to read your writing.

Writing Strategies

A number of strategies are helpful in writing a clearly reasoned, well-organized, well-developed essay that demonstrates a thorough understanding of the assigned topic.

1. **Read the essay topic carefully.** Read it two or three times. Underline the key ideas and words so that you know exactly what you are being asked by the essay prompt. *An essay on a topic other than the one assigned will not be accepted.*

2. **Form a thesis statement.** Since this statement is critical to the organization of the essay, write it down in rough form at the bottom of the test booklet page where you are allowed to make notes. Then form it into a well-crafted representation of your thoughts on the subject chosen.

3. **Order your major supporting points.** *Use the first few minutes of the test to make an outline at the bottom margin of the test booklet after brainstorming several ideas to support your thesis.* You can write the essay more easily if you first make an outline to keep your ideas on track.

4. **Take a stand and relate all your points to it.** Do not digress from your thesis! If you do not maintain your thesis, the scorers will think that your writing is unorganized, lacking in focus, and confused. *You may fail if your essay is not well organized.*

5. **Write or print legibly.** Be as neat as possible. Readers like neat writing because it is easier for them to read. Avoid using excessively large handwriting. Do not skip any lines in the test booklet; do not leave margins wider than approximately an inch on each side of the paper. Indent approximately five spaces at the beginning of each new paragraph.

6. **Proofread your writing during the last five minutes for correct spelling, grammar, and punctuation.** Make sure that you did not unintentionally forget to write down an

important word. Break any run-on sentences into two or more complete sentences. Correct errors as neatly as possible. Although the appearance of your essay is not graded, too many crossed-out or squeezed-in words can be distracting and make it difficult for the evaluator to follow your train of thought.

Stylistic Tips

In addition to these Writing Strategies, bear in mind the following Stylistic Tips when writing your essay. Style is as important in the construction of a good essay as the subject of the essay itself, so be careful to make your style increase the readability of your writing.

1. **Only use words that you know how to spell.** The *Oxford English Dictionary* lists approximately 500,000 words in the English language. This tremendous variety of words makes it possible to write with simple, easily spelled words that are synonyms of more complex words, which may be difficult to spell. When in doubt about the spelling of a difficult word, substitute a word that has the same meaning, but has a familiar spelling.

2. **Use an appropriate tone in your writing.** Try to avoid contractions, slang, colloquialisms, and platitudes, all of which indicate an informal tone. Also, avoid repeating words in close proximity so that your essay displays an interesting variety in vocabulary.

3. **Try to use the active voice rather than the passive voice.** The active voice enhances your writing by making it more direct and straightforward, whereas the passive voice often suggests evasiveness. For example, in the following sentences the active voice (I made a mistake) suggests more honesty and candor than the passive construction of the same idea (A mistake was made).

4. **Keep your verbs in the same tense.** If your topic sentence is in the present tense, then each sentence within that paragraph should also be in the present tense.

5. **Use familiar punctuation that you know.** Colons, semicolons, dashes, parentheses, or ellipsis points are confusing to most people who do not write professionally. Do not use them unless you are absolutely certain that you are using them correctly.

6. **Be careful with your word usage.** Be sure to use I/me, there/they're/their, to/two/too, its/it's, and other easily confused words correctly. If you are unsure how to use a word correctly, rephrase the sentence so that you do not have to use that word.

7. **Use exciting verbs.** Verbs are the key to presenting ideas forcefully and with variety. For example, instead of a simple verb such as go, use *run, hurry, move,* or *stumble.*

8. **Never use swear words, profanity, or derogatory language.**

Essay Scoring

The evaluators who read your essays are experienced teachers who will score your writing holistically; that is, each of your essays will receive a single score based on its overall quality. Holistic scoring is similar to the scoring of individual ice skaters in the Olympics. The skater's performance is ranked by the judges for its overall artistic appeal; however, the performance must also display technical merit. The overall score takes into account both the skater's artistic qualities and technical skills. Holistic scoring for writing means that the evaluators will judge not only the overall quality of your ideas, but also how well and correctly you use language. The organization of your ideas will receive the most weight, just as the judges in the skating competition give more weight to a skater's artistic performance. Nonetheless, it is important to recognize that, just as an excellent artistic performance by an Olympic skater can be hurt by poor technique, a writer with excellent organization and ideas can be hurt by the use of incorrect language. In other words, to receive the highest score on your writing, you must demonstrate both good organization and ideas, as well as correct and effective use of language. (The following section, **Sample Papers and Grading,** illustrates how the grading rubric functions.)

Your essays will be read under very carefully controlled conditions to ensure fairness and reliability. Two readers will score your first essay; two different readers will score your second essay. The evaluators will rate your essay on the Six Primary Traits of Good Writing (described earlier in this chapter):

- Rhetorical Force
- Organization
- Support and Development
- Usage
- Structure and Conventions
- Appropriateness

Each reader will give your essay a score. Individual readers will not see the other scores given to your writing. *Pass* (a score of 4) is the highest rating. *Marginal Pass* (a score of 3) is the second highest rating. *Marginal Fail* means a score of 2; *Fail* means a score of 1 and is the lowest rating.

A Pass is given to an essay that is well formed and communicates effectively a coherent and meaningful message to its audience. In order to receive a Pass, you must demonstrate your proficiency with the Six Primary Traits of Good Writing. First, you must clearly present your thesis statement and maintain your focus on it throughout the essay (Rhetorical Force). Second, the organization of your essay must display a logical and coherent arrangement (Organization). Third, assertions should be supported with specific examples that fully develop your thesis (Support and Development). Fourth, your word choice should highlight your strong vocabulary, and grammar must be used correctly (Usage). Fifth, the sentences should showcase syntactic complexity and variety; the sentences should combine to form coherent paragraphs (Structure and Conventions). Sixth, the essay should respond to the question at hand, and do so in a manner that engages its audience (Appropriateness).

A Marginal Pass essay adequately communicates its thesis to the specified audience, yet it lacks the overall cohesion of a Pass essay. The writer succeeds in presenting a central idea, and the focus of the essay is maintained throughout most of the supporting paragraphs. The organization of ideas is strong and clear, and the meaning of the essay is easy to follow. Assertions are supported with evidence, but the evidence is perhaps not always especially compelling. Word choice and usage are simple and effective; the errors that do exist do not hamper comprehension. If the essay has problems with paragraphing, sentence structure, and/or mechanical conventions, they do not present excessive confusion to the reader. The writer addresses the topic with language and style suitable to the audience.

A Marginal Fail essay inadequately communicates its thesis. Although the writer may declare a thesis in the introductory paragraph, the thesis is lost in the ensuing discussion, and the reasoning is simplistic. The organization and structure of the essay fail to assist the reader in grasping the ideas of the writer. Assertions are presented without clear supporting evidence, and the writer fails to provide meaningful examples. The writer's words are imprecise, and the essay evinces little concern for correct grammar and punctuation. Distracting errors in paragraphing, sentence structure, and/or mechanical conventions result in confusion for the reader. The essay fails to address the question put forth in the assignment; also, it does not communicate to its audience with appropriate language or with an appropriate style.

A failing essay represents an unsuccessful attempt to communicate a message. No central idea or thesis directs the reader's attention. The organization of ideas appears haphazard, and no structure provides support for an overarching argument. Assertions devolve into mere generalizations which cannot be adequately supported and which lack logical meaning. Word choice and usage are too often incorrect, and these errors distract the reader's ability to follow the essay.

Paragraphing, sentence structure, and mechanical conventions are ignored. The response does not appear to engage with the assignment at hand, and the style and language of the essay are inappropriate for its target audience.

Sample Papers and Grading

Analyze the following essays as part of your preparation for the CBEST. As you read each essay, judge it yourself in terms of its Rhetorical Force, Organization, Support and Development, Usage, Structure and Conventions, and Appropriateness. Remember, these Six Primary Traits of Good Writing are the basis for the scoring of an essay.

Topic 1: "Describing how individuals are different is the easier task; discovering how individuals are alike is the more important task."

On the basis of your own experience, explain why you agree or disagree with this statement.

Sample Essay on Topic 1

When I am asked why Janet, my best friend, and I get along so well, I always tell people it is because we are so different. However, the more I think about our relationship, I realize our differences are not the only things that make our friendship so special. Beneath the obvious variations, there are many similarities which make us even more compatible.

In the middle of my sophmore year, my English teacher, Mrs. Estrada, changed the seating chart and I found myself sitting next to a quiet, but pretty black-haired girl named Janet. Being the loquacious person

that I am, I immediately engaged her in a conversation. My lack of shyness, though I did not know it at the time, would create a beautiful friendship.

After I got to know Janet a little better, I became aware that we were very different. She was shy and pretty, and I was forward and gawky. She had a boyfriend and many friends, while I had not yet discovered boys and had few friends. She was from a lower socio-economic class, while I was from an upper socioeconomic class. With all of these differences, I wondered how we could be such good friends.

At first, I thought our friendship was as secure as it was because we contrasted so well. Yet, after we acknowledged that we were best friends and we began to spend more time together, I began to see many similarities. For instance, we both had the same goals and morals. We are both kind, compassionate, and sensitive people, and we both snort when we laugh.

It is very important for individuals to identify how they are different from others, but more difficult and more important is to discover how they are similar. By identifying how I am different from Janet, I was able to keep my individuality and learn about how another person operates, and by discovering our similarities, I was able to form an unbreakable bond with a unique and special individual who I can relate on terms that I understand. Now, when I am asked about why our relationship is so secure, I tell them it is because we are very different yet so very similar.

Analysis of the Essay

The preceding essay, which answers the first topic, fits the Pass criteria. The organization of the essay is very strong. If you superimpose the summary for multi-paragraph essays from earlier in this review, you see that the first topic essay is well structured. The opening paragraph includes the thesis statement: "Beneath the obvious variations, there are many similarities which make us even more compatible." This statement agrees with the essay prompt, which fulfills the assignment of choosing to agree or to disagree with the prompt. The style and tone of the writing are appropriate for an audience of teachers and graders. The illustrations from the area of values, socio-economic background, physical appearance, and politics support the thesis statement and capture the attention of the reader. The supporting paragraphs each explore a point implied in the introductory paragraph or provide support for the thesis. The first supporting paragraph tells the ways in which the writer and Janet are different. The second supporting paragraph elaborates on how their characteristics differ. The third supporting paragraph emphasizes the importance of recognizing similarities. The concluding paragraph summarizes the importance of such similarities in relating to other people. It also brings in the uniqueness of individuals as a strong link to the topic sentence in the opening paragraph; in this return to the ideas of the introduction, the conclusion expands upon these initial ideas, rather than just repeating the thesis. This essay meets the criteria of a Pass because it is clearly reasoned, well organized, and well developed; it also demonstrates a thorough understanding of the question it is answering.

In addition to the strong presentation of a thesis statement and the superior organization of supporting and concluding paragraphs, the writer also demonstrates familiarity with Usage (the writer's precision in word choice) and Structure and Conventions (the writer's avoidance of errors in syntax and mechanics). Only minor flaws appear in the essay which detract from its readability, such as overusing the word "friendship," failing to hyphenate "socio-economic" in the third paragraph, mistakenly using "a" rather than "an" before "unbreakable" in the fifth paragraph, and writing "individual who" rather than "individual to whom" in the fifth paragraph. These few flaws, however, do not detract from the essay's overall excellent use of language. Furthermore, the sentences are interesting and developed with variety. The verbs are in the active voice and primarily in the present tense. Spelling errors do not handicap the flow of ideas. No run-on sentences impede comprehension, and the punctuation is correct. This essay exhibits the writer's ability to communicate effectively and to construct sentences with precision, variety, and complexity.

This essay completes all the tasks set by the assignment. The writer expressed an opinion in response to the prompt. The writer used personal experience and observations to explain the reasons for agreeing with the quotation. It is important to note that personal experience and observation are useful tools for providing compelling reasons to support your thesis, but one could also cite experiences and observations gained from other sources.

Topic 2: Describe two incidents in your life that significantly influenced your decision to choose the career you are pursuing.

Sample Essay on Topic 2

Throughout my life, I have made many decisions concerning my career goals. I wanted to do a variety of things, ranging from engineering to teaching, but certain circumstances and realizations discouraged me from carrying out those plans. My decision to be a psychologist was final after two incidents that occurred during high school.

During my sophomore year, my boyfriend was arrested and sent to a continuation high school. I was a sheltered girl with a high sense of values, and so this bewildered and angered me. Soon this anger was channeled into concern. We remained friends and I

tried to be supportive. I discovered many reasons why he was delinquent, but I felt helpless because I couldn't do very much for him. I realized that many people have frustrations and other problems that drive them to hurt themselves. Recognizing this, I wanted to help others with their problems.

In the same year, my mother took me to a psychologist. I was going to see one because I have problems with my friends and I was very depressed and pessimistic about my life. Right away, I felt uncomfortable with the lady. When I explained the situations that were bothering me, she seemed to always tell me that I was feeling as all teenagers do. I felt as though she was citing from a textbook, readily willing to lump me into a stereotypical group. This made me more determined to counsel people. I am a person who can see others as individuals and I learned that this is necessary to work with people.

I have always had an awareness and concern for others and these incidents helped me realize my calling. I love talking and being with people but it is painful and confusing to see the strife people inflict upon themselves and on others. Psychology is a field where I will be working directly with people and actually help them; it also represents a continuing learning process for me and will encourage me to keep growing.

Analysis of the Essay

This essay, which answers the prompt for the second topic, also fits the criteria of a Pass. The organization of this essay is very strong and adheres nicely to the guidelines for multi-paragraph essays, described earlier in this review. The thesis statement, located in the opening paragraph, declares that "My decision to be a psychologist was final after two incidents that occurred during high school." This sentence fulfills the assignment because it speaks of two experiences that changed the writer's perception of career choices. The two supporting paragraphs elaborate on the attitudes and events that support the key statement in the opening paragraph. The second and third paragraphs describe these critical incidents and the impact they had on the writer's career decisions. The fourth paragraph addresses goals in life and the steps in finalizing a career choice; it also summarizes the changes that took place because of the two experiences and again underscores their great influence. Furthermore, the conclusion does not merely restate the thesis; it amplifies upon the thesis and delineates its greater significance. This essay meets the criteria of a Pass score because it is clearly reasoned, solidly organized, and well developed; also, it demonstrates a clear understanding of the assignment.

Note, too, the skilled manner in which the writer handles issues both of Usage and of Structure and Conventions. The sentences are interesting and developed with variety. The verbs use the active voice in the past tense. The writer uses a variety of words. The style, although slightly informal, holds the attention of the reader; if the style had been more casual or conversational, the essay would have been inappropriate for its audience of teachers. There are no run-on sentences, and the punctuation is error-free (although some grammarians would advocate commas to separate clauses both in the last sentence of the third paragraph and the second sentence of the final paragraph). This essay demonstrates that the writer uses language effectively to construct an essay of interest and complexity.

Sample Writing Topic

You should practice some of the strategies and techniques described in this review. Compare your writing to the essays in this review; then analyze your own writing with the Six Primary Traits of

Good Writing. For your practice writing, be sure to time yourself and to limit your writing time to 30 minutes.

Essay Prompt: Describe the major qualities you feel have led to the success of the person you most admire.

Once you have completed this practice essay, ask another person, preferably an experienced teacher or perhaps a tutor at your college writing lab, to read and criticize your work against the criteria in this review.

Practice Test 1

The Second of Three Full-Length Practice Tests

DIRECTIONS: One or more questions follow each statement or passage in this test. The question(s) are based on the content of the passage. After you have read a statement or passage, select the best answer to each question from among the five possible choices. Your answers to the questions should be based on the stated (literal) or implied (inferential) information given in the statement or passage. Mark all answers on your answer sheet. **Note: You will encounter some passages with numbered sentences, blank spaces, or underscored words and phrases. These cues are provided on the CBEST for your reference in answering the questions that follow the relevant passages.**

Questions 1 and 2 refer to the following passage:

America's national bird, the mighty bald eagle, is being threatened by a new menace. Once decimated by hunters and loss of habitat, this newest danger is suspected to be from the intentional poisoning by livestock ranchers. Authorities have found animal carcasses injected with restricted pesticides. These carcasses are suspected to have been placed to attract and kill predators such as the bald eagle in an effort to preserve young grazing animals. It appears that the eagle is being threatened again by the consummate predator, humans.

1. One can conclude from this passage that

(A) the pesticides used are beneficial to the environment.
(B) ranchers believe that killing the eagles will protect their ranches.
(C) ranchers must obtain licenses to use illegal pesticides.
(D) poisoning eagles is good for livestock.
(E) pesticides help to regulate bird populations.

2. The author's attitude is one of

(A) uncaring observation.
(B) concerned interest.
(C) uniformed acceptance.
(D) suspicion.
(E) unrestrained anger.

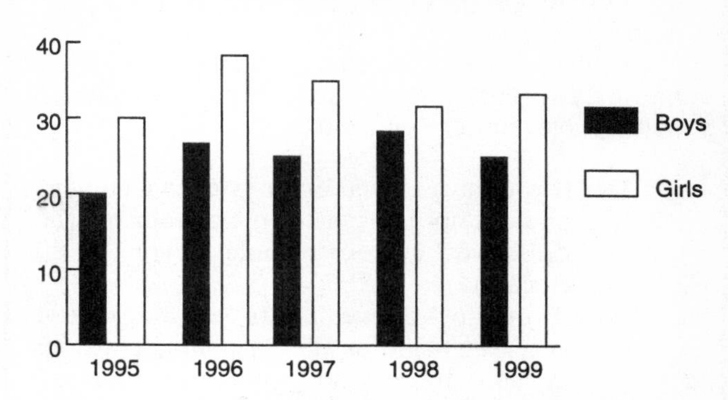

Questions 3 and 4 refer to the graph above:

3. In what year was the involvement in scouting closest to being equal between girls and boys?

(A) 1999
(B) 1995
(C) 1996
(D) 1998
(E) 1997

4. How much of a difference was there between the number of boys and the number of girls involved in scouting in 1997?

(A) 10 million
(B) 1 million
(C) 5 million
(D) .1 million
(E) 100 million

Question 5 refers to the following statement:

The <u>disparaging</u> remarks about her performance on the job made Alice uncomfortable.

5. The word <u>disparaging</u> is closest in meaning to

(A) congratulatory.
(B) immoral.
(C) whimsical.
(D) tantalizing.
(E) insulting.

GO ON TO THE NEXT PAGE

Questions 6–8 refer to the following passage:

INSTRUCTIONS FOR ABSENTEE VOTING

These instructions describe conditions under which voters may register for or request absentee ballots to vote in the November 5 election.

(1) If you have moved on or prior to October 7, and did not register to vote at your new address, you are not eligible to vote in this election.
(2) If you move after this date, you may vote via absentee ballot or at your polling place, using your previous address as your address of registration for this election.
(3) You must register at your new address to vote in further elections.
(4) The last day to request an absentee ballot is October 29.
(5) You must be a registered voter in the county.
(6) You must sign your request in your own handwriting.
(7) You must make a separate request for each election.
(8) The absentee ballot shall be issued to the requesting voter in person or by mail.

6. A voter will be able to participate in the November 5 election as an absentee if he or she

(A) planned to register for the next election.
(B) requested an absentee ballot on November 1.
(C) voted absentee in the last election.
(D) moved as a registered voter on October 13.
(E) moved on October 7, 1999.

7. On October 21, Mr. Applebee requested an absentee ballot for his daughter, a registered voting college student, to enable her participation in the election process. Mr. Applebee will not be successful because of which of the following instructions?

(A) 3
(B) 2
(C) 6
(D) 7
(E) 5

8. You can vote in future elections if you

(A) register at your new address.
(B) registered at your previous address.
(C) request a registration form in your own handwriting.
(D) moved after October 29.
(E) registered as a Republican.

Questions 9 and 10 refer to the following passage:

The atrophy and incapacity that occurs when a broken bone is encased in plaster and immobilized clearly demonstrates what a sedentary lifestyle can do to the human body.

9. In the passage above, atrophy refers to

(A) a strengthened condition brought about by rest.
(B) a decrease in size and strength.
(C) a type of exercise and rehabilitation.
(D) rest and recuperation.
(E) the effects of convalescence.

10. Which of the following statements best paraphrases the author's view of sedentary living?

(A) It's good to relax and take it easy.
(B) A sedentary lifestyle is a healthy lifestyle.
(C) A body responds well to a sedentary lifestyle.
(D) Sedentary living increases mobility.
(E) Mobility is affected by lifestyle.

Questions 11–15 refer to the following passage:

Frederick Douglass was born Frederick Augustus Washington Bailey in 1817 to a white father and a slave mother. Frederick was raised by his grandmother on a Maryland plantation until he was eight. It was then that he was sent to Baltimore by his owner to be a servant to the Auld family. Mrs. Auld recognized Frederick's intellectual acumen and defied the law of the state by teach-

GO ON TO THE NEXT PAGE

ing him to read and write. When Mr. Auld warned that education would make the boy unfit for slavery, Frederick sought to continue his education in the streets. When his master died, Frederick, who was only sixteen years of age, was returned to the plantation to work in the fields. Later, he was hired out to work in the shipyards in Baltimore as a ship caulker. He plotted an escape but was discovered before he could get away. It took five years before he made his way to New York City and then to New Bedford, Massachusetts, eluding slave hunters by changing his name to Douglass.

At an 1841 anti-slavery meeting in Massachusetts, Douglass was invited to give a talk about his experiences under slavery. His impromptu speech was so powerful and so eloquent that it thrust him into a career as an agent for the Massachusetts Anti-Slavery Society.

Douglass wrote his autobiography in 1845, primarily to counter those who doubted his authenticity as a former slave. This work became a classic in American literature and a primary source about slavery from the point of view of a slave. Douglass went on a two-year speaking tour abroad to avoid recapture by his former owner and to win new friends for the abolition movement. He returned with funds to purchase his freedom and to start his own anti-slavery newspaper. He became a consultant to Abraham Lincoln and throughout Reconstruction fought doggedly for full civil rights for freedmen; he also supported the women's rights movement.

11. According to the passage, Douglass's writing of his autobiography was motivated by

(A) the desire to make money for the anti-slavery movement.
(B) his desire to become a publisher.
(C) his interest in authenticating his life as a slave.
(D) his desire to educate people about the horrors of slavery.
(E) his desire to promote the Civil War.

12. The central idea of the passage is that Douglass

(A) was instrumental in changing the laws regarding the education of slaves.
(B) was one of the most eminent human rights leaders of the nineteenth century.
(C) was a personal friend and confidant to a president.
(D) wrote a classic in American literature.
(E) was an advocate of women's rights.

13. According to the author of this passage, Mrs. Auld taught Douglass to read because

(A) Douglass wanted to go to school like the other children.
(B) she recognized his natural ability.
(C) she wanted to comply with the laws of the state.
(D) he needed to be able to read so that he might work in the home.
(E) she was obeying her husband's wishes regarding education.

14. The title that best expresses the ideas of this passage is

(A) The History of the Anti-Slavery Movement in America.
(B) The Outlaw Frederick Douglass.
(C) Reading: A Window to the World of Abolition.
(D) Frederick Douglass's Contributions to Freedom.
(E) Frederick Douglass's Oratorical and Literary Brilliance.

15. In the context of the passage, impromptu is the closest in meaning to

(A) unprepared.
(B) nervous.
(C) angry.
(D) loud.
(E) elaborate.

Questions 16 and 17 refer to the following passage:

Acupuncture practitioners, those who use the placement of needles at a strategic location under the skin to block pain, have been tolerated by American physicians since the 1930s. This form of Chinese treatment has been used for about 3,000 years and until recently has been viewed suspiciously by the West. New research indicates that acupuncture might provide relief for sufferers of chronic back pain, arthritis, and recently, pain experienced by alcoholics and drug addicts as they kick the habit.

GO ON TO THE NEXT PAGE

16. According to the passage, acupuncture has been found to help people suffering from all of the following except

(A) arthritis.
(B) recurring back pain.
(C) alcoholics in withdrawal
(D) liver disease.
(E) drug addicts in withdrawal.

17. According to the passage, acupuncture has

(A) been enthusiastically embraced by American physicians.
(B) been used to alleviate chronic migraine headaches.
(C) always been available only in the Far East.
(D) been used since the 1930s.
(E) received tepid support from American physicians.

Question 18 refers to the following passage:

Commercial enterprises frequently provide the backdrop for the birth of a new language. When members of different language communities need to communicate or wish to bargain with each other, they may develop a new language through a process called "pidginization." A pidgin language, or pidgin, never becomes a native language; rather, its use is limited to business transactions with members of other language communities. Pidgins consist of very simple grammatical structures and small vocabularies. They have tended to develop around coastal areas where seafarers first made contact with speakers of other languages.

18. The passage suggests which of the following about pidgins?

(A) We could expect to hear pidgins along the coast of Africa and in the Pacific Islands.
(B) Pidgins are a complex combination of two languages.
(C) Pidgins develop in inland mountain regions.
(D) Pidgins become native languages only after several generations of use.
(E) Pidgins are the language of the seafarer.

Question 19 refers to the following passage:

There are two ways of measuring mass. One method to determine the mass of a body is to use a beam-balance. By this method, an unknown mass is placed on one pan at the end of a beam. Known masses are added to the pan at the other end of the beam until the pans are balanced. Since the force of gravity is the same on each pan, the masses must also be the same on each pan. When the mass of a body is measured by comparison with known masses on a beam-balance, it is called the gravitational mass of the body.

The second method to determine the mass of a body is distinctly different; this method uses the property of inertia. To determine mass in this way, a mass is placed on a frictionless horizontal surface. When a known force is applied to it, the magnitude of the mass is measured by the amount of acceleration produced upon it by the known force. Mass measured in this way is said to be the inertial mass of the body in question. This method is seldom used because it involves both a frictionless surface and a difficult measurement of acceleration.

19. Which of the following statements can best be supported from the passage?

(A) The gravitational and inertia mass methods measure different properties of the object.
(B) The masses are equal when the weights are equal and cause the beam to be balanced.
(C) Gravitational inertial measurements do not give the same numerical value for mass.
(D) The same result for a beam-balance method cannot be obtained at higher altitudes.
(E) The mass of a body depends on where it is located in the universe.

Question 20 refers to the following passage:

Her introductory remarks provided a segue into the body of the speech.

20. In the context of this passage, the word "segue" means

(A) rendition.
(B) performance.
(C) transition.
(D) plausible.
(E) critique.

GO ON TO THE NEXT PAGE

Questions 21–23 refer to the following passage:

One of the many tragedies of the Civil War was the housing and care of prisoners. The Andersonville prison, built by the Confederates in 1864 to accommodate 10,000 Union prisoners, was not completed when prisoners started arriving. Five months later, the total number of men incarcerated there had risen to 31,678.

The sounds of death and dying were not diminished by surrender of weapons to a captor. Chances of survival for prisoners in Andersonville were not much better than in the throes of combat. Next to overcrowding, inadequate shelter caused unimaginable suffering. The Confederates were not equipped with the manpower, tools, or supplies necessary to house such a population of captives. The prisoners themselves gathered lumber, logs, anything they could find to construct some sort of protection from the elements. Some prisoners dug holes in the ground, risking suffocation from cave-ins, but many hundreds were left exposed to the wind, rain, cold, and heat.

The sheer numbers of prisoners exhausted daily food rations, and this situation resulted in severe dietary deficiencies for the incarcerated men. The overcrowding, meager rations, and deplorable unsanitary conditions resulted in rampant disease and high mortality rates. The consequences of a small scratch or wound could result in death in Andersonville. During the prison's 13-month existence, more than 12,000 prisoners died and were buried in the Andersonville cemetery. Most of the deaths were caused by diarrhea, dysentery, gangrene, and scurvy that could not be treated due to inadequate staff and supplies.

21. What is the central idea of the passage?

(A) The major problem for the Confederates was finding proper burial spaces in the cemetery.
(B) The prison was never fully completed.
(C) Prison doctors were ill-equipped to handle emergencies.
(D) Andersonville prison was not adequate to care for three times as many prisoners as it could hold.
(E) Many prisoners died as a result of shelter cave-ins.

22. From this passage, the author's attitude toward the Confederates is one of

(A) endorsement.
(B) objectivity.
(C) scorn.
(D) insensitiveness.
(E) contradiction.

23. The first sentence of the second paragraph of this passage can best be described as

(A) an homage.
(B) a deviation.
(C) a tentative assumption.
(D) an anecdote.
(E) an irony.

Questions 24–27 refer to the following passage:

When William Wordsworth implies that the "mind [is] an aesthetic object," he is validating the human narcissistic capacity to impose such a judgment in the first place. And if this is so, then is romantic poetry merely self-serving, or is it responding to social, political, economic, and theological anxieties, tensions, and issues?

24. What does the term narcissistic mean?

(A) Naïveté
(B) Intelligent
(C) Self-centered
(D) Foolish
(E) Impulsive

25. What does Wordsworth mean when he implies that the mind is "an aesthetic object"?

(A) It is lovely to look at.
(B) It creates beauty.
(C) It wants beauty.
(D) It lacks beauty.
(E) It smells funny.

26. The passage suggests which of the following about romantic poetry?

(A) It is art for art's sake.

(B) It is beauty, and beauty is truth.
(C) It can represent and/or encompass significant contemporary issues.
(D) It is only about love and love lost.
(E) It has the capacity to impose judgment.

27. What does the term <u>aesthetic</u> mean?

(A) Thoughtful
(B) Intelligent
(C) Empty
(D) Artistic
(E) Arrogant

Questions 28–30 refer to the following index sample:

28. To which page(s) would one turn for information on how to install a grinding wheel?

(A) 126–140
(B) 136–138
(C) 130
(D) 126–129
(E) 129–140

29. Which of the following best describes the organizational scheme used to index the section dealing with grinding wheel selection and use?

(A) by type of wheel
(B) by physical characteristics
(C) by task
(D) by type of drill
(E) by order of appearance

30. On which page(s) would you find information on grinding a rounded edge on metal stock?

(A) 136–138
(B) 131–133
(C) 126–129
(D) 126–140
(E) 127

Questions 31–35 refer to the following passage:

Jonathan Edwards's lineage was comprised of a prestigious line of clergymen. His parents were the Rev. Timothy Edwards, pastor of the Congregational Church of East Windsor for 64 years, and his mother was Esther Stoddard, daughter of the Rev. Solomon Stoddard, pastor of the Congregational Church of Northampton for more than 50 years. Edwards received his Master of Arts from Yale in 1723. In 1727 he became his grandfather's colleague in the church at Northampton, whereby, "upon the death of his grandfather, Edwards became the sole proprietor of the Northampton pulpit." Edwards soon became renowned for a series of powerful sermons. Enthusiastic sermonizing such as *Justification by Faith Alone* (1734), contributed to a great spiritual <u>grassroots revival</u>, known throughout the colonies as the Great Awakening. In the winter and spring of 1734-35, Edwards's subsequent report, *A Faithful Narrative of the Surprising Works of God* (1737) made a profound impression in America and Europe. Needless to say, Edwards <u>correlated the nuances</u> of religious discourse, politics, and rhetoric fluently.

GO ON TO THE NEXT PAGE

31. What does the phrase <u>grassroots revival</u> mean?

(A) People spoke to one another outside, in parks and squares, instead of meeting halls and other public buildings.
(B) People brought their concerns to the politician and he was able to address their needs.
(C) It personifies Jonathan Edwards as a natural outdoorsman, thereby making him easier for the common man to relate to.
(D) It is a social resurgence of philosophical values that stems from the common man upward.
(E) It suggests that public figures like Edwards plant the philosophical seeds and their agendas grow from there.

32. The author's attitude toward the subject is

(A) angry.
(B) impartial.
(C) apologetic.
(D) lamenting.
(E) propitious.

33. From the information provided by the passage, it can be inferred that Jonathan Edwards was

(A) gregarious and debonair.
(B) prominent and devoted.
(C) auspicious and adamant.
(D) ancillary and dejected.
(E) deceitful and hypocritical.

34. In the context of the passage, what does <u>correlated the nuances</u> mean?

(A) Connected the differences
(B) Ordered the similarities
(C) Utilized the subtleties
(D) Deplored the differences
(E) Assimilated the correlations

35. According to the passage, Edwards made a profound impact on both Europe and America after the release of a report published in

(A) 1737.
(B) 1734.
(C) 1735.
(D) 1723.
(E) 1727.

Questions 36–40 refer to the following passage:

Life in seventeenth-century England was <u>tempestuous</u> indeed. It was a time of religious and secular confrontations resulting in new social abstractions, symbolism, paradoxes, and ironies. Explorers such as Galileo Galilei (1564–1642), the Italian astronomer and physicist, challenged the formal dogma of the day by mindfully watching the heavens and questioning conventional reality, thereby threatening established theological doctrine. Galileo was the first person to use a telescope to study the constellations in 1610. He was an outspoken advocate of Copernicus's theory, which states that the sun, and not the earth, forms the center of the universe. This blasphemy led to Galileo's persecution and finally to his imprisonment by the Inquisition of 1633.

________________, philosophers, essayists, courtiers, clergymen, scholars, laborers, and statesmen such as Francis Bacon (1561–1626) were "pleading for science in an age dominated by religion," while their counterparts such as Sir Thomas Browne were "pleading for religion in an age which was beginning to be dominated by science."

The age of religious sovereignty was coming to a close. Protestant reformers began to challenge sovereign sacrament during the reign of Queen Elizabeth I, 1558–1603, and those responsible for instigating the friction came to be known as Puritans. These "nonconformists" wanted greater reorganization and simplicity within the Episcopal and Anglican branches of the Church of England, ostensibly to purify it from "elaborate ceremony" and "regal formalities," which they saw as major distractions from religious meditations and moral purity. Moral purity was closely linked with the practice of ritual purity, that is, ritual free from ostentatious display. ________________, ritual purity from this perspective precipitated Puritan conceptions of human impurity connected with disorder, since they involve uncontrolled bodily emissions, fluids, and death.

36. From the information in the above passage it can be deduced that the seventeenth century was a time of

(A) anger and resentment due to economic hierarchy.
(B) social tranquility due to religious and scientific conflicts.

GO ON TO THE NEXT PAGE

(C) social agitation due to scientific and religious conflicts.
(D) social controversy due to a woman on the throne.
(E) peace, prosperity, and social harmony due to scientific advancements.

37. What is the meaning of the word <u>tempestuous</u>?

(A) Jocund
(B) Disinterested
(C) Impoverished
(D) Turbulent
(E) Progressive

38. According to the information in the passage, Galileo went to prison because he

(A) used a new invention to see something he shouldn't have.
(B) did not pay his taxes at the appropriate time.
(C) questioned contemporary scientific and religious doctrine.
(D) questioned the authority of the monarchy.
(E) wrote a pamphlet that some thought to be propaganda.

39. Which of these grouped words or phrases, if inserted *in order* into the passage's blank lines, would address the logical sequencing of the narrative?

(A) Nonetheless; However
(B) Concomitantly; Thus
(C) However; Consequently
(D) Therefore; Disturbingly
(E) Meanwhile; Interestingly

40. The central idea of the passage is that the seventeenth century was a time of

(A) artistic expression.
(B) religious freedom.
(C) religious and scientific controversy.
(D) social oppression.
(E) legal maneuvering.

Questions 41–44 refer to the following passage:

In order to categorize the fourteenth-century narrative verse *The Alliterative Morte Arthure* (*AMA*) as an <u>epic</u>, one must first determine the criteria by which the piece is to be evaluated. Therefore, for the purposes of this argument, when referring to the conventions of the *epic*, I refer to a long narrative poem on a serious subject matter, told in a formal or elevated style. Concurrently, epic conventions include adventure. Adventure centered around a heroic <u>protagonist</u> or quasi-divine figure of great national or cosmic significance; a figure upon whose decisions and actions hinged the fate of a clan, tribe, nation, or even (as in the case of Milton's *Paradise Lost*) the entire human race.

The <u>topography</u> plays an important role in epic narrative. It is usually of a grand scale as in the *Iliad*. The epic territory can be worldwide, or even larger, as in the representation of Mt. Olympus or purgatory. It might well include ancient worlds personified as real (i.e., Camelot as an entity or a haunted house as an antagonist), surreal (as in the domain of Grendel's mother), or completely imaginary (as in Dante's *Divine Comedy*). The topography is relevant because it provides the adventurer with both physical and emotional challenges, as well as establishing a stylized ambiance.

41. According to the passage, an <u>epic</u> is defined as

(A) a long narrative poem, on a monotonous subject matter, told in an elevated or formal style.
(B) a long narrative poem, on a serious subject matter, told in an elevated or formal style.
(C) a long alliterative poem, on a lyrical subject matter, told in an elevated or formal style.
(D) a long poem, on any subject, told any way the poet feels appropriate.
(E) a poem that talks about the topography in an elevated or formal manner.

42. What does <u>topography</u> mean?

(A) Terrain
(B) Alchemy
(C) Language
(D) Heroics
(E) Movement

43. The topography is important because it provides the adventurer with

(A) a difficult challenge that he must overcome to become king.

GO ON TO THE NEXT PAGE

(B) both physical and emotional challenges, as well as establishing a stylized atmosphere.
(C) rewards both physical and emotional, as well as establishing social status.
(D) a long road which must be traversed in order for the hero to succeed.
(E) makes for a more believable atmosphere.

44. The meaning of <u>protagonist</u> is

(A) the landscape.
(B) a villain.
(C) the central character.
(D) a quest.
(E) the lust for adventure.

Questions 45–47 refer to the following passage:

1 Henry Wadsworth Longfellow's "The Village Blacksmith" is a direct descendent of the emblem poem. **2** Although the basic emblem format existed as early as medieval times, its popularity peaked in the seventeenth century with poets like Francis Quarles (1592-1644) and his book, *Emblems, Divine and Moral* (1635), the most popular-selling book of the century. **3** Emblem poetry consisted of a picture, illustrating some "moral or divine truth," which might be a proverb, a psalm, or any terse quote of scripture. **4** The picture was followed by a relevant scriptural citation. **5** Then a poem of approximately 40 to 50 lines would further elaborate on the scripture. **6** The poem then culminates with a concluding epigram.

7 The poems commonly have six to eight lines in a stanza, and relatively simple variations of the standard *abab* rhyme scheme. **8** They employ couplets, and/or alliterative, melodic rhymes. They are typically composed in iambic meter, but any meter that allows for ample substitutions of feet, beats, and additions of light lyrical syllables would suffice. **9** The goal was to make them melodic, simple, and, therefore, attractive, versatile, and memorable. **10** Their subject matter was conventional and non-threatening, not classical, ominous, stoic, or otherwise foreboding, and, thereby, forgettable.

45. According to the passage, the most popular selling book of the seventeenth century was

(A) Longfellow's "The Village Blacksmith."
(B) Francis Quarles.
(C) *Emblems, Divine and Moral.*
(D) emblem poems by Quarles.
(E) *Moby Dick.*

46. The ultimate goal of the emblem poem was to make it

(A) complicated, versatile, and, therefore, attractive and worth memorizing.
(B) melodic, simple, and, therefore, attractive, versatile, and memorable.
(C) lyrical, monosyllabic, and, therefore, attractive, versatile, and memorable.
(D) conventional, oblique, and, therefore, addictive, versatile, and memorable.
(E) genuine, austere, and, therefore, attractive, variable, and memorable.

47. Which of the following numbered sentences of the passage best characterizes the subject matter that typified emblem poems?

(A) Sentence 5
(B) Sentence 7
(C) Sentence 8
(D) Sentence 10
(E) Sentence 9

Questions 48–50 refer to the following passage:

Christina Rossetti's "Goblin Market" is actually a traveling farmer's market, selling an abundance of "orchard [fresh] fruits, nuts" and produce. The caravan is owned and operated by grotesque and unscrupulous businessmen or "merchant men," who impose their wares of "orchard fruits" upon the female inhabitants of a rural community. Despite the conspicuous absences of fellow residents, the poem's insistence on consumerism, with its resounding commercial <u>mantra</u> of "come buy, come buy" is indicative of the dilemma faced by burgeoning market towns and provincial communities that grew in relationship to England's industrial economy. Urban commercialism brought domestic convenience and leisure, as well as vice and corruption, to traditionally established rural communities.

GO ON TO THE NEXT PAGE

48. What does the author feel is the overall idea of the poem?

(A) Urban commercialism brought both convenience and wealth to traditionally established rural communities.
(B) Urban commercialism brought both produce and textiles to traditionally established rural communities.
(C) Merchants brought affordable wares to traditionally established rural communities.
(D) Urban commercialism brought both convenience and vice to traditionally established rural communities.
(E) Urban commercialism brought businessmen and farmers to traditionally established rural communities.

49. What is meant by the term mantra?

(A) Profiteering
(B) Redundancy
(C) Shopkeepers
(D) Indebtedness
(E) Incantation

50. The author's tone in writing the passage is

(A) aggressive.
(B) laughable.
(C) promiscuous.
(D) assertive.
(E) impartial.

PRACTICE TEST 1

ANSWER KEY

Section 1: Reading Comprehension

1. (B)
2. (B)
3. (D)
4. (A)
5. (E)
6. (D)
7. (C)
8. (A)
9. (B)
10. (E)
11. (C)
12. (B)
13. (B)
14. (D)
15. (A)
16. (D)
17. (E)
18. (A)
19. (B)
20. (C)
21. (D)
22. (B)
23. (E)
24. (C)
25. (B)
26. (C)
27. (D)
28. (C)
29. (C)
30. (B)
31. (D)
32. (B)
33. (B)
34. (C)
35. (A)
36. (C)
37. (D)
38. (C)
39. (E)
40. (C)
41. (B)
42. (A)
43. (B)
44. (C)
45. (C)
46. (B)
47. (D)
48. (D)
49. (E)
50. (E)

Detailed Explanations of Answers

PRACTICE TEST 1

SECTION 1: Reading Skills

1. **B**

The ranchers believe that killing the eagles will protect their ranches. This is understood by the implication that "attract[ing] and kill[ing] predators…in an effort to preserve young grazing animals" will protect their ranches.

2. **B**

The author's use of words such as "mighty bald eagle" and "threatened by a new menace" supports concern for the topic. For the most part, the author appears objective; thus, concerned interest is the correct answer.

3. **D**

In 1998, the difference between boys and girls was a minimal half percent.

4. **A**

In 1997, the difference between the two was 10 million: 25 million for boys and 35 million for girls.

5. **E**

Insulting is the correct definition. The other terms are either antonyms or incorrect interpretations.

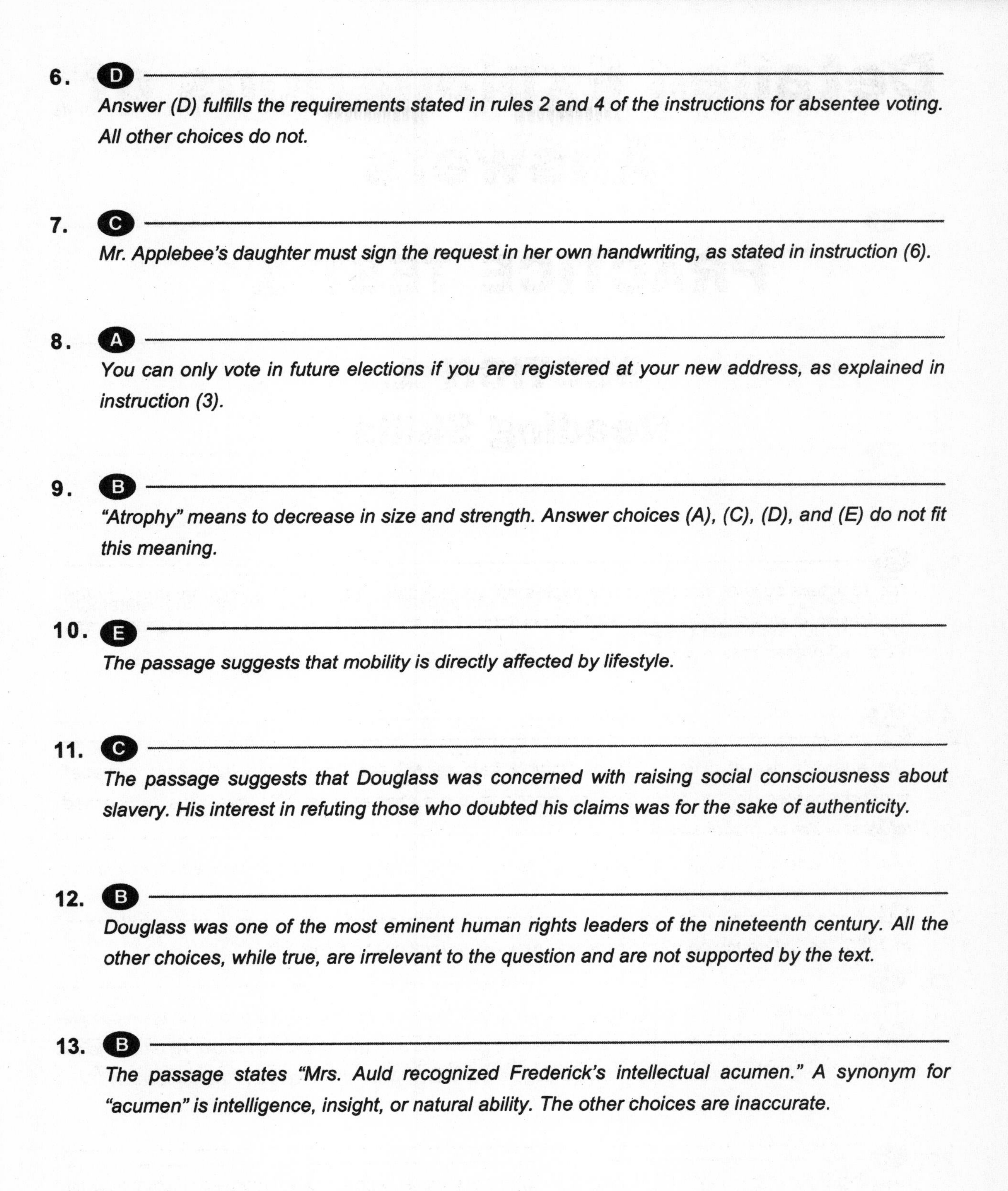

6. **D**

Answer (D) fulfills the requirements stated in rules 2 and 4 of the instructions for absentee voting. All other choices do not.

7. **C**

Mr. Applebee's daughter must sign the request in her own handwriting, as stated in instruction (6).

8. **A**

You can only vote in future elections if you are registered at your new address, as explained in instruction (3).

9. **B**

"Atrophy" means to decrease in size and strength. Answer choices (A), (C), (D), and (E) do not fit this meaning.

10. **E**

The passage suggests that mobility is directly affected by lifestyle.

11. **C**

The passage suggests that Douglass was concerned with raising social consciousness about slavery. His interest in refuting those who doubted his claims was for the sake of authenticity.

12. **B**

Douglass was one of the most eminent human rights leaders of the nineteenth century. All the other choices, while true, are irrelevant to the question and are not supported by the text.

13. **B**

The passage states "Mrs. Auld recognized Frederick's intellectual acumen." A synonym for "acumen" is intelligence, insight, or natural ability. The other choices are inaccurate.

14. (D)

Choices (A), (B), and (C) are too vague or ill-defined. Choice (E) is too finite and limited in its relevance to the entire passage. Thus, choice (D) is correct.

15. (A)

An "impromptu" speech is one given extemporaneously, or off the cuff.

16. (D)

Liver disease is never mentioned. All the other choices are.

17. (E)

The passage states that American physicians "have...tolerated" acupuncture.

18. (A)

The passage tells us to expect to hear pidgins in coastal communities. All the other statements are contradicted by the passage.

19. (B)

None of the other statements is supported by the text.

20. (C)

Although musical in origin, a "segue" has now come to refer to a transition between two information and/or reference points.

21. (D)

The passage tells us that Andersonville prison was built to accommodate 10,000 prisoners; upon completion there were 31,678. This is three times as many prisoners as it was designed to hold. All other choices are discussed, but the main focus of the passage is the overcrowded conditions and the tragic results.

22. (B)

The author remains objective (impartial) rather than (D) insensitive. Answers (A), (C), and (E) are contradictory by definition.

23. **E**

One definition of irony is a result that is the opposite of what might be expected, anticipated, or appropriate. Thus, "the sounds of death and dying were not diminished by surrender," as one might expect them to be. That is, surrender was no guarantee of survival.

24. **C**

Based upon the Greek mythological figure Narcissus, who fell in love with his own reflection, the word "narcissistic" means self-centered.

25. **B**

By definition, the adjective "aesthetic" suggests something beautiful, cultured, or artistic. Thus, Wordsworth is suggesting that the mind is able to create beauty, rather than (A) looks beautiful, (C) wants beauty, or (D) lacks beauty.

26. **C**

Because the passage asks us if romantic poetry is capable of "responding to social, political, economic, and theological issues," there is an implied sense that (C), it can represent and/or encompass significant contemporary issues.

27. **D**

The word "aesthetic" means artistic.

28. **C**

Choice (A), "Grinding operations, 126–140," would be expected to discuss how the grinders are operated, but "grinding wheels" is too general in the context of the question posed. Choice (E), pages 129–140 ("Grinding wheel selection and use"), essentially suffers from the same weakness as Choice (A). Pages 136–138 (B) describe an unrelated function. Choice (D), "Grinding wheels,126–129," is overly broad, particularly when considered alongside choice (C), which proves to be the best choice because it specifically uses the phrase "installing the wheel."

29. (C)

While the extract is surely arranged alphabetically, there is another pattern that emerges—one governed by task. This is clear by the preponderance of task-oriented descriptors (e.g., "grinding," "sharpening," "truing and dressing," etc.). Choice (B), "Physical characteristics," addresses a level of detail that does not figure to any appreciable extent in the passage. Thus, choice (C) is the best answer.

30. (B)

Choice (A) is incorrect because finding information on grinding a rounded edge is not relevant to the idea of sharpening a chisel. Choice (C), "grinding wheels," gives no particular indication of holding the answer. Choice (D), while pointing generally to the answer, proves inferior when juxtaposed with choice (B) because the latter contains some of the specific language sought in the extract (i.e., "grinding metal stock"). Choice (E), of course, is completely irrelevant.

31. (D)

The term "grassroots" is synonymous with the common people, especially those of rural or non-urban areas, thought of as best representing essential political interests or fundamental sources of support.

32. (B)

The author's attitude toward the subject is impartial, stating facts as facts without excessive emotional intrusions.

33. (B)

From the information provided by the passage, such as the "profound impression [Edwards made] in America and Europe" and prolific spiritual writings, it can be determined that he was both prominent (eminent) and devoted (dedicated).

34. (C)

Edwards, we are told, utilized or incorporated the subtleties of discourse and rhetoric fluently. (A), (B), (D), and (E) suggest similar discourse techniques but they are not the definition suggested by the passage.

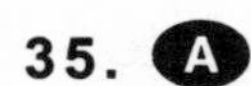

35. A

The passage tells us that after A Faithful Narrative *was published in 1737, it "made a profound impression in America and Europe."*

36. C

The declaration in the second paragraph of the passage states that a variety of seventeenth-century socio-political figures were "pleading for science in an age dominated by religion" and vice versa. Thus, social agitation was predicated on the conflicts between those two disciplines. Answers (A), (B), (D), and (E) are erroneous.

37. D

The meaning of "tempestuous" is turbulent.

38. C

The passage states that Galileo supported Copernicus's theory, which was considered blasphemy at the time. Thus, answer (C), questioned contemporary scientific and religious dogma (doctrine), is the correct answer.

39. E

Only choice (E) properly addresses the logic and flow of the passage. All the other responses are appropriate to only one of the blank lines or to neither.

40. C

The overall theme of the passage states that the social controversy of the period raged over religious and scientific conflicts.

41. B

The passage tells us that an epic is a long narrative poem, on a serious subject, told in an elevated or formal style. While answers (A), (C), (D), and (E) contain components of the formula, only (B) contains all three elements.

42. (A)

"Topography" refers to the terrain.

43. (B)

The last sentence of the passage states that the topography is relevant (important) because "it provides…both physical and emotional challenges, as well as establishing a stylized ambiance." Thus, (B) is the correct answer.

44. (C)

A "protagonist" is (C), the central character.

45. (C)

The first paragraph of the passage states that Francis Quarles wrote Emblems, Divine and Moral *in 1635, "the most popular-selling book of the century." Therefore, (C) is the correct answer.*

46. (B)

The second paragraph maintains that "the goal [of the emblem poems] was to make them melodic, simple, and, therefore, attractive, versatile, and memorable." (B) is the appropriate answer.

47. (D)

Choice (D), Sentence 10, describes the subject matter unambiguously and concisely.

48. (D)

The passage tells us that the paradox of commercialism is that it "brought domestic convenience and leisure, as well as vice and corruption, to traditionally established rural communities." Answers (A), (B), (C), and (E) allude to individual components brought about by the advent of consumerism, but only answer (D) states both the pros and cons.

49. (E)

The term "mantra" means song, chant, or incantation.

50. (E)

The author's tone is one of impartiality. (A), aggressive, suggests hostility, (B), laughable, suggests humor, and (C), promiscuous, implies indiscretion, while (D), assertive, suggests a sense of moderate aggression.

DIRECTIONS: Each of the questions or incomplete statements below is followed by five suggested answers or completions. Select the one that is best in each case.

1. Simplify the following expression: $6 + 2(x - 4)$

(A) $4x - 16$
(B) $2x - 14$
(C) $2x - 2$
(D) $-24x$
(E) $4x$

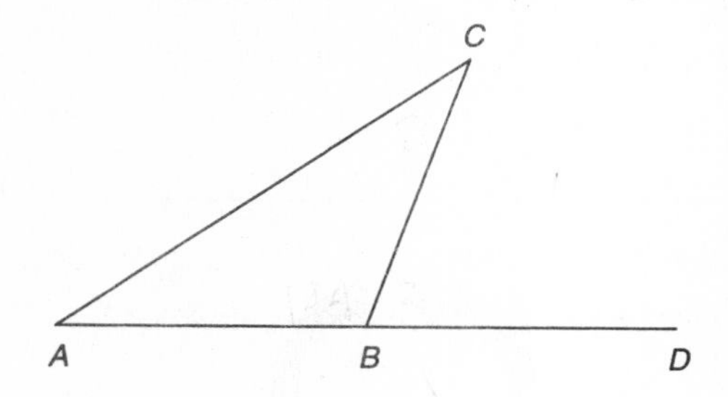

2. Referring to the figure above, if the measure of $\angle C$ is 20° and the measure of $\angle CBD$ is 36°, then what is the measure of $\angle A$?

(A) 16°
(B) 20°
(C) 36°
(D) 56°
(E) 144°

3. If six cans of beans cost $1.50, what is the price of eight cans of beans?

(A) $.90
(B) $1.00
(C) $1.60
(D) $2.00
(E) $9.60

4. Bonnie's average score on three tests is 71. Her first two test scores are 64 and 87. What is her score on test three?

(A) 62
(B) 71
(C) 74
(D) 151
(E) 222

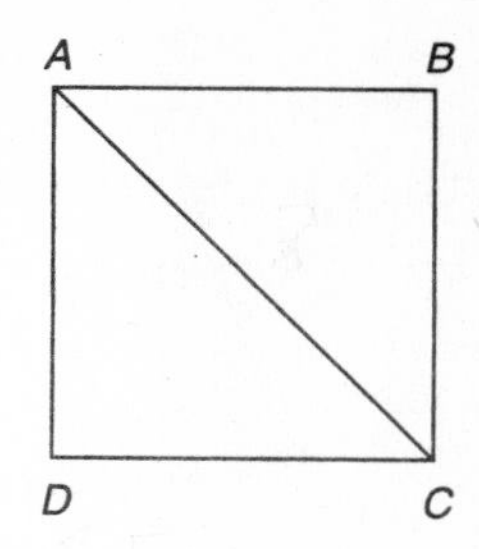

5. In the figure above, what is the perimeter of square ABCD if diagonal AC = 8?

(A) 32
(B) 64
(C) $4\sqrt{2}$
(D) $16\sqrt{2}$
(E) $8\sqrt{3}$

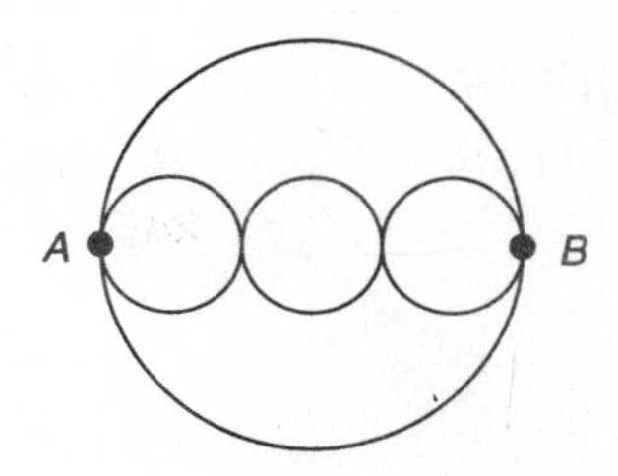

6. Three small circles, all the same size, lie inside a large circle as shown above. The diameter *AB* of the large circle passes through the centers of the three small circles. If each of the smaller circles has area 9π, what is the circumference of the large circle?

(A) 9
(B) 18
(C) 18π
(D) 27π
(E) 54π

7. A jar contains 20 balls. These balls are labeled 1 through 20. What is the probability that a ball chosen from the jar has a number on it that is evenly divisible by 4?

GO ON TO THE NEXT PAGE

(A) $\frac{1}{20}$ (D) 4

(B) $\frac{1}{5}$ (E) 5

(C) $\frac{1}{4}$

8. If $2x^2 + 5x - 3 = 0$ and $x > 0$, then what is the value of x?

(A) $-\frac{1}{2}$ (D) $\frac{3}{2}$

(B) $\frac{1}{2}$ (E) 3

(C) 1

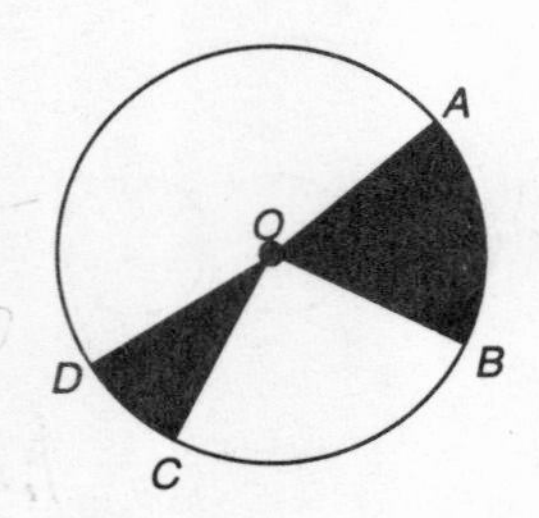

9. The center of the above circle is the point O. What percentage of the circle is shaded if the measure of arc AB is 65° and the measure of arc CD is 21.4°?

(A) 86.4% (D) 27.4%
(B) 50% (E) 24%
(C) 43.6%

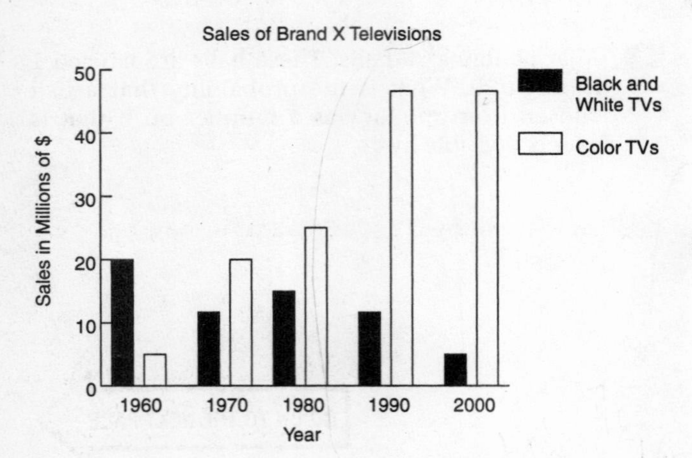

10. According to the chart, in what year was the total sales of Brand X televisions the greatest?

(A) 1960 (D) 1990
(B) 1970 (E) 2000
(C) 1980

11. Ten cards are drawn, without replacement, from a deck of 52 cards. What is the probability that both cards are diamonds?

(A) $\frac{1}{17}$ (D) $\frac{1}{5}$

(B) $\frac{1}{16}$ (E) $\frac{1}{4}$

(C) $\frac{1}{8}$

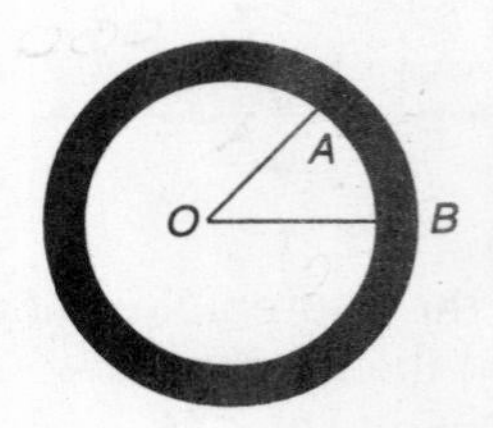

12. Two concentric circles are shown in the figure above. The smaller circle has radius $OA = 4$ and the larger circle has radius $OB = 6$. Find the area of the shaded region.

(A) 4π (D) 36π
(B) 16π (E) 100π
(C) 20π

13. Solve the following inequality for x: $8 - 2x \leq 10$

(A) $x \leq 1$ (D) $x \geq -1$

(B) $x \geq -9$ (E) $x \leq \frac{5}{3}$

(C) $x \leq -1$

14. Working alone, John needs four hours to paint a fence, whereas Linda only needs three hours for this task. If both work together, how many hours will be needed to complete this task?

GO ON TO THE NEXT PAGE

(A) 1 (D) $2\frac{1}{7}$

(B) $1\frac{5}{7}$ (E) $2\frac{2}{3}$

(C) 2

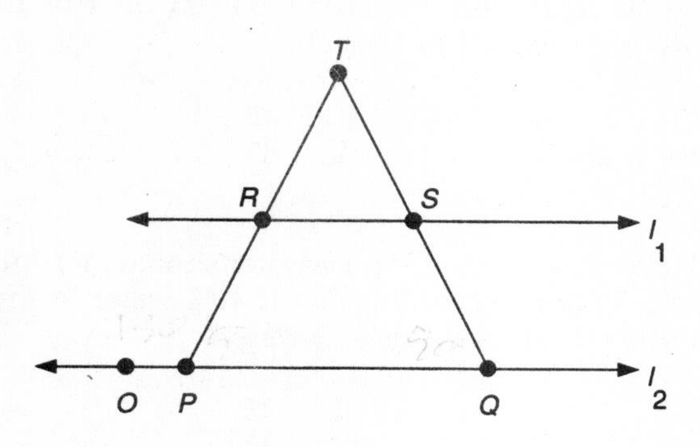

15. In the figure above $l_1 \parallel l_2$, ΔRTS is an isosceles triangle, and the measure of $\angle T = 80°$. Find the measure of $\angle OPR$.

(A) 50° (D) 105°
(B) 80° (E) 130°
(C) 100°

16. Four apples and five pears cost a total of $5.30. If each apple costs 65 cents, what is the cost of two pears?

(A) $0.54 (D) $1.08
(B) $0.58 (E) $1.18
(C) $0.76

17. The ratio of men to women at University X is 3:7. If there are 6,153 women at University X, how many men are at University X?

(A) 879 (D) 2,637
(B) 1,895 (E) 14,357
(C) 2,051

18. Marie works a 35-hour week and earns $9.00 per hour. If her raise gives her weekly earnings of $333.90, what percent raise did she receive?

(A) 19 (D) 9
(B) 16 (E) 6
(C) 13

19. Linda bought a jacket on sale at a 25% discount. If she paid $54 for the jacket, what was the original price of the jacket?

(A) $72.00 (D) $40.50
(B) $67.50 (E) $36.00
(C) $54.00

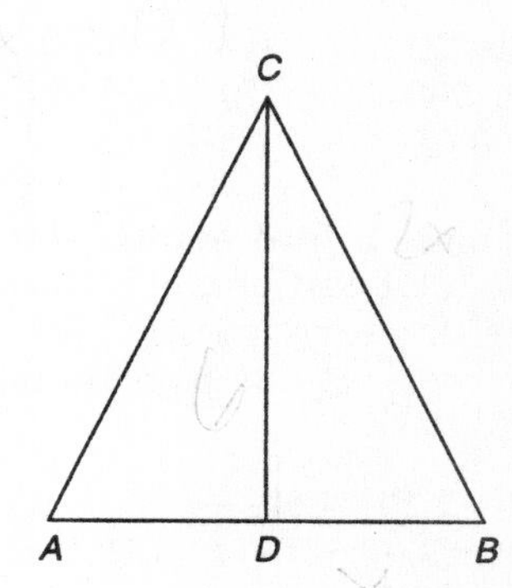

20. Assume that ΔABC above is an equilateral triangle. If $CD \perp AB$ and $CD = 6$, what is the area of ΔABC?

(A) $3\sqrt{3}$ (D) 18
(B) 12 (E) 36
(C) $12\sqrt{3}$

$$F = \frac{9}{5}C + 32$$

21. The formula relating the Celsius (C) and the Fahrenheit (F) scales of temperature is given in the box above. Find the temperature in the Celsius scale when the temperature is 86° F.

(A) 25° (D) 124.6°
(B) 30° (E) 188.6°
(C) 105°

22. In the number 72,104.58, what is the place value of the 2?

GO ON TO THE NEXT PAGE

(A) Thousands (D) Tenths
(B) Millions (E) Thousandths
(C) Ten thousands

23. Mrs. Wall has $300,000. She wishes to give each of her six children an equal amount of her money. Which of the following methods will result in the amount that each child is to receive?

(A) $6 \times 300{,}000$ (D) $6 - 300{,}000$
(B) $6 \div 300{,}000$ (E) $300{,}000 - 6$
(C) $300{,}000 \div 6$

24. For three children, two adults, and four senior citizens, the total cost of movie tickets is $32.50. Each child's ticket costs $4.50. Which one of the following represents the expression for each senior citizen's ticket?

(A) $(32.50 - 2.50 - 4.50) \div 4$
(B) $[32.50 - (3)(2.50) - (2)(4.50)] \div 4$
(C) $(32.50 - 2.50 - 4.50) \div 9$
(D) $[32.50 - (3)(2.50) - (2)(4.50)] \div 9$
(E) $32.50 \div 9 - 2.50 - 4.50$

25. Bob wants to bake some cupcakes. His recipe uses $2\frac{2}{3}$ cups of flour to produce 36 cupcakes. How many cups of flour should Bob use to bake 12 cupcakes?

(A) $\frac{1}{3}$ (D) $1\frac{2}{9}$
(B) $\frac{8}{9}$ (E) $1\frac{2}{3}$
(C) 1

26. The area of rectangle *EFGH* above is 120 and *EF* is twice as long as *EH*. Which of the following is the best approximation of the length of *EH*?

(A) 7 (D) 12
(B) 8 (E) 15
(C) 10

27. Ricky drove from Town A to Town B in 3 hours. His return trip from Town B to Town A took 5 hours because he drove 15 miles per hour slower on the return trip. How fast did Ricky drive on the trip from Town A to Town B?

(A) 25.5 (D) 45
(B) 32 (E) 52
(C) 37.5

28. How many ounces of pure water should be added to a 30-ounce solution that is 40% water to produce a solution that is 50% water?

(A) 6 (D) 16
(B) 8 (E) 18
(C) 12

I. If $x > y$, then $x^2 > y^2$.
II. If $x > y$, then $x + z > y + z$.
III. If $x > y$, then $x - y > 0$.
IV. If $x > y$, then $xz > yz$.

29. Given that *x*, *y*, and *z* are any real numbers, which of the above statements are true?

(A) I and II only (D) I, II, and III only
(B) II and III only (E) II, III, and IV only
(C) II and IV only

30. Round the following number to the nearest hundredths place: 287.416

(A) 300 (D) 287.41
(B) 290 (E) 287.42
(C) 287.4

$$\frac{x^2 \times x^7}{x}$$

31. Simplify the above expression.

(A) x^6 (D) x^{10}
(B) x^7 (E) x^{13}
(C) x^8

GO ON TO THE NEXT PAGE

$$\frac{1}{9}, \frac{2}{15}, \frac{3}{21}$$

32. List the fractions shown above from least to greatest.

(A) $\frac{1}{9}, \frac{2}{15}, \frac{3}{21}$

(B) $\frac{2}{15}, \frac{3}{21}, \frac{1}{9}$

(C) $\frac{3}{21}, \frac{1}{9}, \frac{2}{15}$

(D) $\frac{1}{9}, \frac{3}{21}, \frac{2}{15}$

(E) $\frac{2}{15}, \frac{1}{9}, \frac{3}{21}$

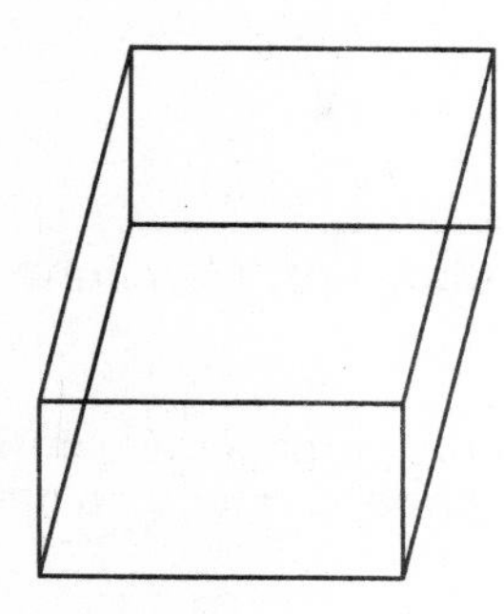

33. A rectangular box with a square base is shown above. If the volume of the box is 256 cubic feet and the height of the box is one-half the length of a side of the base, find the height of the box.

(A) 4 feet
(B) 6 feet
(C) 8 feet
(D) 10 feet
(E) 12 feet

34. If $x = -3$, then find the value of $-x^2 + 2x$.

(A) –15
(B) –3
(C) 3
(D) 6
(E) 15

35. If $a = b^3$ and $a = \frac{1}{8}$, what is the value of b?

(A) $\frac{1}{512}$

(B) $\frac{1}{8}$

(C) $\frac{3}{8}$

(D) $\frac{1}{2}$

(E) $\frac{3}{2}$

36. In a barn there were cows and people. If we counted 30 heads and 104 legs in the barn, how many cows and how many people were in the barn?

(A) 10 cows and 20 people
(B) 16 cows and 14 people
(C) 18 cows and 16 people
(D) 22 cows and 8 people
(E) 24 cows and 4 people

$$\frac{12}{x-1} = \frac{5}{6}$$

37. Solve for x in the proportion given above.

(A) 14.6
(B) 15.4
(C) 16
(D) 16.6
(E) 16.8

38. Sharon and Ellen are office typists. Sharon makes 1 mistake every 30 minutes, whereas Ellen makes 4 mistakes every 45 minutes. If Sharon types for 5 hours, and Ellen types for 3 hours, how many total mistakes will be made?

(A) 20
(B) 20
(C) 26
(D) 33
(E) 40

39. Which one of the following fractions lies between $\frac{19}{90}$ and $\frac{13}{60}$?

(A) $\frac{8}{45}$

(B) $\frac{7}{30}$

(C) $\frac{29}{120}$

(D) $\frac{77}{360}$

(E) $\frac{59}{270}$

GO ON TO THE NEXT PAGE

40. If X is a negative number and Y is a positive number, which one of the following *must* be a negative number?

(A) $X + XY$
(B) $Y - XY$
(C) $Y - X$
(D) $2X + Y$
(E) $Y + X$

41. Suppose P and Q are true statements, and R is a false statement. Which one of the following *must* be a false statement?

(A) (P implies Q) or R
(B) R implies (P and Q)
(C) (P or R) implies Q
(D) Q or (P implies R)
(E) P and (Q implies R)

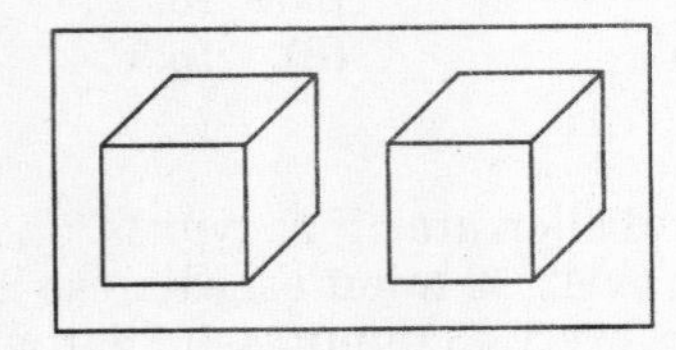

42. Sal has a set of blocks. If 8% of this collection is shown in the box above, how many blocks did Sal have?

(A) 8
(B) 16
(C) 25
(D) 64
(E) 100

43. Solve the following problem: $|x - 3| < 2$

(A) $-5 < x < 5$
(B) $x = -5$ or 5
(C) $x < 5$
(D) $1 < x < 5$
(E) $x = 5$

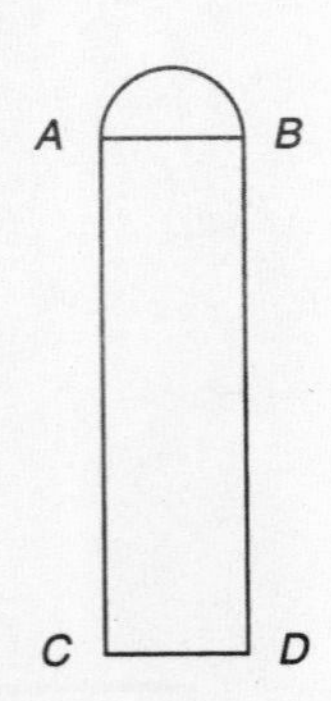

44. In the figure, a semicircle is attached to the top of rectangle $ABCD$. If $AB = 4$ and $AC = 6$, what is the total area enclosed by the figure?

(A) 26π
(B) 40π
(C) $20 + 4\pi$
(D) $24 + 16\pi$
(E) $24 + 2\pi$

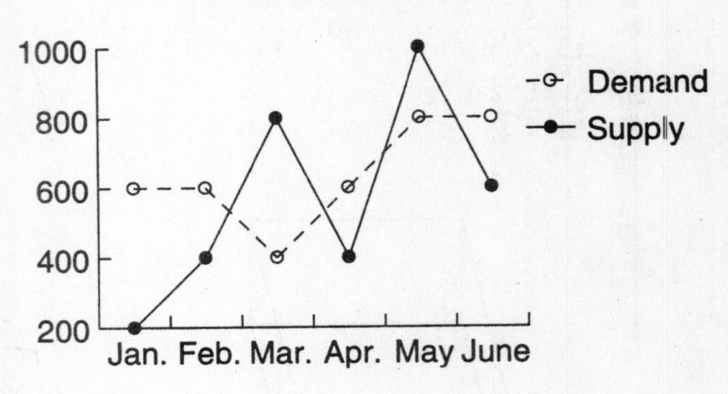

45. According to the graph above, during how many months was supply greater than demand?

(A) 0
(B) 1
(C) 2
(D) 3
(E) 4

Year	# of Inmate Lawsuits	# of Total Lawsuits
1997	640	2,780
1998	600	2,140
1999	470	2,820

46. What was the approximate percent increase in lawsuits filed by inmates from 1997 to 1998, based on the data presented above?

(A) 5
(B) 6
(C) 7
(D) 8
(E) 9

GO ON TO THE NEXT PAGE

47. For the entire three-year period, what percent of all lawsuits were filed by inmates, based on the data presented above?

(A) 16
(B) 18
(C) 20
(D) 22
(E) 24

48. How many negative integers are between –9 and 5?

(A) 13
(B) 10
(C) 9
(D) 8
(E) 6

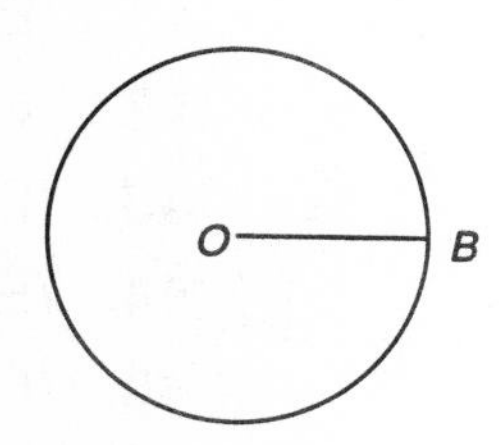

49. The area of the circle above is 144π square feet. If $\overline{OB}$ is increased by 2 feet, what is the area of the new circle (in square feet)?

(A) 4π
(B) 121π
(C) 146π
(D) 169π
(E) 196π

50. In the above figure, $AB \perp BC$, $AC = 10$, and $AB = 6$. What is the area of ΔABC?

(A) 24
(B) 48
(C) 121
(D) 240
(E) 480

PRACTICE TEST 1

ANSWER KEY

Section 2: Mathematics

1. (C)
2. (A)
3. (D)
4. (A)
5. (D)
6. (C)
7. (C)
8. (B)
9. (E)
10. (D)
11. (A)
12. (C)
13. (D)
14. (B)
15. (E)
16. (D)
17. (D)
18. (E)
19. (A)
20. (C)
21. (B)
22. (A)
23. (C)
24. (B)
25. (B)
26. (B)
27. (C)
28. (A)
29. (B)
30. (E)
31. (C)
32. (A)
33. (A)
34. (A)
35. (D)
36. (D)
37. (B)
38. (C)
39. (D)
40. (A)
41. (E)
42. (C)
43. (D)
44. (E)
45. (C)
46. (A)
47. (D)
48. (D)
49. (E)
50. (A)

Detailed Explanations of Answers

PRACTICE TEST 1

SECTION 2: Mathematics

NOTATION: m $\angle PQR$ will represent "the measure of angle PQR."

1. **(C)**

When simplifying algebraic expressions, always work from left to right. First, perform all multiplications and divisions. Once this is done, start again from the left and do all additions and subtractions.

SUGGESTION: It can be helpful to translate the algebraic statement to English. For example, $6 + 2(x - 4)$ is "six plus two times the quantity x minus 4." The word "times" indicates multiplication, so we must first perform $2(x - 4)$ by using the distributive property $a(b - c) = ab - ac$:

$$6 + 2(x - 4) = 6 + 2 \cdot x - 2 \times 4 = 6 + 2x - 8.$$

Then we perform the subtraction to combine the terms 6 and 8:

$$6 + 2x - 8 = 2x + (6 - 8) = 2x - 2.$$

Note that we did not combine the 2x term with the other terms. This is because they are not like terms. Like terms are terms that have the same variables (with the same exponents). Since the terms 6 and 8 have no variable x, they are not like terms with 2x.

2. **(A)**

The sum of the measures of the interior angles of a triangle is 180°. Therefore,

$$\angle A + m\,\angle ABC + m\angle C = 180°.$$

We also know that $m\angle C = 20°$, so if we substitute this into the previous equation, we have

$m\angle A + m\angle ABC + 20° = 180°.$

Subtracting 20° from both sides of this equation gives us

$m\angle A + m\angle ABC = 160°$ or $m\angle A = 160° - m\angle ABC.$

Therefore, if we know $m\angle ABC$, we are done! To find $m\angle ABC$, notice that $\angle ABD$ is a straight angle and, thus, $m\angle ABD = 180°$. But

$m\angle ABC + m\angle CBD = m\angle ABD.$

So, using the facts that

$m\angle CBD = 36°$ and $m\angle ABD = 180°$, and substituting, we have

$m\angle ABC + 36° = 180°$ or $m\angle ABC = 180° - 36° = 144°$. Hence,

$m\angle A = 160° - m\angle ABC = 160° - 144° = 16°.$

3. **D**

Let x be the cost of one can of beans. Then 6x is the cost of six cans of beans. So 6x = \$1.50. Dividing both sides of the equation by 6, we get x = \$.25 and, hence, since 8x is the cost of eight cans of beans, we have 8x = 8 x \$.25 = \$2.00.

4. **A**

Let t_1, t_2, t_3 represent Bonnie's scores on tests one, two, and three, respectively. Then the equation representing Bonnie's average score is

$$\frac{t_1 + t_2 + t_3}{3} = 71.$$

We know that $t_1 = 64$ and $t_2 = 87$. Substitute this information into the equation above:

$$\frac{64 + 87 + t_3}{3} = 71$$

Combining 64 and 87 and then multiplying both sides of the equation by 3 gives us

$$3 \times \frac{151 + t_3}{3} = 3 \times 71 \text{ or } 151 + t_3 = 213.$$

Now subtract 151 from both sides of the equation so that

$t_3 = 213 - 151 = 62.$

5. **D**

Let s be the length of each side of square ABCD. Since triangle ADC is a right triangle, we can use the Pythagorean Theorem to solve for s. We have $AD^2 + DC^2 = AC^2$ or $s^2 + s^2 = 8^2$.

Simplifying the equation, we get: $2s^2 = 64$. *Now divide both sides of the equation by two:*

$$s^2 = 32 \text{ so } s = \sqrt{32} = \sqrt{16} \times \sqrt{2} = 4\sqrt{2}.$$

Therefore, the perimeter of square ABCD is

$$P = 4s = 4 \times 4\sqrt{2} = 16\sqrt{2}.$$

6. **C**

Let r be the length of the radius of each of the small circles and let R be the length of the radius of the large circle. Then, $R = 3r$. *The area of each of the small circles is* $\pi r^2 = 9\pi$. *Now divide both sides of the equation by* π:

$r^2 = 9 \rightarrow r = 3$. *Then,*

$R = 3r = 3 \times 3 = 9.$

Therefore, the circumference of the large circle is

$C = 2\pi R = 2\pi \times 9 = 18\pi.$

7. **C**

Note that the numbers 4, 8, 12, 16, and 20 are the only numbers from 1 through 20 that are evenly divisible by 4. The probability that a ball chosen from the jar has a number on it that is evenly divisible by 4 is given by

$$\frac{\text{total number of balls with numbers that are evenly divisible by 4}}{\text{total number of possible outcomes}} = \frac{5}{20} = \frac{1}{4}.$$

8. **B**

To solve the equation $2x^2 + 5x - 3 = 0$, *we can factor the left side of the equation to get* $(2x - 1)(x + 3) = 0$. *Then use the following rule (sometimes called the Zero Product Property): If* $a \times b = 0$, *then either* $a = 0$ *or* $b = 0$. *Applying this to our problem gives us*

$2x - 1 = 0$ or $x + 3 = 0$.

Solve these two equations:

$$2x - 1 = 0 \rightarrow 2x = 1 \rightarrow \frac{1}{2} \text{ or } x + 3 = 0 \rightarrow x = -3.$$

But $x > 0$, *so* $x = \frac{1}{2}$.

9. **E**

$\angle AOB$ and $\angle COD$ are central angles, meaning that their vertices are at the center of a circle. The measure of a central angle is equal to the measure of its intercepted arc. Hence, since arc AB and arc CD are the intercepted arcs of $\angle AOB$ and $\angle COD$, respectively, $m\angle AOB = 65°$ and $m\angle COD = 21.4°$. So,

$$m\angle AOB + m\angle COD = 86.4°.$$

Therefore, since one revolution of a circle is 360°, the shaded portion of the circle is represented by the following:

$$\frac{86.4}{360} = 0.24 = 24\%$$

10. **D**

First find the total sales for each year by reading the graph for the sales of (i) black and white televisions and (ii) color televisions. Then combine these numbers:

1960	*\$20,000,000 + \$5,000,000*	=	*\$25,000,000*
1970	*\$10,000,000 + \$20,000,000*	=	*\$30,000,000*
1980	*\$15,000,000 + \$25,000,000*	=	*\$40,000,000*
1990	*\$10,000,000 + \$45,000,000*	=	*\$55,000,000*
2000	*\$5,000,000 + \$45,000,000*	=	*\$50,000,000*

The greatest total sales occurred in 1990.

11. **A**

The probability that first card is a diamond is $\frac{13}{52} = \frac{1}{4}$. There are now 51 cards remaining, of which 12 are diamonds; thus $\frac{12}{51} = \frac{4}{17}$ is the probability that the second card is a diamond. Finally, $\left(\frac{1}{4}\right)\left(\frac{4}{17}\right) = \frac{1}{17}$ is the probability that both cards are diamonds.

12. **C**

The area of the shaded region is equal to the area of the large circle (which has $\overline{OB}$ as a radius), minus the area of the smaller circle (which has $\overline{OA}$ as a radius). Since the area of a circle with *radius r is $A = \pi r^2$, the area of the shaded region is:*

$\pi (OB)^2 - \pi (OA)^2 = 36\pi - 16\pi = 20\pi$.

13. **D**

To solve this inequality, we shall use the following rules:

(i) If $a \le b$ and c is any number, then $a + c \le b + c$.

(ii) If $a \le b$ and $c < 0$, then $ca \ge cb$.

The goal in solving inequalities, as in solving equalities, is to change the inequality so that the variable is isolated (i.e., by itself on one side). So, in the equation $8 - 2x \le 10$, we want the term $-2x$ by itself. To achieve this, use rule (i) above and add -8 to both sides, obtaining $8 - 2x + (-8) \le 10 + (-8)$ or $-2x \le 2$. Now we use rule (ii) and multiply both sides of the inequality by $-\frac{1}{2}$ as follows: $-\frac{1}{2} \times 2x \ge -\frac{1}{2} \times 2$ or $x \ge -1$.

14. **B**

In 1 hour, John will have painted $\frac{1}{4}$ of the fence and Linda will have painted $\frac{1}{3}$ of the fence. Then $\frac{1}{4} + \frac{1}{3} = \frac{7}{12}$ of this fence will be painted in 1 hour. To complete the entire fence requires $1 \div \frac{7}{12} = 1\frac{5}{7}$ hours.

15. **E**

Since $\angle OPQ$ is a straight angle, $m\angle OPQ = 180°$. But

$m\angle OPQ = m\angle OPR + m\angle RPQ$, so

$m\angle OPR + m\angle RPQ = 180°$ or $m\angle OPR = 180° - m\angle RPQ$.

Thus, we need to find $m\angle RPQ$. Since, $l_1 \parallel l_2$, $mRPQ = m\angle TRS$, since $\angle RPQ$ and $\angle TRS$ are corresponding angles. Recall that corresponding angles are two angles that lie on the same side of the transversal (i.e., a line intersecting other lines; in this case, line TP is a transversal since it intersects both line l_1 and l_2), are not adjacent, and one is interior ($\angle RPQ$ in this problem) while the other is exterior ($\angle TRS$). Also, we know that the sum of the measures of the interior angles of a triangle is 180° and

$m\angle T = 80°$, so $m\angle TRS + m\angle RST = 180° - m\angle T = 100°$.

But $m\angle TRS = m\angle RST$ since ΔRTS is isosceles. Thus, $m\angle TRS = 50°$. Therefore,

$m\angle RPQ = 50°$ and $m\angle OPR = 180° - m\angle RPQ = 180° - 50° = 130°$.

16. D

Four apples cost (.54) (4) = \$2.60. Five pears cost 5.30 – 2.60 = \$2.70. Each pear costs \$2.70 ÷ 5 = \$0.54, so two pears would cost (2) (0.54) = \$1.08.

17. D

Let m = the number of men at University X. Then we have the following proportion:

$$\frac{3}{7} = \frac{m}{6{,}153}.$$

To solve this equation, we isolate the variable (i.e., get m by itself) by multiplying both sides of the equation by 6,153 to get

$$\left(\frac{3}{7}\right)6{,}153 = \left(\frac{m}{6{,}153}\right)6{,}153 \text{ or } m = 2{,}637.$$

18. E

(35) (\$9) = \$315.00. Then 333.90 – 315.00 = \$18.90. Finally, 18.90 ÷ 315.00 = 6%.

19. A

Let p be the original price of the jacket. Linda received a 25% discount, so she paid 75% of the original price. Thus, 75% of p equals 54. Writing this in an equation, we get:

$$0.75p = 54 \text{ or } \frac{3}{4}p = 54.$$

To solve this equation, multiply both sides of the equation by the reciprocal of $\frac{3}{4}$, which is $\frac{4}{3}$. This will isolate the variable p.

$$\frac{4}{3}\left(\frac{3}{4}p\right) = \left(\frac{4}{3}\right)54 \text{ or } p = \frac{216}{3} = 72.$$

20. **C**

The area of $\Delta ABC = \frac{1}{2}$(base)(height) = $\frac{1}{2}$ (AB)(CD) = $\frac{1}{2}$(AB)(6) = 3(AB). So we need to find AB. Let s = AB. Since ΔABC is equilateral (i.e., all the sides have the same length), BC = s. Also, since ΔABC is equilateral, D is the midpoint of AB so DB = $\frac{s}{2}$. Now $CD \perp AB$, so ΔCDB is a right triangle and we can use the Pythagorean Theorem: $(CD)^2 + (DB)^2 = (BC)^2$. As CD = 6, this equation becomes $6^2 + \left(\frac{s}{2}\right)^2 = s^2$, or $36 + \frac{s^2}{4} = s^2$. To solve for s, subtract $\frac{s^2}{4}$ from both sides:

$$36 = s^2 - \frac{s^2}{4} = \frac{3}{4}s^2.$$

Now multiply both sides of the equation by the reciprocal of $\frac{3}{4}$ which is $\frac{4}{3} \therefore \frac{4}{3}(36) = s^2$ or $s^2 =$ 48. Hence, $s = \sqrt{48} = \sqrt{16} = \sqrt{3} = 4\sqrt{3}$. The area of $\Delta ABC = 3s = 3\left(4\sqrt{3}\right) = 12\sqrt{3}$.

21. **B**

Substituting F = 86 into the formula $F = \frac{9}{5}C + 32$, we get: $86 = \frac{9}{5}C + 32$. To solve for C, first subtract 32 from both sides:

$$86 - 32 + \frac{9}{5}C + 32 - 32 \text{ or } 54 = \frac{9}{5}C.$$

Now multiply both sides of this equation by the reciprocal of $\frac{9}{5}$, which is $\frac{5}{9}$:

$$\left(\frac{5}{9}\right)54 = \left(\frac{5}{9}\right)\frac{9}{5}C \text{ or } \frac{270}{9} = C \text{ or } C = 30.$$

22. **A**

72,104.58 is read "seventy-**two thousand**, one hundred four and fifty-eight hundredths."

23. **C**

Another way to phrase the second sentence is: She wants to divide her money equally among her six children. Therefore, each child is to receive 300,000 ÷ 6.

24. B

For the adults and children, total cost = (2) (4.50) + (3) (2.50) = 16.50. Then 32.50 – 16.50 = $16. Each senior citizen's ticket = 16 ÷ 4 = $4.00.

25. B

Bob wants to bake 12 cupcakes. The recipe is for 36 cupcakes. Therefore, Bob wants to make $\frac{12}{36}$ or $\frac{1}{3}$ of the usual amount of cupcakes. Thus, Bob should use $\frac{1}{3}$ of the recipe's flour or $\left(\frac{1}{3}\right)\left(\frac{8}{3}\right) = \frac{8}{9}$. Note we used $\frac{8}{3}$ since $2\frac{2}{3} = \frac{8}{3}$.

26. B

Let x be the length of EH, then the length of EF is 2x. The area of a rectangle is length (EF) times width (EH). So we have

$(2x)(x) = 120$ or $2x^2 = 120$.

To solve for x divide both sides of the equation by 2 to get $x^2 = 60$. Note that $49 < x^2 < 64$, so $\sqrt{49} < \sqrt{x^2} < \sqrt{64}$ or $7 < x < 8$. But 60 is closer to 64 than it is to 49, so 8 is the best approximation of x which represents the length of EH.

27. C

Let s_1 and s_2 be Ricky's speed (rate) on the trip from A to B and the return trip from B to A, respectively. Then, since he drove 15 miles per hour slower on the return trip, $s_2 = s_1 - 15$. Recall that rate times time equals distance. So the distance from A to B is $(s_1)3 = 3s_1$ and the distance from B to A is $(s_2)5 = 5s_2 = 5(s_1 - 15) = 5s_1 - 75$. Since the distance from Town A to Town B is the same as the distance from Town B to Town A, we have the following equation:

$3s_1 = 5s_1 - 75$. To solve this equation, first add 75 to both sides of the equation:

$3s_1 + 75 = 5s_1 - 75 + 75$ or $3s_1 + 75 = 5s_1$.

Now to isolate the variable, subtract $3s_1$ from both sides:

$3s_1 + 75 - 3s_1 = 5s_1 - 3s_1$ or $75 = 2s_1$.

To finish the problem, divide both sides of the equation by 2:

$$s_1 = \frac{75}{2} = 37.5.$$

Thus, Ricky drove 37.5 miles per hour on his trip from Town A to Town B.

28. **A**

Let x = required amount. (30) (.40) + x = (30 + x) (.50) 12 + x = 15 + .50x Solving, x = 6.

29. **B**

Statement I is not always true. For example, let x = 2 and y = –3. Then x > y but $x^2 = 4$ and $y^2 = 9$ so $x^2 < y^2$. Statement IV is not always true. For example, let x = 5, y = 1, and z = –2. Then xz = –10 and yz = –2 so that xz < yz. Statements II and III are true.

30. **E**

The 1 is in the hundredths place. If the number to the immediate right of the 1 (i.e., the number in the thousandths place) is greater than or equal to 5, we increase 1 to 2, otherwise, do not change the 1. Then we leave off all numbers to the right of the 1. In our problem, 6 is in the thousandths place, so we change the 1 to a 2 to get 287.42 as our answer.

31. **C**

Recall the following Laws of Exponents:

$$x^p \times x^q = x^{p+q} \text{ and } \frac{x^p}{x^q} = x^{p-q}.$$

So, $x^2 \cdot x^7 = x^{2+7} = x^9$. Hence, $\frac{x^2 \times x^7}{x} = \frac{x^9}{x^1} = x^{9-1} = x^8$.

32. **A**

We need to write the three fractions with the same denominator. So, find the least common multiple (LCM) of 9, 15, and 21. $9 = 3^2$, $15 = 3 \times 5$, and $21 = 3 \times 7$. Therefore, the LCM is $3^2 \times 5 \times 7 = 315$. Then $\frac{1}{9} = \frac{5 \times 7}{5 \times 7} \times \frac{1}{9} = \frac{35}{315}$, $\frac{2}{15} = \frac{3 \times 7}{3 \times 7} \times \frac{2}{15} = \frac{42}{315}$, and $\frac{3}{21} = \frac{3 \times 5}{3 \times 5} \times \frac{3}{21} = \frac{45}{315}$.

Clearly, $\frac{35}{315} < \frac{42}{315} < \frac{45}{315}$ and, hence, in order from least to greatest, we have: $\frac{1}{9}, \frac{2}{15}, \frac{3}{21}$.

33. **A**

The volume of a rectangular box is the area of the base times the height. So if we let s be the length of each side of the base (it is a square), the area of the base is s^2. The height of the box is one-half the length of a side of the base, thus, the height is $\frac{1}{2}s$. The volume is then $V = s^2 \times \frac{1}{2}s$ $= \frac{1}{2}s^3$. But the volume is given as 256. Substituting this into the equation $V = \frac{1}{2}s^3$ gives us:

$$256 = \frac{1}{2}s^3.$$

Now multiply both sides of the equation by 2 to get: $2 \times 256 = 2\frac{1}{2}s^3$ or $512 = s^3$. But, $512 = 8^3$ so that we have $8^3 = s^3$ or $s^3 = 8$. The height of the box is $\frac{1}{2}s = \frac{1}{2} \times 8 = 4$ feet.

34. A

If $x = -3$, then $-x^2 + 2x = -(-3)^2 + 2(-3) = -(9) + (-6) = -15$.

35. D

If $a = b^3$ and $a = \frac{1}{8}$, then substituting into the first equation we have:

$$\frac{1}{8} = b^3 \text{ or } \left(\frac{1}{2}\right)^3 = b^3 \text{ so } b = \frac{1}{2}.$$

36. D

Let x be the number of people in the barn. Then, since each person and cow has only one head, the number of cows must be $30 - x$. Since people have two legs, the number of human legs totals $2x$. Similarly, since the number of legs each cow has is 4, the total number of cow legs in the barn is $4(30 - x)$. Thus, we have this equation:

$$2x + 4(30 - x) = 104.$$

To solve this equation, use the distributive property: $a(b - c) = ab - ac$. We get:

$$4(30 - x) = (4 \times 30) - (4 \times x) = 120 - 4x.$$

Our equation reduces to:

$$2x + 120 - 4x = 104 \text{ or } 120 - 2x = 104.$$

Now subtract 120 from both sides or the equation to get $-2x = 104 - 120 = -16$. Dividing both sides of the equation by -2: $x = 8$. Therefore, there were 8 people and $30 - 8 = 22$ cows in the barn.

37. **B**

To solve the proportion $\frac{12}{x-1} = \frac{5}{6}$, multiply both sides of the equation by 6 and by (x – 1) so that we have:

$$6(x-1) \times \frac{12}{x-1} = 6(x-1) \text{ or } 72 = 5(x-1).$$

Now, use the distributive property: $a(b - c) = ab - ac$ to get $72 = 5x - 5$. Add 5 to both sides of the equation: $77 = 5x$ and then divide both sides by 5:

$$x = \frac{77}{5} = 15.4.$$

38. **C**

In 5 hours, Sharon makes $(5)\left(\frac{60}{30}\right) =$ mistakes. In 3 hours, Ellen makes $(4)\left(\frac{180}{45}\right) = 16$ mistakes. The total is 26 mistakes.

39. **D**

If all selections were changed to a common denominator of 1080, they would read (from A to E) as:

$$\frac{192}{1080}, \frac{252}{1080}, \frac{261}{1080}, \frac{231}{1080}, \text{ and } \frac{236}{1080}.$$

The original two fractions of $\frac{19}{60}$ and $\frac{13}{60}$ become $\frac{228}{1,080}$ and $\frac{234}{1,080}$, respectively. Only choice D would lie between the original fractions.

40. **A**

XY must be negative, since it is the product of a negative and positive number. Then X + XY represents the sum of two negative numbers, which must yield a negative number.

41. **E**

Q implies R becomes "true implies false," which is false. Since P is true, choice E becomes "true and false," which is false.

42. **(C)**

Let 2 be the number of blocks that Sal has. Then, 8% of x is 2, according to the given figure. Thus, we have the equation:

$$.08x = 2 \text{ or, dividing both sides by } .08,\ x = \frac{2}{.08} = \frac{2}{.08} \times \frac{100}{100} = \frac{200}{8} = 25.$$

43. **(D)**

$|x - 3| < 2$ is equivalent to $-2 < x - 3 < 2$. To solve this double inequality, we must add 3 to all three sides: $3 + -2 < x - 3 + 3 < 2 + 3$ or $1 < x < 5$.

44. **(E)**

We must find the areas of the rectangle and semicircle. The area of the rectangle is length times width or $6 \times 4 = 24$. The area of the semicircle is one-half the area of a circle with diameter AB or $\frac{1}{2} \times \pi r^2$, where r is one-half the length of the diameter AB. So $r = 2$ and the area of the semicircle is $\frac{1}{2}\pi(2)^2 = 2\pi$. Thus, the total area is $24 + 2\pi$.

45. **(C)**

According to the graph, the supply was greater than the demand in March and May only.

46. **(A)**

$\frac{640}{2,780} \approx .23 \quad \frac{600}{2,140} \approx .28 \quad$ *Then $.28 - .23 = 5\%$.*

47. **(D)**

Total lawsuits = 2,780 + 2,140 + 2,820 = 7,740.

Total inmate lawsuits = 640 + 600 + 470 = 170.

Then $\frac{1,710}{7,740} \approx 22\%$.

48. **D**

The list of all the negative integers between –9 and 5 is: –8, –7, –6, –5, –4, –3, –2, –1.

49. **E**

The area of a circle is πr^2, where r is the radius. In the given circle, $\overline{OB}$ is the radius and A = 144π. So, $144\pi = \pi r^2$ so that r = 12. If we increased the radius by 2 feet so that now r = 14, the area of the new circle is $A = \pi (16)^2 = 196\pi$.

50. **A**

Since $AB \perp BC$, we know that ΔABC is a right triangle and, thus, we may use the Pythagorean Theorem to find the length of BC (let x be the length of BC): $AC^2 = AB^2 + BC^2$ or $(10)^2 = 6^2 + x^2$ or $100 = 36 + x^2$. To solve this, subtract 36 from both sides of the equation to get: $64 = x^2$ so that x = 8. The area of ΔABC =

$$\frac{1}{2}(AB)(BC) = \frac{1}{2}(6)(8) = 24.$$

DIRECTIONS: Carefully read the two writing topics below. Plan and write an essay on each, being sure to cover all aspects of each essay. Allow approximately 30 minutes per essay.

Topic 1

The minimum wage in America has been the subject of debate for many years. Many people argue that we should be careful about sharp increases in the minimum wage because of the resulting inflation (higher labor costs equal higher consumer prices) and layoffs. Others believe the minimum wage is too low to support a family and should be raised to keep up with the cost of living.

Write an essay analyzing and evaluating these opposing views on the minimum wage. You may include personal experience, knowledge, or observations.

Topic 2

Popular psychology tells us that "habit" is a powerful force, compelling us to live out our lives with basically the same behaviors we learned as we grew up. Write an essay in which you discuss a significant habit of yours that you'd like to change. Speculate on why this may be difficult for you.

GO ON TO THE NEXT PAGE

Detailed Explanations of Answers

PRACTICE TEST 1

SECTION 3: Writing

SAMPLE SCORED ESSAYS WITH EXPLANATIONS

Topic 1 Sample Answers

Essay #1—Pass (Score = 4)

There is no doubt that minimum wage laws are necessary for the well-being of workers and their families. It had always been the policy for most businesses to pay laborers less than they deserve. Minimum wage laws are one of the only ways workers can be protected from management; without them they are fair game to whatever exploitation the employer can manage.

Many argue against the minimum wage, protesting that it is too high. The fact is, even with raises in the rate, it still does not meet the needs of the laborers because of the increases in inflation and the basic cost of living. At present, it would be extremely difficult, or even impossible, to support a family on a salary as low as $5.00 an hour. There is no person (or family) in my experience who survives on minimum wage; teenagers who have financial help from their parents, might find a minimum wage adequate, but no "head of a household" would. If anything, the current minimum wage rate is too low.

Another argument against minimum wage, especially sharp increases, is the possibility of inflation due to higher labor costs which might cause higher consumer prices. The problem with this is management. Workers do not cause inflation, businesses and corporations do. If the leaders of these companies were not so money hungry, workers could have higher salaries without causing an increase in the price of goods and services. It is quite possible to do this because products are extremely overpriced. Most businesses, however, look to short-term, easy money instead of long term stability. A raise in the minimum wage would actually help the business in the long-run because workers would be happier and thus, productivity would be increased. The only way a raise in the minimum wage would cause inflation would be if the companies themselves let it.

The final point made by those opposed to minimum wage is the possibility of inflationary pressures resulting in worker lay-offs. As was discussed earlier, inflation in this situation is not a given. For the moment however, let's just theorize on the possibilities of workers being fired. Those most likely to be laid off are the teenagers, minorities, seniors, and the disabled. Although this seems like the course of action many businesses would take, it is not if the companies are smart. First, firing workers would not be tolerated by unions. Next, even in non-union companies, laying off workers would cost the business money in the long run; with less workers, productivity is diminished and when there is a need for more workers they will have to be paid at the same wage as were the ones who were fired. There is little chance that businesses would make decisions that would cost them money.

It would be ridiculous to say that minimum wage is a panacea for the laborers of the world. It barely makes a dent, even with the recent increases in their bills. What it does do, though, is give the worker a guarantee that he will get paid no less than is mandated; this, in many cases, is enough.

Scoring Explanation for Essay #1—Pass

This essay is thoughtful and well-organized, and it introduces several interesting arguments supporting the minimum wage. The author obviously has some knowledge about and experience with the effect that minimum wage legislation bears on businesses and their employees. The essay attempts to debunk arguments that a minimum wage necessarily entails inflation, higher costs, and layoffs. The writer presents his/her views straightforwardly and clearly, although the opinions may not be popular (or accurate) from an employer's perspective.

Still, the author systematically addresses the most typical arguments against the minimum wage and reaches a realistic conclusion. In other words, he/she does not argue that the minimum wage is a panacea; rather, the position advanced is that it is a valuable support to low-wage workers. In addition, the syntax assists the flow of the argument, and the text is easy to follow. The few grammatical mistakes do not markedly distract from the writer's ideas. Considering the time constraints of the exam, the essay pursues its thesis consistently, answers all aspects of the prompt, and develops its argument with lucid prose. For these reasons, the essay earns a "4."

Essay #2—Marginal Pass (Score = 3)

The issue of minimum wage for American workers is definitely a controversial one. Since there are so many aspects of this issue, many conflicting opinions are held concerning what constitutes a fair minimum wage. Because the cost of living changes so frequently in society, minimum wage should definitely change with it.

Some people argue that raising minimum wage constantly will harm, rather than benefit society. They believe that "higher labor costs would be reflected in higher consumer prices," thereby causing unnecessary inflation. They feel that many workers would be needlessly laid off, due to the fact that their employers would not be able to pay higher wages to many workers. Consequently, there are some people who vehemently oppose the raising of minimum wage and cannot see how it would benefit society.

While these arguments are somewhat understandable, the fact still remains that living conditions change over the years, and the average cost of living only continues to grow.

Although people may have survived on a lower salary many years ago, it is entirely unrealistic to think that this same salary will be adequate for those living in the 1990's. For those who are raising a family, it is crucial that they receive a reasonable salary so that their family can function and survive today's standards. Minimum wage should be raised whenever necessary, for people cannot be expected to manage properly unless they are receiving wages which reflect the current cost of living.

The minimum wage for American workers has consistently risen, so it is evident that Congress had seen the changes in society and raised the minimum wage accordingly. It becomes more expensive daily to live comfortably by today's standards. It is obvious that many people feel the need to earn more money, since the cost of living today is so high.

In order for society to continue functioning efficiently, it must adequately meet the growing needs of its people. One such need is to provide a fair minimum wage for workers which coincides with their cost of living.

Scoring Explanation for Essay #2—Marginal Pass

This essay is generally coherent and satisfactorily written, but it offers much less specific information than most typical passing essays. It relies on the repetition of its points rather than their full explication. Thus, the writer's chief problem lies in his/her development of the argument. The essay does more asserting than analyzing; it assumes the reader will accept, without question, its assertions.

The writer concludes, in reasonable fashion, that the cost of living continues to rise and that the minimum wage should correspondingly increase. Rather than presenting specific evidence that it is difficult for workers to keep up with inflation or demonstrating that the minimum wage should periodically increase, the writer merely asserts that these things are true. A personal anecdote or observation could help to illustrate this key point. Nevertheless, the essay reads well and shows an acceptable command of written English. Although it suffers from many distracting problems, they are not sufficiently detrimental to the essay to earn it a score of marginal fail, and thus the essay marginally passes.

Essay #3—Marginal Fail (Score = 2)

The baby begins to cry as the father enters the run-down apartment. He dodges the dripping ceiling and proceeds over to help his wife who is caught between the bargain dinner and the crying child. After soothes the child he goes onto explain that on account of his low wage, there will not be any hot water for a while. We can't have everything, it was either that or the streets.

I don't believe that the minimum wage is high. It is not fair, some people should be expected to live such a low standard. The Adult work force should be given a more fair and reliable wage to support themselves. Then they would gain a better self esteem and, in turn, give their children a better outlook on life.

The minimum wage does not have to be raised for the teenagers. I believe there should be separate minimums for minors and adults. This way a business owner does not have to pay extra for a teenagers incompetence, and the adult worker who is struggling to support a family is much better.

The poverty levels of this country is increasing more and more. If the minimum wages would be lifted for adults it may aliviate some of the poverty. It may also solve some problems for many struggling families who are going homeless, and once your homeless, the minimum wage doesn't matter any more.

Scoring Explanation for Essay #3—Marginal Fail

This essay begins with a compelling vignette that describes the human difficulties of surviving while earning the minimum wage. The writer gives his/her essay a unique and personal feel which interests the reader in the argument. Unfortunately, the rest of the essay does not maintain the promise of the introductory paragraph.

The organization and development of the remainder of the essay lack focus. The author jumps from topic to topic, arguing that the minimum wage is too low, that teenage workers do not need to have the minimum wage raised, and that poverty is increasing throughout the land. None of these topics is adequately explored to support an argument for raising the minimum wage. For example, the essay should address the potential difficulties of having two separate minimum wages, one for teenagers and the other for adults.

Many errors in punctuation and syntax hinder the reader from readily understanding the writer's ideas. Capital letters and spelling provide problems for the writer, and sentences such as "We can't have everything, it was either that or the streets" highlight the writer's difficulty with combining sentences correctly. The writer displays a clear sense of style in this essay, but inadequate development and frequent grammatical errors result in a failing grade.

Essay #4—Fail (Score = 1)

Todays american economy and cost of-living index has change dramatically within the past years. For the value of the dollar has weaken compared to what it was worth in the early 1900 's; thus making the cost of living for low income and disabled people much more difficult than what it was already. Minimum wage law was created to prevent Americans form becoming poor and homeless by raising the minimum wage for to coincid with todays living standards. But now, the standards of living are very difficult and the minimum wage law has become controversial. People feel the law might enuse inflation and consumer prices. But this is not so.

The minimum wage does not pose a threat and should be raise. We live in a low income society. But since minimum wage was raised more have a chance for college.

Minimum wage gives us americans a chance to live a better and enjoyible life; one of the things that makes this country so great. It makes us americans feel as though we are here to live a life, not just survive and never expand beyond what our life could be.

Many people claim that the raise in minimum wage might cause inflation. But before the minimum increased the prices and inflation were at a high. That is why many of us americans demanded a increase.

Scoring Explanation for Essay #4—Fail

This essay does not adequately support its thesis that the minimum wage should be raised. The author reiterates this point several times but never provides compelling reasons why the current minimum wage is too low. The author should develop his premise that raising the minimum wage would allow more people to attend college or to enjoy a better life; as it now stands, the essay's analysis of this complex issue is too simplistic to warrant a passing score. Thus, because the essay makes many claims that are awkward, confusing, and poorly supported, we never get a full view of the issue's true significance.

Furthermore, the essay teems with grammatical and syntactic errors that cause a great deal of difficulty for the reader. Spelling errors abound, and the writer experiences real difficulty in attempting to write complex sentences. Problems with verb tenses are evident. Due to the serious weaknesses in the essay's organization and development, as well as its problems with grammar and syntax, the essay receives a failing score.

Topic 2 Sample Answers

Essay #1—Pass (Score = 4)

As people grow older, they begin to look at themselves and examine who they are. They look at their life and how they go about living it. These introspections can be very reassuring for a person, revealing many strong qualities that provide them with much comfort. However, some people are able to go further and examine every aspect of their lives—including the things they are uncomfortable with.

As I reflect on my life, I am able to discover many positive qualities which I can be very proud of. On the other hand, I am also able to realize some things about myself which I am not comfortable with and would like to change. One such thing is a bad habit I developed in my youth. Ever since I can remember, I've had trouble letting people know what it is I want to do.

Many times I've let people get away with things just because I'm afraid to tell them how I feel or what I want. For some reason, it's always been hard for me to speak my mind. This inability to communicate my inner feelings has led to many difficulties. In many situations I have wanted to tell someone how I feel but was afraid to. For example, I ended up attending a party where drugs were being used because I wasn't strong enough to tell my friends I didn't want to go. I didn't want to be thought of as a "nerd." Fortunately, I was able to leave the party without incident.

At times dealing with my parents has been difficult because I won't always let them know what I'm thinking. The same thing occurs in relations with teachers, friends and members of the opposite sex. Perhaps if I could be more open, future difficulties could be avoided.

It's difficult to ascertain the source of this problem. Maybe it's because I grew up under the impression that "real men" don't show emotions. Maybe it's just because I'm a quiet person. Whatever the reason, I'd like to change it, and I have been trying. Lately, I've been more able to tell people how I feel and not hold back. I may have finally realized that people aren't going to laugh at me when I tell them how I feel. It's becoming easier to express myself, but it's still difficult. Perhaps as I grow older the problem will disappear. That is my hope, but I intend to continue my periodic, introspective self-analysis to make sure I don't slip.

Scoring Explanation for Essay #1—Pass

The writer begins this essay by speculating about the value of examining one's life and concludes on a similar note. In the body of the essay, the writer explores a habit that he is uncomfortable with and would like to change. The discussion of this problematic habit is well developed and specific, offering both generalizations and illustrations of the ways in which the habit manifests itself.

The writer also attempts to address the origin of the habit, providing several possible reasons for its existence. The essay prompt asks the writer to speculate why changing the habit might be difficult, and the author addresses this topic in the concluding paragraph. In sum, the writer offers a reasonable response that is also a sincere investigation of a personal issue. Few grammatical errors appear, and the sentence structure is relatively complex at times. For all of its positive features, the essay earns a passing score.

Essay #2—Marginal Pass (Score = 3)

In developing habitual behaviors or tendencies one may find himself limited or restrained. One's habits limit the diversity he is able to experience and develop. They, habits, limit your ability to change, learn and experience novelties by always acting in one particular manner.

I find I have various habits that limit my growth as an individual. One specific habit is that of not speaking my thoughts or opinions amongst family and friends. This habit, although its seemingly minor, often limits the capacity and development of a relationship. All the burdens and pressures of planning, "what we should do," are thrown on the shoulders of the individual. The burdens I create can easily be eased by my own input or opinion. No matter how insignificant the input may be, it still causes more of a "mutual agreement."

This habit will be difficult to break since it takes all the pressure off me. Forcing another to decide everything may make my part of the relationship easier. I have grown so accustomed to not giving input that it will be hard for me to start deciding because of the added pressure. However, I believe if *I* take some pressure, my relationships will develop fully and concretely.

Scoring Explanation for Essay #2—Marginal Pass

This essay contains elevated diction and sophisticated, complex sentences. Although these features often characterize good writing, this writer uses them to mask the weaknesses of his essay. Pompous phrasings attempt to conceal a discussion that is too abstract to make its points clearly.

The author's implied promise to discuss the habit of "not speaking [his] thoughts or opinions amongst family and friends" is never completely fulfilled. The reader is offered few specific examples of the habit, so the writer's speculations about the burdens he creates are less powerful than if they were well illustrated with specific cases in point. The reader is left wondering what precisely is meant by the "burdens and pressures of planning" and how these burdens create problems for the writer.

Similarly, the writer mentions the difficulty involved in altering the habit (because it's easier not to), but this section is obtuse and generalized. The writer has a firm grip on grammar and syntax, and this strength in communication saves the essay from losing its grounding entirely. The ideas suffer from being overly abstract, but they are presented with sufficient clarity to earn a marginally passing score.

Essay #3—Marginal Fail (Score = 2)

Popular psychology tell us that "habit" is a powerful force, compelling us to live out our lives with basically the some behaviors we learned as we grew up. Reassurance in decision making is a significant habit, I'd like to change. In this essay, I will discuss why this may be difficult.

Since the time I could remember, I would always ask my mother or sister, Alex, to help me. In making a decision; for example, clothes I bought, the University I wanted to attend or whether to cut my hair or not. Some of these decision makings, life did not depended on, but asking for their advice-in trying to make my decision—I was assured that I was right.

I know I need to break this habit, but it is difficult for me. Many times I tell myself that I need to make my own decisions. Because Alex and my mother are not going to be there all the time. One of the reasons it is difficult for me is because I always need someone to approve. Someone to say, "yes, you're making the right choice."

Now in college I am begin to make my own decisions without their consents; but I still need to work on it. I am beginning to force myself to do what I want to do whether someone likes it or not. Although I am trying to break away from this habit, it will take a long time to break completely from it. This is because, although I am making some decisions with out their consent, there are other decisions I make in which I feel I need reassurance.

Scoring Explanation for Essay #3—Marginal Fail

The writer reiterates the question to open this rather ordinary response. A specific example is offered to illustrate the difficulty the writer has in making decisions, but it appears in the middle of a sentence wracked with various grammatical errors. The writer has difficulty with punctuation and syntax, and she/he inadvertently creates many awkward and incomplete sentences. In paragraph two, the reader must struggle with "In making a decision; for example, clothes I bought, the University I wanted to attend or whether to cut my hair or not." Still, the writer does attempt to address the question and mentions his/her need for approval as the impediment to change. Rather than exploring this issue, however, the writer merely reasserts it as the conclusion to the essay. The combination of a superficial response with little development and numerous grammatical errors results in a marginally failing essay.

Essay #4—Fail (Score = 1)

A habit becomes a heartbeat that lets us live on. By this, I mean, that it becomes voluntary; once we start that habit until we end it. A habit that I have and I would like to change is massaging and cracking my nuckles when I am nervous.

It is a significant habit because I start massaging my hand and once I finished, it feels relaxed, but what I realized is that it makes my hand shake more. Sometimes I am so nervous, for example when I am about to give speech in Public Speaking class, that I massage my hand so hard - it turns red and swollen. I cause myself a lot of pain!

I finished massaging my hand, Well, what can I do now? I then start cracking my nuckles(fingers). I know one day I am going to end up with arthritus if I keep on doing this! Sometimes when I do it, it feels good, but other times I over do it. I usually over do it by cracking my fingers so much that they don't want to crack no more. Then they start hurting very much.

I guess I don't realize what pain I am causing myself with this habit. For me it has become a heartbeat. I can't stop it This is how this habit works. Maybe I forget about being nervous. Because I am feeling pain - That is what I think, maybe.

Somehow I think it will be difficult to stop this habit. I don't think when I massage and crack my fingers It just happens. It became - something to do when I am nervous. A painful Heartbeat that will probably go on forever until I die. By then the doctors would of cut of my hands or maybe I cut them of. Who knows what will happen with this habit of mine.

Scoring Explanation for Essay #4—Fail

This essay describes a habit of the author; beyond this surface gesture, however, it does not engage with the essay prompt. The essay is confusing and does not develop any thesis other than describing the author cracking his/her knuckles. Since the thesis itself is so trivial, the author cannot develop a compelling response to the topic at hand.

Frequent grammatical mistakes make the essay very difficult to follow. Sentences such as "By then the doctors would of cut of my hands or maybe I cut them of" make very little sense and do not contribute to building an effective piece of writing. In the frequent metaphoric comparisons between cracking knuckles and a heartbeat, the author repeatedly attempts to bring a poetic style into the essay, but the endless repetitiveness of this move stifles any life it would allow the essay. A poor thesis, little development, and excessive grammatical mistakes result in a failing grade.

Practice Test 2

The Third of Three Full-Length Practice Tests

DIRECTIONS: One or more questions follow each statement or passage in this test. The question(s) are based on the content of the passage. After you have read a statement or passage, select the best answer to each question from among the five possible choices. Your answers to the questions should be based on the stated (literal) or implied (inferential) information given in the statement or passage. Mark all answers on your answer sheet. **Note: You will encounter some passages with numbered sentences, blank spaces, or underscored words and phrases. These cues are provided on the CBEST for your reference in answering the questions that follow the relevant passages.**

Questions 1–3 refer to the following passage:

The teaching apprentice initiated the discussion in a clear and well-prepared manner. To ____________ the lecture topic the teaching apprentice utilized overhead transparencies of both lexicon and abstract representation to better ____________ the theories behind various <u>pedagogical</u> concepts. The class culminated whereby students established enthymemes extrapolated from the class discussion. The class maintained integrity and continuity.

1. Which of these grouped words, if inserted *in order* into the passage's blank lines, would address the logical sequencing of the narrative?

(A) refute; criticize
(B) conflate; discern
(C) laud; consider
(D) support; illustrate
(E) undermine; explain

2. The definition of the term <u>pedagogical</u> as used in the sentence means

(A) intelligent.
(B) abstract.
(C) meaningless.
(D) obtuse.
(E) academic.

3. The passage suggests that the author's classroom experience was

(A) a needless waste of time and energy.
(B) intelligible and pragmatic.
(C) haphazard and disorderly.
(D) too advanced and complicated.
(E) superfluous and derogatory.

Questions 4–6 refer to the following passage:

To receive an "A" on a paper in this class one must write sophisticated prose. The criteria will be based on the complexity of both content and expression. The grade will require a demonstration of obvious familiarity with primary texts, as well as additional readings of the course and secondary materials and research sources. An effective combination of personal opinion and outside sources will also be required. Proficiency in organizational skills, format, rhetoric, grammar, syntax, and sentence structure is a must. An additional requirement is a thoroughly proofread essay resulting in no distracting mechanical errors with the possible exception of occasional arguable usage.

4. To receive an "A" grade in the above class, the student must

(A) turn in a proofread paper with no punctuation errors and demonstrate an understanding of the reading material.
(B) write an effective paper without mistakes and with an abundance of secondary source materials.
(C) turn in a thoughtful paper with no corrections as well as demonstrate a proficiency of organizational skills, such as format, rhetoric, and grammar.
(D) write an intelligent paper without regard for grammar, syntax, or rhetorical strategies, with the possible exception of occasional arguable usage.
(E) write about arguable strategies and demonstrate an understanding of secondary source materials and research sources.

5. What does the author mean by "sophisticated prose"?

(A) A readable text that does not make sense.
(B) A readable text made up of knowledgeable or thoughtful language.
(C) A readable text consisting of pompous or ostentatious language.
(D) A readable text made up of poetic metaphor.
(E) A readable text that reflects the author's antecedents.

GO ON TO THE NEXT PAGE

6. When the author of the passage refers to the "primary texts," he means

(A) the reference materials, such as the dictionary, encyclopedia, thesaurus, etc.
(B) the primary note pages, works cited page, or preliminary rough draft page.
(C) the source or principal text in the assignment.
(D) the first text written about a certain subject.
(E) the beginning text in a numbered series of texts.

Questions 7–10 refer to the following passage:

Language not only expresses an individual's ideology, it also sets perimeters while it persuades and influences the discourse in the community that hears and interprets its meaning. Therefore, the language of failure should not be present in the learning environment (i.e., the classroom) because it will have a prohibitive impact on the students' desire to learn as well as a negative influence on the students' self-esteem.

The *Oxford English Dictionary* defines *failure* as a fault, a shortcoming, a lack of success, a person who turns out unsuccessfully, becoming insolvent, etc. We as educators might well ask ourselves if this is the sort of doctrine that we want to permeate our classrooms. Perhaps our own University axiom, *mens agitat molem* (the mind can move mountains), will help us discover if, indeed, the concepts of failure are really the types of influences we wish to introduce to impressionable new students. Is the mind capable of moving a mountain when it is already convinced it cannot?

One must remain aware that individuals acquire knowledge at independent rates of speed. Certainly no one would suggest that one infant "failed" the art of learning to walk because she acquired the skill two months behind her infant counterpart. Would anyone suggest that infant number one *failed* walking? Of course not. What would a mentor project to either toddler were he to suggest that a slower acquisition of walking skills implied failure? Yet we as educators feel the need to suggest student A failed due to the slower procurement of abstract concepts then student B. It is absolutely essential to shift the learning focus from failure to success.

7. Which of the following statements best conveys the meaning of the passage?

(A) Learning is something that happens at different speeds and is, therefore, natural.
(B) Instructors need to be sensitive to students' individual needs.
(C) Instructors need to shift the educational focus from failure to success in learning environments.
(D) Failure is a potential hazard in the classroom and should be avoided at all costs.
(E) Too much emphasis is placed on grades and not enough on education.

8. As stated in the context of the passage, what does University axiom mean?

(A) University Latin
(B) University motto
(C) University rhetoric
(D) University sophomore
(E) University legend

9. According to the passage, what will have a negative effect on student self-esteem?

(A) The rhetoric of diction
(B) The slower procurement of abstract concepts
(C) The learning focus from failure to success
(D) The language of failure
(E) The *Oxford English Dictionary*

10. According to the passage, what does language do besides aid individual expression?

(A) It establishes individual thought and tells of individual philosophies.
(B) It paints visual images and articulates individual declaration.
(C) It suggests individual axioms and community philosophy.
(D) It persuades and influences the discourse in the community that hears and interprets its meaning.
(E) It manipulates the truisms and reiterates ideologies.

GO ON TO THE NEXT PAGE

Questions 11–13 refer to the following passage:

Life in seventeenth-century England was tempestuous indeed. It was a time when religious and secular confrontations resulted in new social abstractions, paradoxes, and ironies. The poet-pastor Robert Herrick (1591-1674) illustrates the ability of lyric poetry to serve not only as an adornment of the era, but as social communiqué, as well. Herrick's Mayday celebration poem "Corinna's Going A-Maying" serves as both an argument against conservative religious dogma and as a response to specific Puritan manifestos. Herrick incorporates abundant Greco-Roman tropes into "Corinna" in order to construct a stylized response to Puritanism based upon traditional structure, symmetry, and thematic representation.

11. The author's attitude toward the subject is one of

(A) lethargy.
(B) apathy.
(C) objectivity.
(D) intensity.
(E) synergy.

12. The passage fundamentally suggests that

(A) Puritanism is based upon a traditional structure, symmetry, and thematic representation.
(B) lyric poetry has the ability to serve not only as an adornment of an era, but also as social communiqué.
(C) life in seventeenth-century England was tempestuous indeed.
(D) the seventeenth century was a time of religious and secular confrontations, resulting in new social abstractions, paradoxes, and ironies.
(E) the poet-pastor Robert Herrick was a critic of Puritanism.

13. As used in the passage, the word trope means

(A) a group of people, animals, etc., such as a herd, a flock, a band, and so on.
(B) a style of writing in the Greek or Roman language.
(C) a desire to travel to Greece or Rome.
(D) the use of a word in a figurative sense; a figure of speech; figurative language.
(E) Italian philosophy, ideology, heritage, culture, etc.

Questions 14–17 refer to the following passage:

A Critic can be equivalent to "a person who pronounces judgement; especially a *Censurer.*" Since the late sixteenth century, the title of Critic has embodied implied meanings such as "professionalism" and "a person *skilled* in textual criticism." Thereby, the title insinuates a distinction of hierarchy among laborers, craftsmen, and the "working class" in general. "Censure" has etymological connotations that date back to the late Middle Ages, "critical recension or revision (along with) expression(s) of disapproval, to give opinion, assess critically, find fault, reprove, blame, pronounce sentence," and "condemnatory (especially ecclesiastical) judgement, opinion, correction," which all furthermore suggest a rather antagonistic posture in relationship to the Humanities. The position of critic is tenuous, as they can serve both as censure or social analyst and commentator. Subsequently, the word is loaded with negative innuendoes, but also innuendoes that denote authority, repression, and judicial propriety. In essence, the Critic who chooses to take the point-of-view of the Censure, sits on the mountaintop, not for a better view of literature, but to establish a false sense of superiority over it in relationship to the Author (as well as the reader for that matter).

14. The passage suggests that

(A) critics are good for the social order.
(B) the position of critic is tenuous as they can serve both as censure or social analyst and commentator.
(C) critics attempt to establish a false sense of superiority over the author and the reader as well.
(D) humanitarians do not make good critics as they are too emotional and not callous or impartial enough.
(E) critics do not serve any valuable social function and, therefore, the position should be eliminated.

15. The passage indicates that the art of criticism

(A) is a modern phenomenon.
(B) is a socially destructive force.
(C) is a thought-provoking entity.

GO ON TO THE NEXT PAGE

(D) began at around the same time as the Civil War.
(E) dates back to the Middle Ages.

16. Which of the following would make the best title for the passage you just read?

(A) Critical Analysis Ruins Literature for the Rest of Us
(B) Critics Assume a False Superiority Thereby Rendering Critical Judgement Null and Void
(C) The Implications and Connotations of the Critic as Author
(D) Criticism is Synonymous with Censorship
(E) The Critic as Both Judge and Jury

17. What does the term etymological mean as it is used in the passage?

(A) The history of the Middle Ages
(B) The history of a word
(C) The history of critical analysis
(D) The history of literature
(E) The history of censorship

Questions 18–20 refer to the following passage:

The early decades of the fifteenth century were a period in our history when English took a "great (linguistic) vowel shift" by redistributing the vowel pronunciation and configuration. Each vowel changed its sound quality, but the distinction between one vowel and the next was maintained. There was a restructuring of the sounds and patterns of communication, as well. One has to conclude that a concurrent stress and exhilaration was occurring within the perimeters of the literate society as well. Musicians, artists, poets, and authors all must have relished the new freedom and experimentation that was now possible with the new-found linguistic shifts.

18. The passage tells about

(A) a shift in vowel pronunciation and configuration.
(B) a fifteenth-century renaissance for musicians, artists, poets, and authors.
(C) a new-found linguistic freedom from conventional sound and linguistic structure.
(D) various vowel stresses and their effect on artistic expression.
(E) the early decades of the fifteenth century.

19. What is the meaning of the word linguistic as used in the passage?

(A) Artistic freedom
(B) Verbal or rhetorical
(C) Social or expressive
(D) Vowel configuration
(E) Historical or archaic

20. Because "each vowel changed its sound quality"

(A) there was a restructuring of the sounds and patterns of communication.
(B) language could never be spoken in the same way again.
(C) artists had to develop new means of expression.
(D) communication went through a divergent change of status and culture.
(E) Shakespeare could write sonnets in Middle English and not Old English.

Questions 21–24 refer to the following passage:

Lead poisoning is considered by health authorities to be the most common and devastating environmental disease of young children. According to studies, it affects 15% to 20% of urban children and from 50% to 75% of inner-city, poor children. As a result of a legal settlement in July 1991, all California MediCal-eligible children, ages one through five, will now be routinely screened annually for lead poisoning. Experts estimate that more than 50,000 cases will be detected in California because of the newly mandated tests. This will halt at an early stage a disease that leads to learning disabilities and life-threatening disorders.

21. Lead poisoning among young children, if not detected early, can lead to

(A) physical disabilities.
(B) heart disease.
(C) liver disease.
(D) social disease.
(E) learning disabilities and death.

GO ON TO THE NEXT PAGE

22. The new mandate to screen all young children for lead poisoning is required of

(A) all young children in California.
(B) all children with learning disabilities.
(C) all MediCal-eligible children, ages one through five, in California.
(D) all minority children in inner cities.
(E) all school-age children.

23. The percentages suggest that more cases of lead poisoning are found among

(A) children in rural areas.
(B) inner-city children.
(C) immigrant children.
(D) upper-middle class children.
(E) adopted children.

24. The ultimate goal of the newly mandated tests is to

(A) bring more monies into inner-city medical programs.
(B) bring more health care professionals into California's inner cities.
(C) alleviate over-crowding in California's public schools.
(D) screen more test subjects to develop more accurate statistical data.
(E) halt at an early stage a disease that leads to learning disabilities and life-threatening disorders.

Questions 25 and 26 refer to the following passage:

The social ostracizing of male hairdressers and ballet dancers, versus the female mechanic or construction worker, presents the case that society classifies individuals by gender. But are these boundaries really changing? That is, what are the implications of a woman in a traditionally male career, who is "surprised" by another female in a traditional male career? What does that say about gender roles?

25. The passage asks the reader to

(A) ostracize various individuals who step outside conventional gender roles.
(B) change social boundaries by taking on non-traditional jobs.
(C) accept people who take on jobs traditionally occupied by the opposite sex.
(D) classify individuals by gender.
(E) question whether traditional gender boundaries are changing or not.

26. As it is used in the passage, what does social ostracizing mean?

(A) Social acceptance
(B) Social pressure
(C) Social traditions
(D) Social alienation
(E) Social examination

Questions 27 and 28 refer to the following passage:

The paradigm of a universal rational mind implies a form of stagnation, rigidity or at the very least, an intellectual elitist form of hierarchy. It suggests that everyone in a discourse community is of an equal mind, or should be. If members of a rhetorical community are not of the same equal mind, then there is an implication that their thinking is skewed by the clutter of culture, politics, and commitment. Additionally, it insinuates a discourse community predicated upon a single universal agenda. Because, after all, rhetoric is argumentation with an agenda.

27. The passage implies that

(A) discourse communities allow for individual thought and freedom of expression.
(B) everyone in a discourse community is of a similar mind, and is, therefore, suspect.
(C) members of a rhetorical community are more liberal than those of a discourse community.
(D) rhetoric is argumentation with an agenda and is, therefore, valuable.
(E) rhetoric is void of agenda and is biased.

28. What does the term paradigm mean?

(A) Model or standard
(B) Group or community
(C) Language or rhetoric
(D) Apathy or agenda
(E) Social order or intellectual

GO ON TO THE NEXT PAGE

Questions 29 and 30 refer to the following passage:

A 150-million-year-old allosaurus skeleton that appears to be intact was found on September 9, 1991, by a Swiss team in north-central Wyoming. This Zurich-based company sells fossils to museums. They were digging on private property, but the fossil actually showed up on federal land.

Immediately, the federal government sealed off the site along the foot of the Big Horn Mountains in Wyoming and deployed rangers from the Bureau of Land Management to prevent vandalism. Paleontologists believe that this discovery could lead them to a vast dinosaur graveyard.

29. The passage you just read can best be utilized by a classroom teacher in

(A) reading.
(B) mathematics.
(C) biology.
(D) zoology.
(E) literature.

30. The main idea of the passage is

(A) government intervention into private matters.
(B) world communities working together in a chosen field.
(C) private versus public ownership of historical artifacts.
(D) dinosaurs once lived in Wyoming.
(E) this discovery could lead to a vast dinosaur graveyard.

Questions 31–33 refer to the following passage:

Looking specifically at animal symbols and what they represent allows one to see a diversified menagerie of animal representations as social commentary, along with their implications of metaphors, like the aristocratic lion, the perfunctory alley cat, and the domesticated dog. Each creature in its own way serves as a metaphor for British imperialistic progressions and colonial expansion. That is, *imperialism* as capitalistic encroachment and *colonialism* as territorial usurpation with governmental despotic autonomy.

31. The main idea of the passage is

(A) literary animal representations can serve as social symbols.
(B) animal symbols are British in nature and are, therefore, aristocratic.
(C) government organizations manifest themselves in literature as a pack of animals.
(D) literary lions are metaphors for perfunctory alley cats.
(E) colonial expansion and imperialism are mainly terms that apply to dogs and cats.

32. What is a metaphor?

(A) A sentence that ends in a question
(B) A theory of colonialism
(C) A figure of speech containing an implied comparison
(D) Two words that mean the same thing
(E) An abstract sentence where the verb comes before the noun

33. In the passage, imperialism and colonialism are defined, respectively, as

(A) territorial arrangement and economic organization.
(B) economic wealth and territorial abundance.
(C) financial infringement and territorial confiscation.
(D) financial freedom and territorial generosity.
(E) land development and economic liberation.

Questions 34 and 35 refer to the following passage:

San Francisco was named the world's favorite travel destination in the prestigious 1991 *Condé Nast Traveler* magazine poll. It was considered the best city in the world that year, beating out Florence, Italy (No. 2), and London and Vienna, which tied for No. 3. A red-carpet gala in the City Hall rotunda is planned in which Mayor Agnos will laud the city's 60,000 tourism-industry workers, including hotel maids, taxi drivers, bellhops, and others in the local hospitality industry.

GO ON TO THE NEXT PAGE

34. An appropriate title for the preceding passage might be

(A) San Francisco: The World's Favorite Travel Destination
(B) A Celebration for Tourism Workers
(C) San Francisco Mayor to Applaud Industry Workers
(D) San Francisco's Tourism Industry Workers are the Best in the World
(E) London, Florence, and Vienna: Favorite Travel Destinations

35. A paraphrase of the above passage might be

(A) industry workers are better in San Francisco than in London or Italy.
(B) tourism is more popular in U. S. cities than in European cities.
(C) San Francisco's mayor is sensitive to the needs of industry workers.
(D) industry workers are responsible for San Francisco's increase in tourism.
(E) every year *Condé Nast Traveler* magazine polls tourists and selects a favorite destination spot based upon the result of those polls.

Questions 36–38 refer to the following passage:

Results of a recent study released show that by 2005, the majority of California's high school graduates will be non-white and that by 2006, one-third of all the nation's students will be from minority groups. It is also predicted that, nationally, the total non-white and Hispanic student population for all grade levels will increase from 10.4 million in 2006–2007 to 13.7 million in 2005–2006. The figures suggest that now, more than ever, equal educational opportunity for all students must be our nation's top priority.

36. The preceding passage suggests that

(A) the nation's educational system is working just fine.
(B) something needs to be done to reduce the growing numbers of minority students in the school system.
(C) urgent educational reform is needed to provide equal opportunity for all students.
(D) a single language system is necessary.
(E) students require additional help with studies outside the classroom.

37. The passage suggests that

(A) if the trend continues, most students will be native speakers of English by the year 2000.
(B) if the trend continues, most students will want to speak English as their language of choice.
(C) English will not be spoken in the California public school system.
(D) all minority groups will absorb English.
(E) English and English as a Second Language programs will need to be instigated accordingly.

38. What does the passage suggest the "number one priority" facing schools must be?

(A) More minority students and more classrooms
(B) More qualified teachers to deal with the influx of minority students
(C) More bilingual teachers to deal with the influx of minority students
(D) Equal time spent on bilingual and multicultural education and instruction
(E) Equal educational opportunities for all students

Questions 39–41 refer to the following passage:

John W. Quinney's speech is a declaration not of independence but a declaration of reproach seeking recompense. Quinney's oratory style is as concise as his language is laconic. He leaves no room for misinterpretation as he opens his address referring to the constituents as a race "of people, who occupy by conquest, or have usurped the possession of the territories of my fathers, and have laid...a train of terrible miseries."

Articulate and powerful, *Quinney's Speech* is not only a caustic political editorial upon the state of the Americas circa 1854, it is also poignant and dignified commentary on the effort put forth by the assimilated Native Americans to preserve their land, their nations, their heritage, and their traditions.

GO ON TO THE NEXT PAGE

39. The author's style in addressing the issues in the passage is

(A) biased.
(B) acrimonious.
(C) impertinent.
(D) dulcet.
(E) objective.

40. The passage suggests Quinney's speech is about

(A) Americans preserving their lands, their nations, their heritage, and their traditions.
(B) American's caustic political views.
(C) an assertion of condemnation seeking compensation.
(D) Americans helping indigenous native peoples.
(E) a series of speeches given to appease and explain America's usurpation of territories.

41. What does <u>laconic</u> mean?

(A) Depressed
(B) Concise
(C) Apologetic
(D) Sentimental
(E) Incensed

Questions 42–44 refer to the following passage:

The Matsushita Electric Industrial Company in Japan has developed a computer program that can use photographs of faces to predict the aging process and, also, how an unborn child will look. The system can show how a couple will look after 40 years of marriage and how newlyweds' future children will look. The computer analyzes facial characteristics from a photograph based on shading and color difference, and then creates a three-dimensional model in its memory. The system consists of a personal computer with a program and circuit board and will soon be marketed by the Matsushita Company.

42. The main idea in the passage is

(A) a computer will be able to show the aging process.
(B) a computer program will choose the right mate.
(C) a computer program will predict the number of children a couple will spawn.
(D) a computer program will predict the look of unborn children and the aged look of their parents.
(E) a computer program will analyze photographs accurately.

43. The program works by

(A) darkening shaded areas of a photograph.
(B) creating a three-dimensional model in the computer's memory.
(C) clairvoyantly predicting the future.
(D) circuit boards and chips.
(E) understanding concepts of aging via color shading.

44. What will result from this new computer system developed in Japan?

(A) The U.S. will follow up by developing an even more sophisticated digitally enhanced computer scanning program.
(B) Competition among computer manufactures will become even more intense.
(C) Japan's economy will skyrocket.
(D) Law enforcement agencies will incorporate this new computer technology into their crime-fighting techniques.
(E) The passage does not suggest any information about what effects this technology will have.

Questions 45 and 46 refer to the following:

On September 17, 1991, a communications power failure brought New York's three major airports to a virtual stop for several hours. Air traffic control centers communicate with planes through a network of radio towers linked to them by telephone. __________ this power failure, local air traffic control centers could not communicate properly amongst themselves or with other U.S. airports.

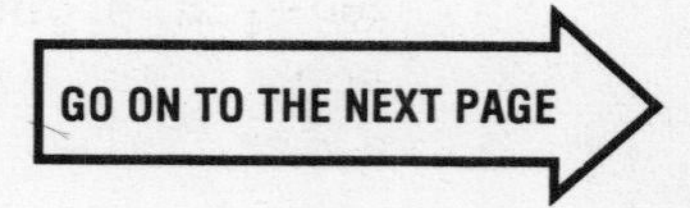

45. Which of these grouped words or phrases, if inserted into the passage's blank lines, would address the logical sequencing and progression of the narrative?

(A) Despite
(B) Notwithstanding
(C) Because of
(D) In lieu of
(E) Vis-à-vis

46. What is the main idea of the passage?

(A) Air traffic control centers could not communicate properly, thus disrupting airport operations.
(B) Air traffic control centers are high-stress environments, thus leading to frequent airport disruptions.
(C) Airports cannot function properly without assistance from air traffic control centers.
(D) Airports can be shut down at any moment, so allow for alternate means of transportation.
(E) Airports can be shut down for hours, so allow for extra time when making air travel plans.

Questions 47–50 refer to the following passage:

New health research shows that regular vigorous exercise during the middle and late years of life not only keeps the heart healthy, but may also protect against colon cancer, one of the major killers in the United States. The researchers in the study compared the rate of colon cancer among those who were physically inactive with those who were either active or highly active. The study covered 17,148 men age 30 to 79. Among the men judged to be inactive, there were 55 cases of colon cancer; among those moderately active, there were 11; and only 10 cases of colon cancer were found among the very active ones.

47. Which of the following would make an appropriate title for the passage?

(A) Colon Cancer, the Deadly Killer
(B) Findings on Colon Cancer: Bleak at Best
(C) Regular Exercise May Prevent Colon Cancer
(D) Latest Results of Colon Cancer Research
(E) Various Ways to Prevent Colon Cancer

48. What is the main idea of the passage?

(A) American men do not exercise enough.
(B) Americans are overweight and that leads to heart disease.
(C) Regular vigorous exercise should be limited to the later stages of the adult male's life.
(D) Regular vigorous exercise is only beneficial after the age of 30.
(E) Vigorous exercise during the middle and late years of life may protect against colon cancer.

49. What is the meaning of the term vigorous?

(A) Energetic
(B) Constant
(C) Burning
(D) Lethargic
(E) Languorous

50. What major component is excluded from the study?

(A) It does not clearly define what "vigorous exercise" is.
(B) It does not address other forms of cancer.
(C) It does not include diseases outside the United States.
(D) It does not include women of the same age group.
(E) It does not include ways of living with cancer.

GO ON TO THE NEXT PAGE

PRACTICE TEST 2

ANSWER KEY

Section 1: Reading Skills

1. (D)
2. (E)
3. (B)
4. (A)
5. (B)
6. (C)
7. (C)
8. (B)
9. (D)
10. (D)
11. (C)
12. (B)
13. (D)
14. (B)
15. (E)
16. (C)
17. (B)
18. (A)
19. (B)
20. (A)
21. (E)
22. (C)
23. (B)
24. (E)
25. (E)
26. (D)
27. (B)
28. (A)
29. (D)
30. (E)
31. (A)
32. (C)
33. (C)
34. (A)
35. (E)
36. (C)
37. (E)
38. (E)
39. (E)
40. (C)
41. (B)
42. (D)
43. (B)
44. (E)
45. (C)
46. (A)
47. (C)
48. (E)
49. (A)
50. (D)

Detailed Explanations of Answers

PRACTICE TEST 2

SECTION 1: Reading Skills

1. **D**

A teaching assistant would be expected to lay the foundation for her lecture and the present greater detail by way of example, or as the passage puts it, "illustration." Someone in this position, having set this task for herself, would not be prone to refuting her own lecture notes (A), attempting to cause confusion (B), reciting praise (C), or perhaps least of all, working to subvert the lecture topic she herself had elected to teach.

2. **E**

The definition of the term "pedagogical" is (E) academic. The answers (A) intelligent, (B) abstract, (C) meaningless, and (D) obtuse are incorrect.

3. **B**

The author's classroom experience was (B) intelligible (understandable) and pragmatic (practical or utilitarian). The passage gives credence to this by the author's use of words like "clear and well prepared." Answers (A), (C), and (E) suggest the opposite of a positive experience, and there is no evidence given that the experience was too advanced or complicated (D).

4. **(A)**

The last sentence in these instructions tells the student that the paper must be proofread with no "mechanical" (punctuation) errors. The third sentence states that an understanding of the reading material is required. Answers (B) and (C) contain only a portion of the needed requirements, while (D) and (E) are completely inaccurate. Thus, (A) is the correct answer.

5. **(B)**

As used in the passage, the term "sophisticated prose" means that the student must write a readable paper using thoughtful language, thereby demonstrating a familiarity with the primary text. Answers (A), (C), (D), and (E) all contain language that suggests the opposite of a readable paper.

6. **(C)**

A primary text is the source material, main, or principal text used in an assignment. The remaining answers (A), (B), (D), and (E) refer to either secondary materials or reference sources.

7. **(C)**

The passage suggests that education is primarily based on failure as negative reinforcement and that, in order to create a more productive and positive learning environment, the emphasis must shift to success. While answers (A), (B), and (E) may be correct, they are not the main idea of the passage. (D) is simply a statement that is not based upon any factual evidence whatsoever. Therefore, (C) is the correct answer.

8. **(B)**

An axiom in this case is another word for motto. It can also mean an accepted truism or principle, which would also apply here. Answers (A), (C), (D), and (E) are erroneous definitions and, therefore (B), University motto or principle is the correct answer.

9. **(D)**

The passage states that "the language of failure…will have a prohibitive impact on the students' self-esteem," and, thus, (D) is the correct answer. Answers (A), (B), (C), and (E) do not apply in this case.

10. **D**

The first paragraph of the passage tells the reader that, in addition to personal expression, language also has the power to "persuade and influence." While answers (A), (B), (C), and (E) may indeed be attributes of language, they are not focused upon in the passage.

11. **C**

The author remains objective throughout the passage. That is, he remains impartial and factual. Answer (A), "lethargy," means sluggish, (B), "apathy" means unconcerned. (D), "intensity" means vehement or fierce, and (E), "synergy" means fellowship or union, and thus, these definitions do not apply.

12. **B**

The third sentence suggests that poetry has the ability to serve both as an adornment or embellishment of an era and as a social commentary. The passage fundamentally suggests that poetry is more than just lyrical fluff, it is a means of social analysis, protest, and interpretation. While (A), (C), (D), and (E) are components of the passage, they are not the passage's main topic.

13. **D**

The word trope means that a word is used in a figurative sense. That is, it conjures images of Greco-Roman representations. Answer (A) is a troop; (B), (C), and (E) are types of terminology that do not apply.

14. **B**

The passage suggests that a critic is a viable political force that serves both as a censure and a social commentator. Answers (A), (C), (D), and (E) are subjective answers and are, therefore, inappropriate.

15. **E**

The passage states that the etymology of the word "censure" dates to the Middle Ages, suggesting that it was in use at that time. The passage also states that a critic can also be equivalent to a censurer. It, therefore, could not be (A), a modern phenomenon or (D), developed around the time of the Civil War. Answers (B) and (C) are not addressed in the passage, leaving (E) as the best answer.

16. (C)

The passage addresses both the implications (indications) and the connotations (meaning) associated with the role of the critic as author. Answers (B), (D), and (E) are only alluded to, while (A) is a supposition. Thus, (C) is the correct answer.

17. (B)

Etymology is the study of the history and/or origin of a word. This definition renders the remaining answers false.

18. (A)

The passage tells of the great (linguistic) vowel shift of the early fifteenth century. While the passage speaks of (B) an artistic renaissance, (C) new linguistic freedoms, (D) effects on artistic expression, and (E) the early decades of the century, these are all results of the shift and not the shift itself. The shift is what the passage is about. Thus, (A) is the correct answer.

19. (B)

In this case, linguistic refers to speaking, talking, verbiage, and/or the act of oration. (A), (C), (D), and (E) are not acceptable definitions for the word linguistic. Consequently, (B) verbal or rhetorical is the correct answer.

20. (A)

Answers (B), (C), and (D) are generalized answers resulting from the vowel shift, while (E) is simply extraneous. (A) is a direct result of the shift and is quoted directly from the passage. Therefore, (A) is the correct answer.

21. (E)

The passage states that lead poisoning leads to learning disabilities and possibly even death. Choice (A) is too broad, (B) and (C) are not directly addressed, and (D) is inappropriate, leaving (E) as the correct answer.

22. (C)

The passage states that all California MediCal-eligible children, ages one through five, will now be routinely screened. Answer choices (A) children in California, (B) children with learning disabilities, (D) minority children, and (E) school-age children are generalities not stated in the passage. Only (C) is clearly stated in the passage.

23. B

The statistics suggest that inner-city children are at the greatest risk from lead poisoning. The statistics do not support answers (A), (C), (D), and (E), leaving (B) as the only legitimate answer.

24. E

The last sentence of the passage suggests that testing will catch the disease "at an early stage" and prevent serious disorders. Answers (A), (B), (C), and (D) do not address this ultimate goal of the testing program. Only answer (E) reiterates the program's ultimate purpose.

25. E

The passage asks the reader to question traditional gender issues. The punctuation at the end of the passage affirms this. (A), (B), (C), and (D) do not assert questions. Rather, they suggest a declarative action or stance to be taken regarding social gender issues. Only (E) addresses the passage's questioning of gender roles; therefore, (E) is the correct answer.

26. D

To "ostracize" is to alienate, exile, or banish. (A) acceptance, (B) pressure, (C) traditions, and (E) examination are false definitions and are incorrect.

27. B

The passage states that discourse communities are of similar mindsets, thus making them suspect. (A), (C), (D), and (E) do not address this issue directly. Only (B) reiterates the second sentence of the passage; therefore, it is the correct answer.

28. A

The definition of the noun paradigm is that it is a model, criterion, or standard that others follow or by which they are measured. Thus, (A), model or standard, is the correct answer.

29. D

While the issues surrounding the allosaurus can be applied to several academic disciplines, including (A) reading, (E) literature, and (C) biology, the scientific study of living organisms, (D) zoology, is the appropriate answer.

30. (E)

Answers (A), (B), (C), and (D) are part of, but not the main idea, of the passage. Only (E) encompasses the complete or "main idea" of the passage.

31. (A)

The opening sentence of the passage tells the reader what one might see by "looking specifically at animal symbols and [deciphering] what they represent." With this precept in mind, answer (A) is the only one that restates the idea.

32. (C)

The definition of a metaphor is that it is a figure of speech that contains an implied comparison. Only answer (C) provides the proper definition. The remaining answers are inaccurate.

33. (C)

The last sentence of the passage states that "imperialism [is] capitalistic encroachment and colonialism [is] territorial usurpation." Another word for encroachment is infringement, or intrusion. Another word for usurpation is confiscation, or appropriation, or taking over. Answer (A), arrangement and organization, and (E), development and liberation, would not suffice. Answer (B), wealth and abundance, and (D), freedom and generosity, are the opposite meanings, leaving (C), financial infringement and territorial confiscation, as the correct answer.

34. (A)

The article declares the 1991 winner of the travel magazine poll to be San Francisco. While the other answers are mentioned in the passage, only (A) suggests San Francisco is the year's best travel destination. Therefore, (A) is the appropriate answer.

35. (E)

Answers (A), (B), (C), and (D) are inferences (i.e., suppositions) drawn from the passage's information, while (E) restates the factual information presented by the passage. Since a paraphrase is a restatement, a rephrasing, or an interpretation of the original, (E) is the correct answer.

36. **C**

This is an interesting passage, because while the information suggests that multicultural numbers are on the rise, it simultaneously demonstrates how urgently educational reform is needed to accommodate students of every ethnic background. (C) is the only answer that addresses this agenda. Answers (A), (B), (D), and (E) are simply erroneous.

37. **E**

The passage does not suggest that (A), all students will speak English; its thrust is quite the opposite. Answers (B) and (D) suggest a false choice on the part of students to abandon their native language for English, and again, this is not stated in the passage. (C) is simply untrue, leaving answer (E), which suggests accommodation, as the only correct answer.

38. **E**

The answer to this question is stated in the last sentence of the passage: "equal educational opportunity for all students must be our nation's top priority." Answer (E) is the only answer that repeats this idea in its entirety.

39. **E**

The author's style in addressing the passage is one of (E) objectivity. Answer (A), biased, means prejudiced, and (D), dulcet, means melodious, so neither of these is correct. Answer (C), impertinent (impolite), and (B), acrimonious (sarcastic), clearly have negative connotations which are not present in the passage, thus (E), objective, is the correct answer.

40. **C**

The opening sentence declares Quinney's speech to be one of "reproach seeking recompense." Another word for reproach *is condemnation and a synonym for* recompense *is compensation. Answers (A), (B), (D), and (E) do not include these definitions; therefore, (C) is the correct answer.*

41. **B**

The word "laconic" means (B) concise. The other answers are erroneous.

42. (D)

The passage states that the program's function is to "predict the aging process and [show how] an unborn child will look." While answer (A) does say "show the aging process," it does not address the issue of the projection of the unborn child. (B), (C), and (E) are misleading notions, leaving only (D) as the complete answer.

43. (B)

The passage tells the reader that the program "creates a three-dimensional model in its memory." Answer (E) does address the issue of color shading, as does (A), but neither of them contain the complete answer, (B), which reiterates the passage exactly.

44. (E)

The question asks for information that is not supplied by the passage. Answers (A), (B), (C), and (D) all attempt to provide information that is not in the passage. This is called supposition. Only (E) correctly states that the passage does not give the facts required; thus, (E) is the correct answer.

45. (C)

Air traffic controllers' inability to communicate was directly linked to the power failure, making choice (C) the only logical, accurate response.

46. (A)

The main idea of the passage is the loss of airport operation time due to a communications failure. This precept is stated in the first sentence of the passage. Answers (B), (C), (D), and (E) state assertions not addressed in the passage. Therefore, (A) is the correct answer.

47. (C)

Answers (A) and (B) use exaggerated language to restate the passage. Answers (D) and (E) are too general. This leaves only (C) as the appropriate answer.

48. **E**

Answers other than (E) are inferences or assumptions, while answer (E) is taken directly from the passage.

49. **A**

The definition of the word "vigorous" is energetic, dynamic, or enthusiastic. Thus, (A) is the correct definition.

50. **D**

While the passage looks at various aspects of middle-age male health issues (see Sentence 3), it does not address those of women. While one could argue that (C) is the correct answer, the passage states that it was a test conducted on and by U.S. subjects. (A), (B), and (E) are not questions at issue for the study, so (D) is the correct answer.

DIRECTIONS: Each of the questions or incomplete statements below is followed by five suggested answers or completions. Select the one that is best in each case.

1. A pair of dice is rolled once. What is the probability of rolling a sum of exactly 8?

(A) $\frac{1}{8}$ (D) $\frac{5}{18}$

(B) $\frac{5}{36}$ (E) $\frac{1}{3}$

(C) $\frac{2}{9}$

2. On July 19, a Friday, Dick received a letter to have a class reunion exactly four years from that day. On what day of the week is his reunion?

(A) Monday (D) Thursday
(B) Tuesday (E) Friday
(C) Wednesday

3. An equilateral triangle has a side of 8. What would be the approximate radius of a circle with the same area as this triangle?

(A) 3.39 (D) 2.97
(B) 3.25 (E) 2.83
(C) 3.11

4. How much water should be added to a half-pint of syrup with 60% sugar to obtain a drink with 5% sugar?

(A) 3 pints (B) 2.5 pints
(C) 4 pints (D) 5.5 pints
(E) 7 pints

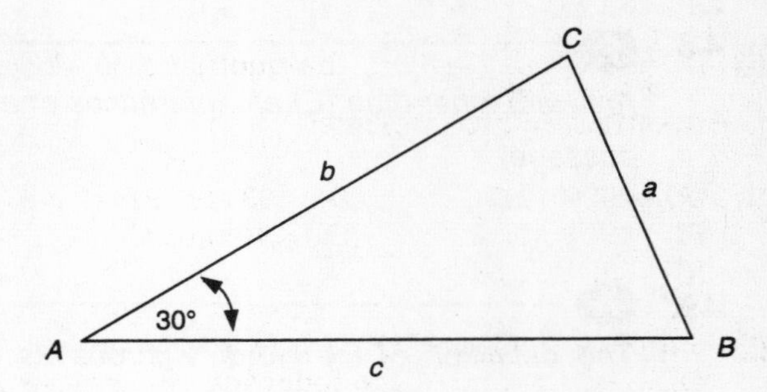

5. Which of the following is true about triangle *ABC*?

(A) Sides *B* and *C* are equal in measurement.
(B) Angle *A* is the smallest angle.
(C) Side *A* is not the longest side.
(D) Angle *B* or *C* must be a right angle.
(E) Side *B* must be greater than side *A* in measurement.

6. If the diameter of circle *A* is twice that of circle *B*, what is the ratio of the area of circle *A* to the area of circle *B*?

(A) 2 to 1 (D) π to 1
(B) 3 to 1 (E) 8 to 1
(C) 4 to 1

7. A solid cube has a volume of 8. What is the volume of the cube whose sides are twice that of this cube?

(A) 16 (D) 36
(B) 28 (E) 64
(C) 32

8. Jack flies from New York to Los Angeles. His plane leaves New York at 2:15 p.m. The flying time is 5 hours and 45 minutes. Since New York is three hours ahead of Los Angeles, what time does he arrive in Los Angeles?

(A) 11:00 p.m. (D) 5:00 p.m.
(B) 8:00 p.m. (E) 4:45 p.m.
(C) 7:45 p.m.

GO ON TO THE NEXT PAGE

9. If $\frac{2}{3}$ is divided by $\frac{8}{11}$, the quotient will lie between which two numbers?

(A) .90 and .91
(B) .91 and .92
(C) .92 and .93
(D) .93 and .94
(E) .94 and .95

10. Suppose "P implies Q" is true and "P and Q" is false. Which one of the following conclusions is valid?

(A) P must be true.
(B) Q must be true.
(C) P must be false.
(D) Q must be false.
(E) "Q implies P" must be true.

11. If ten babies drink a total of ten gallons of milk in ten days, how many gallons of milk will 20 babies drink in 20 days?

(A) 20
(B) 25
(C) 30
(D) 35
(E) 40

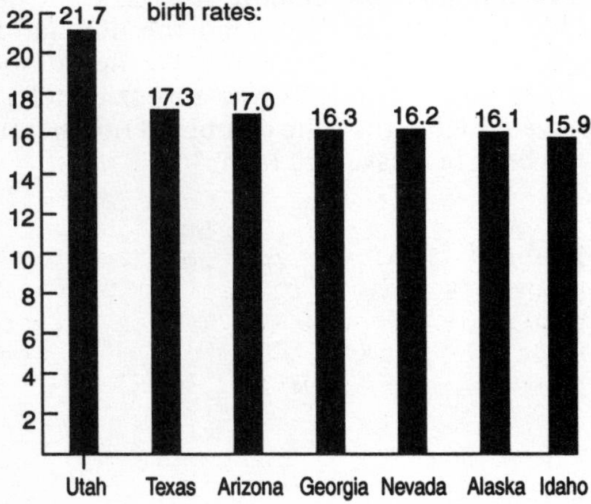

12. In 1999, Georgia's population was 9,000,000. Approximately how many births were there?

(A) 1,467,000
(B) 729,300
(C) 484,300
(D) 484,300
(E) 146,700

13. A parallelogram *ABCD* has all its sides measure 4; one of the diagonals *AC* also measures 4. What is its area?

(A) Its area is 16.
(B) Its area is 32.
(C) Its area is $4\sqrt{3}$.
(D) Its area is $8\sqrt{3}$.
(E) Its area cannot be found; further information is needed.

14. Jack gave one-third of his money to his daughter and one-quarter of his money to his son. He then had $150,000 left. How much money did he have before he gave some away?

(A) $225,000
(B) $250,000
(C) $300,000
(D) $360,000
(E) $400,000

15. In a certain class, there are three exams and two quizzes. Each exam counts 30% and each quiz counts 5% toward a student's final grade. If a student has exam grades of 70, 75, and 90, and a grade of 77 on the first quiz, what score will he need on the second quiz so that his final grade will be exactly 79?

(A) 80
(B) 83
(C) 87
(D) 90
(E) 93

16. If Don and Ron can paint a house in five days, and Ron can paint it alone in seven days, how long will it take Don to paint it alone?

(A) 2 days
(B) 7 days
(C) 17.5 days
(D) 9.75 days
(E) 11.25 days

GO ON TO THE NEXT PAGE

17. If the volume of a cube is 8, how long is its main diagonal (the line segment joining the two farthest corners)?

(A) $2\sqrt{2}$
(B) $3\sqrt{2}$
(C) $2\sqrt{3}$
(D) $3\sqrt{3}$
(E) The length of the main diagonal cannot be found with this information.

18. Norman lives 6 blocks north and 6 blocks east of Bob. The town is made up of all square blocks. How many ways can Bob walk to Norman's house by walking only 12 blocks?

(A) 2 ways
(B) 924 ways
(C) 36 ways
(D) 4,096 ways
(E) Infinitely many ways

19. Donald gave Louie a number of marbles to share with Dewey and Huey. Making sure that he got his share, Louie took one-third of the marbles and hid them. Dewey, after hearing from Donald that he is entitled to one-third of the marbles as well, went and hid one-third of the remaining marbles. Not knowing what was going on, Daisy took two marbles from the pile. When Huey came, there were only 10 marbles left. How many marbles did Donald give to Louie in the beginning?

(A) 18
(B) 21
(C) 24
(D) 27
(E) That number cannot be found with this information.

20. In 1999, Texas' population was 22,000,000 and Utah's population was 3,000,000. About how many more births were there in Texas than in Utah?

(A) 65,100
(B) 148,400
(C) 192,600
(D) 315,500
(E) 390,000

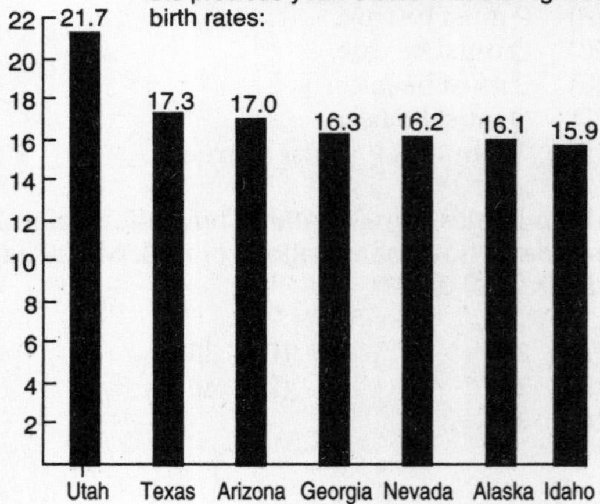

21. The combined population of Alaska and Idaho was 2,500,000 (in 1999), and the population of Arizona was 8,000,000. For 1999, the number of babies born in Arizona was approximately what percent higher than the combined number of babies born in Alaska and Idaho?

(A) 80
(B) 70
(C) 60
(D) 50
(E) 40

GO ON TO THE NEXT PAGE

22. In which of the following are the decimals arranged in order from lowest to highest?

(A) .0009, .0031, .02
(B) .0009, .002, .00031
(C) .0031, .002, .09
(D) .031, .009, .02
(E) .02, .9, .31

23. In 1998, a TV sold for $500. If the price dropped 15% from 1998 to 1999, but then increased in price by 10% from 1999 to 2000, what was the cost in the year 2000?

(A) $425.50
(B) $440.00
(C) $467.50
(D) $475.00
(E) $517.50

24. Sarah bought 10 pounds of apples and nuts. Apples are 89 cents a pound, and nuts are $1.29 a pound. She spent a total of $10.10. How many pounds of nuts did she buy?

(A) 1
(B) 2
(C) 3
(D) 4
(E) 5

25. Jim and Joe were running together. Jim's average speed was 400 meters per minute. Jim started running 4 minutes before Joe. Ten minutes after Joe started, he caught up with Jim. What was Joe's average speed?

(A) 440 meters per minute
(B) 450 meters per minute
(C) 480 meters per minute
(D) 500 meters per minute
(E) 560 meters per minute

26. If 96 chickens and rabbits are put together, they have a total of 312 legs. How many chickens are there?

(A) 36
(B) 60
(C) 72
(D) 24
(E) 42

27. Harold decided to cut down his sugar consumption in coffee, tea, and other drinks. He had been consuming 120 grams of sugar a day. He was determined to cut down 2 grams per week until he no longer used sugar in his drinks. Starting from the first day that he began cutting down his sugar, how much sugar would he have consumed before he arrived at his goal?

(A) 92,160 grams
(B) 10,900 grams
(C) 72,000 grams
(D) 8,200 grams
(E) 24,780 grams

28. What is .05957 rounded off to the nearest thousandths place?

(A) .060
(B) .059
(C) .057
(D) .055
(E) .05

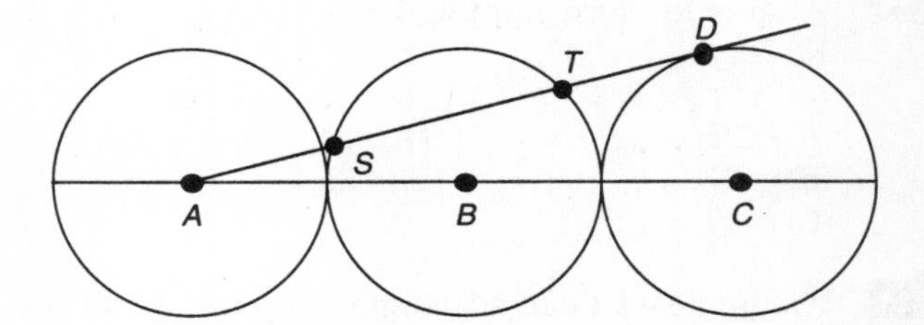

29. Three circles of equal radii with centers *A*, *B*, and *C* are lying on a straight line and tangent to each other as in the figure. A tangent line to circle *C* is drawn from *A*, meeting circle *B* at *S* and *T*, tangent to circle *C* at *D*. What is the ratio of the line segment *ST* to the radii?

(A) $\frac{\sqrt{3}}{2}$
(B) $\frac{3}{2}$
(C) $\sqrt{3}$
(D) 1
(E) $\sqrt{2}$

30. If a number times itself is added to five times itself, the result is 24. What is this number?

(A) 3 or 8
(B) –3 or 8
(C) 3 or –8
(D) –3 or –8
(E) –4 or 6

GO ON TO THE NEXT PAGE

31. A raw score of 110 on a standardized test converts to a standard score of 1.6. If the standard deviation is 2.5, what is the value of the mean?

(A) 98
(B) 103
(C) 106
(D) 109
(E) 114

32. What is the measurement of an angle of a regular pentagon?

(A) 72°
(B) 108°
(C) 100°
(D) 84°
(E) 104°

33. What is the next number in the sequence 4, 5, 8, 13, 20, . . . ?

(A) 25
(B) 27
(C) 29
(D) 31
(E) 33

34. The longest side of a triangle measures 2 and the shortest side measures 1. What cannot be the measurement of the angle between them?

(A) 30°
(B) 60°
(C) 70°
(D) 20°
(E) 90°

35. A rectangular floor measures 20 feet in length and 16 feet in width. If a square rug covers only 45% of the floor, what is the perimeter of the rug (in feet)?

(A) 48
(B) 64
(C) 80
(D) 120
(E) 144

36. If $A*B$ means $A + B^2$, what is the value of $5 * 3$?

(A) 64
(B) 32
(C) 16
(D) 14
(E) 11

37. The expression $\frac{x+1}{x-1} - \frac{x-1}{x+1}$ simplifies to

(A) –1.
(B) 1.
(C) $\frac{2x}{x^2-1}$.
(D) $\frac{4x}{x^2-1}$.
(E) $\frac{x}{x^2-1}$.

38. If an equilateral triangle has area $\sqrt{3}$, what are the lengths of its sides?

(A) 1
(B) $\frac{3}{2}$
(C) 2
(D) $\frac{5}{2}$
(E) 3

39. Jane went shopping. On her first trip, she bought six pairs of shoes, all at the same price, and three pairs of socks, also at the same price (shoes and socks are not necessarily of the same price), and she spent $96. On her second trip, she went to the same shop and bought four more pairs of the same socks and returned a pair of shoes; she spent $2. How much does a pair of her shoes cost?

(A) $10
(B) $12
(C) $14
(D) $16
(E) $18

40. Triangle *ABC* is inscribed in a circle with center *O* at the midpoint of the side *BC*. If angle *B* measures 47°, what is the measurement of angle *C*?

(A) 43°
(B) 47°
(C) 53°
(D) 37°
(E) Insufficient information

GO ON TO THE NEXT PAGE

41. Dan flies north at a speed of 200 miles per hour, and Tom flies east at a speed of 150 miles per hour. Head wind and air resistance all having been taken into consideration, how far apart are they two hours later?

(A) 300 miles
(B) 350 miles
(C) 400 miles
(D) 450 miles
(E) 500 miles

42. The sum of the base and altitude of a triangle is 12 and the area is 16. What are the base and altitude of the triangle?

(A) 2 and 10
(B) 6
(C) 4 and 8
(D) 3 and 9
(E) 5 and 7

43. If 1 kilogram is equivalent to about 2.2 pounds, what is the approximate reduced weight in kilograms of a 120-pound woman who diets and loses 10% of her weight?

(A) 55
(B) 52
(C) 49
(D) 46
(E) 43

44. An isosceles triangle *ABC* is inscribed in a circle with center *O* in such a way that *OBC* forms an equilateral triangle. The measurement of angle *B* is

(A) 80°.
(B) 75°.
(C) 70°.
(D) 65°.
(E) 60°.

For the next two questions, use the pie chart shown here. Assume the population is 2,000,000.

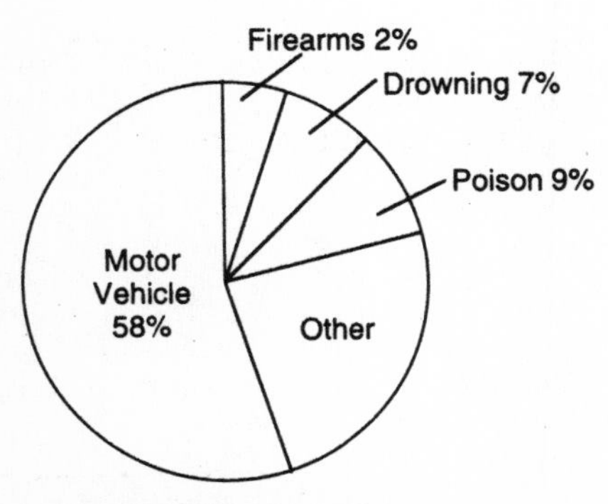

Accidental Deaths by Type

45. How many accidental deaths were attributed to the category "Other"?

(A) 480,000
(B) 740,000
(C) 1,000,000
(D) 1,260,000
(E) 1,520,000

46. How many more deaths were attributable to motor vehicles than to the combined total of firearms, drowning, and poison?

(A) 560,000
(B) 800,000
(C) 1,040,000
(D) 1,280,000
(E) 1,520,000

47. Bob is lending money at 6% simple interest. How much does he need to lend at the beginning of the year to yield $1,000 by the end of the year? (Figure to the nearest dollar.)

(A) $850
(B) $950
(C) $894
(D) $943
(E) $927

48. The expression $x^n - y^n$

(A) can be factored only when n is odd.
(B) can never be factored.
(C) can always be factored.
(D) can be factored only when n is a power of 4.
(E) can be factored only when n is twice an odd integer.

49. If one root of the equation $ax^2 + bx + c = 0$ is 2, the other root must be

(A) $\frac{c}{2}$.
(B) $\frac{c}{2a}$.
(C) $\frac{c}{2b}$.
(D) $\frac{b}{2c}$.
(E) $\frac{a}{2c}$.

GO ON TO THE NEXT PAGE

50. If five gallons of 50% alcohol solution is mixed with three gallons of 20% alcohol solution, what is the alcohol content of the resulting solution?

(A) 38.75%
(B) 37.5%
(C) 35%
(D) 42.25%
(E) 32.25%

PRACTICE TEST 2

ANSWER KEY

Section 2: Mathematics

1. (B)
2. (C)
3. (D)
4. (D)
5. (C)
6. (C)
7. (E)
8. (D)
9. (B)
10. (C)
11. (E)
12. (E)
13. (D)
14. (D)
15. (E)
16. (C)
17. (C)
18. (B)
19. (D)
20. (D)
21. (B)
22. (A)
23. (C)
24. (C)
25. (E)
26. (A)
27. (E)
28. (A)
29. (C)
30. (C)
31. (C)
32. (B)
33. (C)
34. (E)
35. (A)
36. (D)
37. (D)
38. (C)
39. (C)
40. (A)
41. (E)
42. (C)
43. (C)
44. (B)
45. (A)
46. (B)
47. (D)
48. (C)
49. (B)
50. (A)

Detailed Explanations of Answers

PRACTICE TEST 2

SECTION 2: Mathematics

1. **B**

Of the 36 possible outcomes, there are 5 which will give a sum of at least 8, namely 26, 62, 35, 53, 44.

2. **C**

Since his reunion will be $365 \times 4 + 1 = 1{,}461$ days from a Friday, dividing 1,461 by 7 yields a remainder of 5. Therefore, his reunion is 5 days from a Friday, which makes it on a Wednesday.

3. **D**

The area of the triangle is $\frac{8^2}{4}\sqrt{3} \approx 27.713$. Then $27.713 = \pi R^2$, where r = radius. Solving $R^2 \approx 8.82$, so $R \approx 2.97$.

4. **D**

Since the sugar content is 60% of $\frac{1}{2}$ pint and will not be changed after the water is added, we obtain an equation by equating the sugar content before and after adding in x pints of water. The equation is then

$$\left(\frac{1}{2}\right) \times 60\% = \left(\frac{1}{2} + x\right) \times 5\% \text{ or}$$

$$30 = \frac{5}{2} + 5x$$

$$60 = 5 + 10x$$

$$55 = 10x$$

$$\text{and } 5.5 = x.$$

5. **C**

Since the only information we have concerning the triangle is that angle A measures 30°, we know that in a triangle, the largest angle faces the longest side, the sum of the three angles of a triangle is 180°, and a 30° angle is not the largest angle. Therefore, A is not the longest side.

6. **C**

The diameter of circle A is twice that of circle B, so if the radius of B is r, then the radius of A is 2r. Since the area of a circle with radius r is πr^2, *the area of B is* πr^2, *while the area of A is* $\pi(2r)^2 = 4\pi r$.

7. **E**

Since the cube has a volume of 8, its sides have length 2. The cube whose sides are twice that would be of length 4, so the volume of the other cube is $4 \times 4 \times 4 = 64$.

8. **D**

2:15 + 5:45 = 8:00; he arrives in Los Angeles at 8 p.m. New York time. But New York is 3 hours ahead of Los Angeles, so the Los Angeles time of arrival is 5 p.m.

9. **B**

$\frac{2}{3} \div \frac{8}{11} = \frac{22}{24} = .91\overline{6}$, *which lies between .91 and .92.*

10. (C)

If "P implies Q" is true, then the possibilities are (a) P and Q are both true, (b) P and Q are both false, (c) P is false and Q is true. However, since "P and Q" is given as false, this eliminates possibility (a). For either possibility (b) or (c), P must be false.

11. (E)

Since 10 babies drink 10 gallons of milk in 10 days, each baby drinks $\frac{1}{10}$ *gallon of milk per day. Each baby drinks 2 gallons of milk in 20 days, so 20 babies will drink* $2 \times 20 = 40$ *gallons of milk in 20 days.*

12. (E)

$9{,}000{,}000 \div 1{,}000 = 9{,}000$. $9{,}000 \times 16.3 = 146{,}700$.

13. (D)

Draw both diagonals to divide the parallelogram into four equal parts. Each part is a right triangle with hypotenuse measuring 4 and one side measuring 2. Therefore, the other side must measure $2\sqrt{3}$ *by the Pythagorean Theorem. The area of this triangle is* $\left(\frac{1}{2}\right) \times \left(2 \times 2\sqrt{3}\right) = 2\sqrt{3}$, *and the area of the parallelogram is four times that, which is* $8\sqrt{3}$.

14. (D)

Let the amount of money he had before be x. We have $x - \left(\frac{1}{3}\right)x - \left(\frac{1}{4}\right)x = 150{,}000$. *Or,* $\left(\frac{5}{12}\right)x = 150{,}000$. *Therefore,* $x = 360{,}000$.

15. (E)

Let x be the missing grade. Then we get $(70)(.30) + (75)(.30) + (90)(.30) + (77)(.05) + .05x = 79$. *Solving,* $x = 93$.

16. C

Since Don and Ron can paint the house in 7 days, they finish $\frac{1}{5}$ of the job in a day. Ron's contribution in a day is $\frac{1}{7}$ of the job, so $\left(\frac{1}{5}\right)-\left(\frac{1}{7}\right)$ is Don's contribution in a day, which amounts to $\left(\frac{2}{35}\right)$. Therefore, if Don is to do it alone, it will take him $\left(\frac{35}{2}\right)$ = 17.5 days.

17. C

Since the volume of the cube is 8, each side has a measure $2\sqrt{3}$, and the main diagonal is found with the Pythagorean Formula.

18. B

Each way for Bob to walk to Norman's consists of 6 blocks northward and 6 blocks eastward in different orders. The total number of ways of walking is then the same as the number of ways to choose 6 out of 12 things, and the number is $12 \times 11 \times 10 \times 9 \times 8 \times 7$ divided by $6 \times 5 \times 4 \times 3 \times 2$, or 924.

19. D

Let the number of marbles in the beginning be x. We have $x-\left(\frac{1}{3}\right)x-\left(\frac{1}{3}\right)\left(\frac{2}{3}\right)x-2=10.$

Solving the equation, $x = 27$.

20. D

22,000,000 ÷ 1,000 = 22,000. (22,000) (17.3) = 380,600.
3,000,000 ÷ 1,000 = 3,000. (3,000) (21.7) = 65,100.
Finally, 380,600 – 65,100 = 315,500.

21. B

$$(8{,}000{,}000)\left(\frac{17}{1{,}000}\right) = 136{,}000$$

$$(2{,}500{,}000)\left(\frac{32}{1{,}000}\right) = 80{,}000$$

$$\frac{(136{,}000 - 80{,}000)}{80{,}000} = 70\%$$

22. A

$.0009 < .0031 < .02$

23. C

$500 - (.15)(500) = 425$. Then $(425)(1.10) = 467.50$.

24. C

Suppose Sarah bought x pounds of apples and y pounds of nuts. We have the following equations to solve:

$$x + y = 10$$
$$89x + 129y = 1{,}010$$

Solving these equations give $x = 7$, $y = 3$.

25. E

When Joe caught Jim, Jim had been running for $(10 + 4) = 14$ *minutes, at the rate of 400 meters per minute. So the total distance covered was* $(14 \times 400) = 5{,}600$ *meters. But Joe covered this distance in 10 minutes. Thus, his average speed was* $\frac{5{,}600}{10} = 560$ *meters per minute.*

26. A

Since a chicken has two legs and a rabbit has four legs, letting x be the number of chickens and y be the number of rabbits, we have the following equations to solve: $x + y = 96$; $2x + 4y = 312$. *Therefore,* $36 + y = 96$; $y = 60$; $2 \cdot 36 + 4 \cdot 60 = 312$.

27. **E**

In the first week, he consumed 118 grams of sugar daily, in the second week, he consumed 116 grams of sugar daily, etc. We are then to add 118 + 116 + 114 + ... + 2 and, since there are seven days in a week, the result must be multiplied by 7. Observing that 118 + 116 + 114 + ... + 2 = $2 \times (1 + 2 + 3 + \ldots + 59) = 2 \times (1 + 59)\left(\frac{59}{2}\right) = 3{,}540$. *And* $3{,}540 \times 7 = 24{,}780$.

28. **A**

The fourth digit after the decimal point is 5. This requires rounding up the third digit following the decimal point. Since this digit is a 9, we must change the 5 in the hundredths place to a 6. The answer is .060.

29. **C**

If we draw a perpendicular line from B to the tangent line, say BE, then the right-angled triangles ABE and ACD are similar, so BE equals half of CD, the radius. BET is also a right-angled triangle, and BT is a radius. Using the Pythagorean Theorem, ET measures $\frac{\sqrt{3}}{2}$ *of the radius. Thus, ST measures* $\sqrt{3}$ *of the radius.*

30. **C**

Letting this number be x, we have $x^2 + 5x = 24$, *or* $x^2 + 5x - 24 = 0$, *or* $(x + 8)(x - 3) = 0$, *so* $x = 3$ *or* $x = -8$.

31. **C**

$z = \frac{(x - \bar{x})}{s}$, *where z = standard score, x = raw score,* $\bar{x}$ *= mean, s = standard deviation. Then* $\frac{(180° - 72°)}{2} = 54°$. *Solving,* $\bar{x} = 106$.

32. **B**

We do not need to memorize any formula. If we inscribe the regular pentagon in a circle, the angle with the vertex at the center facing each side is $\frac{360°}{5} = 72°$, *and each of the other angles of that triangle must be* $\frac{(180° - 72°)}{2} = 54°$. *Thus, each of the angles is 108°.*

33. **C**

From 4 to 5, the increase is 1. From 5 to 8, the increase is 3. From 8 to 13, the increase is 5. From 13 to 20, the increase is 7. The next increase is 9, so 20 + 9 = 29.

34. **E**

Since a 90° angle must be the largest in a triangle, it must face the longest side, and the angle between the longest side and the shortest side is not facing the longest side.

35. **A**

The area of the rug = (.45) (20) (16) = 144. Then each side of the rug is $\sqrt{144} = 12$ *feet. Finally, the perimeter is* $12 \times 4 = 48$ *feet.*

36. **D**

$5 * 3 = 5 + 3^2 = 5 + 9 = 14.$

37. **D**

The common denominator is $x^2 - 1$*, and the numerator is* $(x + 1)^2 - (x - 1)^2 = 4x$.

38. **C**

Using the Pythagorean Theorem and the formula for the area of a triangle, b = a and $h = \sqrt{a^2 - \left(\frac{1}{2}a\right)^2}$ *where a is the length of the sides.*

$$\frac{1}{2}bh = \text{area}$$

$$\frac{1}{2}a\sqrt{a^2 - \frac{1}{4}a^2} = \sqrt{3}$$

$$\frac{1}{2}a\sqrt{\frac{3}{4}a^2} = \sqrt{3}$$

$$\frac{1}{4}a^2\left(\frac{3}{4}a^2\right) = 3$$

$$a^4 = (3)\left(\frac{16}{3}\right)$$

$$a^2 = 2$$

39. **C**

Let the price for a pair of shoes be x, and let the price for a pair of socks be y. Then, $6x + 3y = 96$, and $4y - x = 2$. Solving these equations, we have $x = 14$.

40. **A**

Since BC is the diameter of the circle, angle A is a right angle. Therefore, angle C is complementary to angle B, i.e., $90° - 47° = 43°$.

41. **E**

Since they travel on the two sides of a right-angled triangle, the Pythagorean Theorem yields $400^2 + 300^2 = 500^2$.

42. **C**

Let b be the base and a be the altitude of the triangle. We have the equations: $a + b = 12$, and $\frac{ab}{2} = 16$. To solve these equations, substitute $b = 12 - a$ into the second equation, we have $a(12 - a) = 32$, or $12a - a^2 = 32$, or $a^2 - 12a + 32 = (a - 8)(a - 4) = 0$; thus, $a = 4$ or 8, and $b = 8$ or 4, respectively.

43. **C**

Her reduced weight in pounds is $(120)(.90) = 108$. To convert to kilograms, divide this figure by 2.2. Then $108 \div 2.2 = 49.\overline{09} \approx 49$.

44. **B**

Since the angle BOC measures 60°, angle BAC measures 30°, angles B and C will be half of

$$\frac{(180° - 30°)}{2} = 75°.$$

45. (A)

Percent for Other = 100 –(58 + 2 + 7 + 9) = 76%. Then .24 × 2,000,000 = 480,000.

46. (B)

(.58) (2,000,000) = 1,160,000

(.02 + .07 + .09) (2,000,000) = 360,000

1,160,000 – 360,000 = 800,000

47. (D)

His principle and interest need to be 1,000, which is 1.06 times his principle. Thus, we divide 1,000 by 1.06 and it is close to 943.

48. (C)

In fact, $x^n - y^n = (x - y)(x^{n-1} + x^{n-2}y + x^{n-3}y^2 + \dots + y^{n-1})$.

49. (B)

The original equation is equivalent to $x^2 + \frac{bx}{a} + \frac{c}{a} = 0$. *The product of the two roots must equal* $\frac{c}{a}$.

50. (A)

The alcohol content is 5 × 0.5 + 3 × 0.2 = 3.1 gallons, and the total amount of solution is 8 gallons. 3.1 ÷ 8 = .3875 = 38.75%.

DIRECTIONS: Carefully read the two writing topics below. Plan and write an essay on each, being sure to cover all aspects of each essay. Allow approximately 30 minutes per essay.

Topic 1

Ideologies, or ways of looking at things, range from very liberal to very conservative views of how lives should be lived and what is good and bad for society. A controversial ideology in our culture holds that women's primary responsibilities are homemaking and child rearing; that men are primarily responsible for the financial support of the family; that women with children should ideally not work outside the home; and that a double standard in these social customs is acceptable.

You may not hold these views personally, but they have pervaded our culture for many years and have influenced everyone to some degree. What is your position on the issue of male and female roles in the home and society?

Topic 2

Sometimes you want something badly, but when you get it, it's not what you want.

GO ON TO THE NEXT PAGE

Detailed Explanations of Answers

PRACTICE TEST 2

SECTION 3:
Writing

SAMPLE SCORED ESSAYS WITH EXPLANATIONS

Topic 1 Sample Answers

Essay #1—Pass (Score = 4)

The ideology that "anatomy is destiny" is completely false. There are, however, explanations for the gap between boys and girls as they take their place in the world as masculine and feminine beings. Different sex role experiences and socializing forces may contribute to the differences in sex in ways far more powerful than the biological ones. The question recognizes ideologies as either liberal or conservative, but doesn't label any as discrimination. There is an unfortunate tradition of women's primary responsibilities as homemaking and child rearing, while men are responsible for the financial support of the family. That is discrimination against both men and women.

The question fails to acknowledge the social changes that have been occurring in contemporary history which have brought about equality and opportunity for women. The ideology of "happy family" is a fast fading one, for in a society of rising divorce rates, single parents, and latchkey kids, women are assuming the roles of sole parent, sole provider, and professional career persons. Beginning with the Voting Rights Act in the 1920s, women have become more independent and more outspoken. Masculine and feminine have become adjectives of the past; fashion has introduced blazers and slacks as the attractive female apparel, rather than the traditional skirts and blouses; the media is introducing a society of "Mr. Mom's" (motherly fathers) on television shows. One final example that proves anatomy is not destiny is the sharp increase in woman professionals. More and more women are assuming managerial (rather than secretarial) positions.

Although I do not share the more traditional views about sex roles, I agree that they have pervaded our culture and influenced everyone to some extent. Thankfully, however, those views are quickly changing, and although women may always possess a certain "feminine" charm, hopefully they won't forever be labeled only mothers, wives, and homemakers, but have the ability and the right to be professional persons as well. And for the men who choose a homemaker's role, there won't be scorn but acceptance.

Scoring Explanation for Essay #1—Pass

This essay demonstrates an understanding of the question that is quite sophisticated, arguing that sex roles, largely determined by society, are, in fact, a form of discrimination. The body of the essay argues for this thesis by demonstrating the ways that both men and women have risen above the stereotypes that tradition has dictated. As evidence for its claim, it offers examples as diverse as style of dress, the depiction of gender roles on television, and changes in business management. The writer gives compelling evidence to support his/her thesis in a readable, reasonable fashion.

The writer's syntax is above average and demonstrates variety and complexity. Grammatical errors are few, the vocabulary is broad and intelligent, and the voice of the writer is compelling. Although the second-to-last sentence runs on in a meandering fashion, such stylistic slips do not detract greatly from the writer's message. Finally, both aspects of the question—sex roles in home and society—are addressed. For its overwhelmingly positive features, the essay earns a Pass.

Essay #2—Marginal Pass (Score = 3)

The society, in which we live, is filled with double standards, none so drastic or common as that between men and women. Throughout my growing up, I have witnessed these contradictions and I have come to find these standards to be unfair.

The programming that children receive, while growing up, is a major cause of established double standards. I have experienced times when my sister and I would be playing together and my father would scold one of us because either I shouldn't be playing with dolls, my sister shouldn't be playing with toy guns. I have also found that at a young age in school, society directs us into boy activities and girl activities. I remember that girls got in trouble for horsing around and boys would get in trouble for playing house. In school we learn that only daddies can be doctors, and that mommies must be nurses.

In high school years, this double standard first becomes challenged by the girls. As teenagers begin dating and going out with friends, I have noticed that guys have less restrictions and later curfews. However the most blatant and offensive double standard, to me, is that over sex. In plain terms, if a guy does it, he is a stud, but if a girl does it, she is a slut. I have observed this happen and have several times been guilty of this thinking myself. Besides the issue of sex, goals following high school also reveals this double standard. It is a common stereotype that guys should go to college or get a job, and that women should go out to raise a family. Despite the fact that increasing numbers of girls go to college and get a good job today, and that it's more common for a father to watch the kids, the double standard still exists.

In the workplace, there is a struggle by women and some men, to shatter the double standards and stereotypes. The typical image of a male boss with a female secretary is being toppled by the rising number of women executives and professionals. The question identifies the double standard of women raising families, and men working to support the family. This is beginning to be permanently altered with the huge efforts to fight that image seen in the business world and family situation every day.

Scoring Explanation for Essay #2—Marginal Pass

This essay largely draws on personal experience from childhood and school years to demonstrate that environmental conditioning in both home and school results in the double standard. While this essay offers a more simplistic treatment of the subject of sex roles than the previous essay, the writer is generally still clear. Although the essay lacks a firm and convincing conclusion, sufficient supporting information illustrates the writer's position and bolsters the authors generalizations of societal conditioning. This essay is a good example of one that takes no risks and relies on commonplace observations; though not exciting or particularly engaging, it is adequate.

The essay's syntax and vocabulary are rather ordinary, and the author has problems with punctuation. The first sentence, for example is over-punctuated; the second sentence of the second paragraph is awkward and ungainly. Despite these problems, the writer succeeds in communicating a message to the reader and, therefore, receives a Marginal Pass.

Essay #3—Marginal Fail (Score = 2)

Societies view points on the role of male and female are often caused by many standards and factors that are put on the male or the female upon birth.

At birth, the infant is placed in one of the categories, if it is a boy, or if it is a girl. Immediately after this is determined, the infant is wrapped in a blue blanket if it is a boy, and a pink blanket if it is a girl. Thus showing that one is taught at a very young age what he/she is *expected* to wear. Children learn early in the home what is right for them.

A point is that a women's primary responsibilities are homemaking and child rearing; that men are responsible for the financial support of the family; that women with children should ideally not work outside the home; and that a double standard in social customs is acceptable. I find that one generation ago this was true, but with todays generation I feel that this passage is not as accurate as it was one generation ago.

From my personal experiences I find the previous statement to be true. I was raised with my mother being a homemaker, my father being responsible for the financial support and there was definately a double standard present. These ideologies range from old customs and beliefs that women are inferior and they have their place in the home.

From my observations, however, I see that the women of today are more independant and defiant to the expectations that are sat upon them from birth. More women are proud to be women and there are not as many girls/women expressing dissatisfaction with the sex they are.

One issue in a family with one boy and one girl is the issue of the double standard. In most families I know, there is always a double standard present on certain issues. (i.e. going out, parties, curfues) The boy usually has more privileges than the girl and the girl is usually the one with the stricter rules. Even though women is trying to be more independent, old habit die hard and protection of their children, especially girls, is always on a parent mind.

The role of a male and a female in todays society is changing from their roles in the past. The female is becoming more independent and don't exactly live up to the expectations sat upon them.

Scoring Explanation for Essay #3—Marginal Fail

This essay draws on personal experience to demonstrate that male and female gender roles are the result of societal influences. The author has less control over organization than is desirable in a brief, analytic essay. The middle paragraphs repeat key points rather than developing them, and no clear transitions assist the reader from paragraph to paragraph. For example, the penultimate paragraph raises the issue of a sex-role double standard for teenagers that allows boys more privileges and less restrictions than girls, but this paragraph more properly belongs earlier in the essay to support the writer's claim that experiences in the home account for the double standard.

The author has inadequate control over punctuation, spelling, and verb tense to a degree that is quite distracting for the audience; these problems are evident in such sentences as "Even though women is trying to be more independent, old habit die hard and protection of their children, especially girls, is always on a parent mind" and "The female is becoming more independent and don't exactly live up to the expectations sat upon them." Sentence fragments also appear. Although the writer attempts to respond to the question put forth in the prompt, severe problems with the development of the thesis and numerous grammatical and punctuation errors earn this essay a score of Marginal Fail.

Essay #4—Fail (Score = 1)

The main point is that ideologies are more effective then the sex of an individual. For centuries traditions influence people more than the sex of a person does. People learn very young, what they think is right from wrong and what they think is sutable for the opposite sex.

Sex should not determine your future. But everyone has the right to their own opinion. Everyone should always do what they think is best for them regardless of what society is used too. Ideologies of many people, especially young people will grow with open minds to what society should be like if everyone does what best for them and work to their full ability.

Customs and traditions are now changing because every individuals are doing whats best for them. Traditions such as women homemaking and men supporting the family has totally changed in some household. Now women are going out and bringing home the bread and men are at home taking care of the home. People are finally starting to realize that customs and traditions are just ideologies.

The new generation is growing up with different views because of what they see is going on our present society. The new generation sees that the idea that man and women can do just about the same. For example, women are now fighting in wars and trying to do just about everything a man could be.

In conclusion, Ideologies are more effective then a persons' sex.

Scoring Explanation for Essay #4—Fail

This writer does not appear to have adequate control of language to communicate his/her ideas. The opening sentence, "The main point is that ideologies are more effective then the sex of an individual," is an unclear and unsophisticated statement of the writer's thesis. This thesis—that tradition determines sex roles—gradually becomes clearer, but the reader must work hard to arrive at this assumption. Also, very little evidence is offered to support the writer's assertions. Without adequate support, the reader is left to wonder why they should see the writer's position as a reasonable response to the question at hand.

Too many errors in diction and spelling make the essay incomprehensible at key points, and several sentences are awkward and confusing, both syntactically and semantically. For example, in the next-to-the-last paragraph, we read: "The new generation sees that the idea that man and women can do just about the same." The reader is left wondering what exactly the writer means by this statement. The essay concludes with a restatement of the thesis ("Ideologies are more effective then a persons' sex") that has not been adequately argued. The many errors in logic and language are impossible to ignore, and the essay, therefore, receives a failing score.

Topic 2 Sample Answers

Essay #1—Pass (Score = 4)

Lee was the most attractive person that I had ever seen. He was tall and well-built, with dark brown hair and piercing hazel eyes. I had had my eye on him for a long, long time. In fact, everytime I went to the dance club, I went to see him. Although it seemed like it had taken forever, the momentous day finally arrived. Just when I least expected it, Lee came up from behind, tapped my shoulder, and asked me to dance. We swayed to the tune of "Take My Breath Away," exchanged telephone numbers, and then left for home. He called the following night at dinner time. Not only did Lee have a terrible sense of timing, but also a very boring personality. All he could talk about was his car. He was obviously not a conversationalist. Much to my disappointment, Lee and I had little in common and had trouble carrying on even a five-minute conversation. He was definitely not the guy that I had expected.

Many people claim that "sometimes when you want something badly and then when you get it, it's not what you expected." Obviously, in my situation, getting to know the "wondrous" Lee was definitely different than what I expected. He had represented a challenge for me and upon overcoming the challenge and actually talking with him, I found myself disappointed and regretful. Why did I feel this way after meeting this once-considered "dreamboat"? I can see two distinct reasons.

To begin with, Lee, after asking me to dance, no longer represented a challenge to me. The high-energy nights of watching and waiting and staring had come to an abrupt end. There was no longer an awe or a mystery to his character—he was a normal human being! The challenge was gone.

Another major reason for the disappointment was the fact that neither Lee, nor any other guy, could ever live up to the image that I had created in my mind of him. In my eyes, Lee could do no wrong. He had the looks of Mel Gibson, the personality of Chevy Chase, and the heart of Mother Theresa. After meeting him and realizing that he seriously lacked in all three areas, it is only obvious that I would be disappointed. True, Lee really did not have a chance, but I was still disappointed.

Disappointment is definitely a factor in wanting something badly and then finally getting it. Maybe because the challenge is gone, maybe because the expectations were too high or maybe because you really thought you would never get it to begin with—whatever the reason, more often than not, finally getting something that was previously desired can definitely be a letdown.

Scoring Explanation for Essay #1—Pass

This personal essay recounts, with much relevant detail, the anticipation of meeting a "dream date" and the subsequent disappointment the writer feels once she knows him better. The writer begins with a very descriptive anecdote of her first interaction with Lee and his failure to live up to her expectations. The writer withholds her thesis until the second paragraph; this approach is atypical, yet effective in this context, and demonstrates a more sophisticated approach than the usual five-paragraph essay structure.

This essay is both well-written and interesting. The writer not only offers a well-developed narrative of her disappointment, but also analyzes her sense of letdown as she speculates that she herself may have caused it by expecting too much. Finally, she uses this specific incident to speculate on the nature of expectation and disappointment in general. Throughout the entire essay, the writing is exceptionally competent, exhibiting sentence variety and a unique overall structure. For these many positive and striking features, the essay merits a Pass.

Essay #2—Marginal Pass (Score = 3)

If anyone where to ask me what my biggest dream in life was, I would have to say it was the hope for a perfect family. When I was young, I lived with only my mom because my father had left my Mom, before I was born.

Together, Mom and I, struggled to find enough money for food, and even a little peace of mind. I had always thought that the answer to our problems would be found in a complete family. By this I mean, I thought a family must consist of a father, mother, brother, and sister. I even included a family dog that would run in the yard that was enclosed by the white picket fence.

As a result of my Mom having to work and worry so hard, we didn't have sufficient time to develop a good relationship. She was having a difficult providing for me, so I had to move in with another family. This family was friends of my mother, so I felt comfortable with them. I thought that this would be the perfect home. It included everything I had ever dreamed of. It had the room, dad, siblings, and pets. I was sure that this family was perfect.

It was not soon before I realized how wrong I really was. This family had their share of problems to. For example, they found it hard to find adequate time together. They were always doing their own thing. I have to admit that initially I was shocked. However, I soon realized that there are many types of families and each of them has their own problems. The families protrayed on T.V. were not how family life really was. Of course it was sometimes difficult, but I now know that what constituts a family is love. It is not always having enough time for each other, or having a white-picket fence. It is not always being understood, or having all members present. It is about love. That love is demonstrated by the family trying to do the best they can.

Scoring Explanation for Essay #2—Marginal Pass

This essay, which focuses on the author's desire for a "perfect" family, is reasonably well-organized and competently written. The writer helps the reader to understand the author's hopes for a perfect family and how these hopes were disappointed, but surprisingly little detail fortifies the narrative. The writer offers a limited description of the problems of living with the author's mother ("my mom having to work and worry so hard") and an equally inadequate discussion of the disappointing new situation ("They were always doing their own thing"). The writer ignores important opportunities to move from the general to the specific, to enliven the essay, and to make it more engaging.

Although some minor grammatical errors distract the reader from the writer's narrative, they do not prohibit the reader from following the writer's message. However, many of the sentences are quite simple in structure, and this dulling simplicity limits the essay to a minimal success. Despite its problems with detail, development, and punctuation, the essay successfully communicates an interesting narrative in response to the essay prompt; it warrants a Marginal Pass.

Essay #3—Marginal Fail (Score = 2)

Growing up, I always wanted to be older. This had a lot to do with my older brothers and sisters. They never would let me play with them. I always looked forward to the following grade. It seemed like that being older had so much more freedom. And excitement.

That is why, after about the age of eight or nine, I couldn't wait til my sweet sixteenth birthday. I would have all the freedom I wanted. I never wanted something so much. I even wanted it more than my cabbage patch kid. When I was six.

I would go to extremes because I wanted my license. When I was fourteen I got caught one evening taking my brother's car for a little spin. Nothing major just a little ride to Carl's Jr. and back. Well the car got a flat on the way back and their was no way of avoiding the inevitable, but to call my parents. I wasn't intellectual enough to call triple A. I got an extreme punishment; that fit my crime perfect.

I was the oldest out of all my classmates because I was held back a year. So out of all my friends I was the luckiest because I would receive—my gold card to freedom—my driver's license.

I turned fifteen and you can bet that I was first in line to getting my permit that foggy cold morning at the DMV. After receiving this I was taxi service everywhere. I had to practice and practice because I wasn't going to fail my driver's test. Everytime I got behind the wheel, shivers tickled across my back. I was so excited be behind the wheel.

Finally, my sixteenth birthday rolled around. I took my drivers test—Passed with a 97. I already had a car waiting in the driveway when I came home. My little Jetta was crying out my name. The first month, I loved it. I could drive anywhere, anytime.

This got old real fast. I was soon driving friends home — home meaning an hour away. Picking up things for the family. I was basically, "slaves incorporated." The worse was having to drive to parties. I sat around watching everybody get drunk. It was not fun. Boy, was I wrong. Two years later, I still won't drive unless its' unavoidable. My friends know that. Now its' there turn to pay the piper.

Scoring Explanation for Essay #3—Marginal Fail

This essay contains many short, choppy sentences and an overwhelming number of errors in grammar and syntax. The writer's sassy and conversational style would be quite engaging if he/she could correctly construct sentences; unfortunately, the many errors frustrate the reader's attempts to comprehend the writer's message. Also, the essay's chronology, which the writer uses as an organizational scheme, confuses rather than assists the reader. Much is made of the author's sixteenth birthday and the subsequent acquisition of a driver's license. But other ages (fourteen and fifteen) are described as "driving years" without needed clarification. This error results in confusion for the reader and the necessity of several readings to achieve coherence. In short, the writer makes the reader work too hard. Although the essay might have been quite effective, since many amusing details pique the reader's interest, the writer's inability to write clearly puts too many demands upon the reader.

The author concludes with the unexpected dismay he/she felt soon after obtaining a driver's license. This section has potential, but it is underdeveloped. As the prompt asks the writer to analyze why this event was so disappointing, the writer should address this key point in extensive detail. The final line ("Now its' there turn to pay the piper") is indicative of the author's lack of control, reliance on inappropriate clichés, and punctuation and spelling errors. The essay receives a Marginal Fail for these reasons.

Essay #4—Fail (Score = 1)

One time when I went to the store I had wanted to by a video cammra. So I went to the department where they were being sold and looked at the different types of cammra. I was surprised at the low prices they were asking. I picked out the one I wanted; and bought it.

When I got home I was messing around with the cammera to see what different type of things it could do. It had a zoom, it had a mic and had many other interesting function. When I was done playing around with it and finding out everything that it could do I went to the park with my little sister. She was only 3 years old I thought I could get some funny pictures. My older sister said that she wanted to go along also; just to watch. When we got to the park I had the cammera no more than 30 seconds and Kelly my older sister wanted to use my cammera. I let her but I said for only a couple. I went to get something to drink and when I came back I saw my cammera being passed around in a group of 15. I asked for it back but all I got was a black eye. Some guy didn't like the way I was trying to get my cammera. As it was being passed around some body dropped it. It broke into a thousand small pieces. I was very upset. I got to use my cammera for about 30 seconds; and I got a black eye.

As you could of told I was very dissappointed; with how much I got to use the cammera. One thing I did learn it if you ever buy a new "toy" than keep it to yourself; or let somebody you can trust.

Scoring Explanation for Essay #4—Fail

Lack of development and errors of many sorts (syntax, grammar, punctuation, and spelling) are, unfortunately, the most memorable features of this essay. The writer begins with an overly simplistic and pedestrian account of the purchase of a "video cammra." The sentences are elementary and surprisingly void of useful detail.

The longest, central paragraph in this too-brief personal essay is a narrative account of the "borrowing," misuse, and destruction of the camera. Although the reader may sympathize for the writer's plight, little effort has been made to make the camera a highly desired or valued object. The story of its untimely demise lacks relevant detail to engage the reader on a meaningful level. The author concludes with a typically awkward sentence: "As you could of told I was very dissappointed; with how much I got to use the cammera." The writer's disengaging style and many errors distance the reader, and the essay fails on these accounts.

Acknowledgments

In addition to our authors, we would like to thank the following people for making this new edition possible:

Dr. Max Fogiel	President, for his overall guidance, which brought this book to completion
Larry B. Kling	Quality Control Manager, for his guidance and management of the editorial staff through every phase of development
Michael Tomolonis	Assistant Managing Editor of Production, for coordinating development of this new edition
Christine Saul	Senior Graphic Artist, for designing the cover
Ellen Gong and Dominique Won	for their editorial contributions
Michael Cote and Wende Solano	for typesetting the manuscript for this new edition and our first edition, respectively

REA's Test Prep Books Are The Best!

(a sample of the hundreds of letters REA receives each year)

“I am writing to congratulate you on preparing an exceptional study guide. In five years of teaching this course I have never encountered a more thorough, comprehensive, concise and realistic preparation for this examination.”

Teacher, Davie, FL

“I have found your publications, *The Best Test Preparation...* to be exactly that.”

Teacher, Aptos, CA

“I am writing to thank you for your test preparation... your book helped me immeasurably and I have nothing but praise for your GRE preparation.”

Student, Benton Harbor, MI

“Your GMAT book greatly helped me on the test. Thank you.”

Student, Oxford, OH

“I recently got the French SAT II Exam book from REA. I congratulate you on first-rate French practice tests.”

Instructor, Los Angeles, CA

“The REA LSAT Test Preparation guide is a winner!”

Instructor, Spartanburg, SC

“This book is great. Most of my friends that used the REA AP book and took the exam received 4's or 5's (mostly 5's which is the highest score!!)”

Student, San Jose, CA

(more on front page)